LABOR AND LIBERTY

The La Follette Committee
and the New Deal

LABOR AND LIBERTY

The La Follette Committee and the New Deal

JEROLD S. AUERBACH

THE BOBBS-MERRILL COMPANY, INC.

INDIANAPOLIS AND NEW YORK

Designed by Joseph P. Ascherl

For Judy

ACKNOWLEDGMENTS

Written history has been called an "Act of Faith." Every historian knows that it is also an act of collaboration—in the fullest scholarly and spiritual sense of the word. I should like to record my obligations to those whose assistance has proved invaluable. The persons named below must, of course, be exonerated from responsibility for the errors and shortcomings that remain.

Dr. Saul Benison of Brandeis University is the intellectual godfather of this book. He suggested the relevance of the La Follette Committee for an understanding of developments in civil liberties during the New Deal. His incisive comments on preliminary drafts immeasurably improved the final product, and his unflagging enthusiasm, which usually surpassed my own, was of inestimable help. In many other ways, too, he made this book possible.

Professor William E. Leuchtenburg of Columbia University, who sponsored an earlier version of the manuscript as a doctoral dissertation, set exacting standards of scholarship for which I am grateful. He rescued me from numerous errors of omission and commission, generously called several items of interest to my attention, and gave the manuscript a critical reading that improved virtually every page. Professor Robert D. Cross and Professor Alan Westin, both of Columbia, and Professor David Brody, now of The Ohio State University, offered sound criticism and went far beyond what I had any right to expect in their efforts to focus my arguments and sharpen my analysis.

I am grateful to Professor Oscar Handlin of Harvard University for his valuable suggestions and for his patience. Dr. Leslie H. Fishel, Jr., director of the State Historical Society of Wisconsin and my undergraduate mentor at Oberlin College, first exposed me to the rigors and rewards of historical study and has prodded and encouraged me ever since; I hope that he finds palatable the fruits of his labor. Professor Leonard W. Levy of Brandeis University manifested unsolicited, and therefore particularly heartening, interest in the fate of the manuscript prior to publication. My friends Frederic C. Jaher of the University of Chicago and James N. Pearlstein of Brooklyn College offered numerous helpful suggestions; in the course of his own research the latter also unearthed archival material for which I am appreciative.

Librarians and archivists made research a pleasure, and I wish to thank those at the following institutions for their assistance: the American Civil Liberties Union, the Catholic University of America, Columbia University, Duke University, the Legislative Reference Library in Madison, Wisconsin, the Manuscript Division of the Library of Congress, the National Archives, the Bureau of Research and Survey of the National Council of the Churches of Christ, the Southern Historical Collection of the University of North Carolina, the New York Public Library, Princeton University, the Franklin D. Roosevelt Library, the State Historical Society of Wisconsin, the Labor History Archives of Wayne State University, and the Workers Defense League. Professor J. Joseph Huthmacher of Georgetown University kindly culled several important letters from the Robert F. Wagner Papers. Various memoirs in the Columbia Oral History Collection were quite useful. Mr. Buford Rowland and his staff in the Legislative Branch of the National Archives, where the papers of the La Follette Committee are deposited, facilitated my research on several occasions.

Many individuals took time from busy schedules to give me the benefit of their oral or written reminiscences of various aspects of the La Follette investigation. Others willingly granted me access to important material in their possession. I should like to thank John J. Abt, Roger Baldwin, Mrs. Ethel Clyde, Thomas I. Emerson, Charles Fahy, Henry H. Fowler, Howard Kester, the late Philip La Follette, Carey McWilliams, Harry L. Mitchell, Boris Shishkin, Norman Thomas, Luke Wilson, and Robert Wohlforth. The late Gardner Jackson graciously invited me to his home, where I spent an enthralling evening listening to his recollections of the thirties.

Two universities bestowed financial aid at critical times. In 1963 Brandeis University appointed me a Florina Lasker Fellow in Civil Liberties and Civil Rights, enabling me to begin work on my dissertation in stimulating and pleasurable environs. An Erb Fellowship granted by Columbia University during 1963–1964 freed me to do virtually all the writing. Editors of *Current History*, the *Journal of American History*, *Labor History*, and the *Wisconsin Magazine of History* kindly gave permission to reprint material that originally appeared in their journals.

No dedication adequately expresses my appreciation for the labor expended on this book and the forbearance extended to its author by my wife, Judith Aaron Auerbach. Her editorial skills ranged from mastery of the intricacies of restrictive clauses to an uncanny ability to ferret out inappropriate semicolons and my favorite clichés. Her tolerance of my excessive demands, while not limitless, far exceeded the bounds of matrimonial obligation. Even her occasional impatience served as a necessary reminder that there was more to life than the La Follette Committee. For that especially I am deeply in her debt.

J. S. A.

Belmont, Massachusetts
March 1966

CONTENTS

Introduction

BETWEEN 1936 and 1940 a subcommittee of the Senate Committee on Education and Labor conducted the most extensive investigation of civil liberties infractions ever undertaken by a congressional committee. It was authorized to investigate "violations of the rights of free speech and assembly and undue interference with the right of labor to organize and bargain collectively." That subcommittee, known as the La Follette Civil Liberties Committee, is the subject of this book. The La Follette Committee's investigation of the relationship between labor organization and civil liberties in the New Deal decade poses several preliminary questions: the functions of a congressional investigating committee; the role played by its chairman; the meaning of "labor" and "civil liberties" in the milieu of the 1930's; and the sensitivity of the New Deal to the Bill of Rights. Analysis of these and related problems provides a framework for the chapters that follow.

Since 1792 investigating committees have aided Congress in discharging its responsibilities. Only in the recent past, however, have analysts probed the scope and exercise of investigative power. Prior to the New Deal, congressional inquiries were deemed legitimate when they obtained information that assisted Congress in legislating or when they supervised the Executive branch. But during the thirties congressional committees assumed still another role: influencing public opinion to mobilize support for administration programs. "One of the outstanding investigatorial developments since 1933," wrote M. Nelson McGeary in 1940, "has been the demonstration of the extent to which Congressional inquiries may become useful tools of an Administration."[1] The avowedly political purposes of many congressional investigations have by now been granted legitimacy. Most investigating committees, concludes one writer, "are primarily means of altering the power position of interest groups. . . ."[2] A congressional investigation, writes another analyst, "is not a scientific fact-finding expedition; it is a political instrument."[3]

[1] McGeary, *The Developments of Congressional Investigative Power*, p. 49.

[2] David B. Truman, *The Governmental Process*, p. 384.

[3] Edward H. Levi, Foreword, "Congressional Investigations," *University of Chicago Law Review*, XVIII (Spring 1951), 421. Changing attitudes toward the roles of con-

1

The congressional investigating committee as political instrument reached its apogee during the New Deal. Not only the La Follette investigation but also the Pecora, Nye, Black, and Dies probes either mustered support for New Deal measures or wrangled with the Roosevelt administration. The political potential of a congressional investigation was revealed as early as 1932–1933, in the interregnum between Franklin D. Roosevelt's election and his inauguration, when the Senate Banking and Currency Committee, led by counsel Ferdinand Pecora, investigated stock-exchange and banking practices. The Pecora investigation produced a spate of banking and securities legislation and may have convinced New Dealers of the virtues of congressional committees. It yielded impressive legislative results at the same time that it isolated a convenient target for New Deal verbal onslaughts.[4]

As the Pecora inquiry exposed the "money changers," so the Nye Committee's investigation of the munitions industry sought to expose the "merchants of death." Although the committee failed to establish the existence of an international munitions conspiracy, its investigation facilitated the enactment of important neutrality legislation. It, too, dabbled in partisan politics: when it impugned the integrity of Woodrow Wilson, it left many Democrats uneasy. Like the Pecora investigation, the Nye Committee served a dual purpose: it exerted political leverage while gathering information for Congress to utilize in drafting new legislation.[5]

A highly partisan investigation began while the Nye inquiry was still in progress. In 1935 the Senate appointed a special committee to investigate the utilities lobby. This probe, chaired by Hugo Black of Alabama, represented an administration attempt to counter the lobbying campaign that power companies had directed against the Wheeler-Rayburn bill to regulate holding companies, particularly its "death sentence" provision. Once again, a congressional committee discovered a villain and proceeded to pillory him. This time it was Howard C. Hopson, who controlled Associated Gas and Electric, a pyramid of more than 160 utility companies. Throughout the investigation, one historian has concluded, Senator

---

gressional committees may be found in Marshall E. Dimock, *Congressional Investigating Committees;* McGeary, *Developments of Congressional Investigative Power;* Telford Taylor, *Grand Inquest.*

[4] Taylor, *Grand Inquest,* p. 67.

[5] John E. Wiltz, *In Search of Peace: The Senate Munitions Inquiry, 1934–36,* pp. 23, 231; William E. Leuchtenburg, *Franklin D. Roosevelt and the New Deal, 1932–1940,* pp. 217–219.

Black behaved like a "relentless prosecuting attorney," eager not for justice but for convictions.[6]

In 1938 New Dealers discovered that the weapon of a congressional investigation could also cut against the administration grain. The House of Representatives created a Committee on Un-American Activities, chaired by Martin Dies of Texas. The Dies Committee was empowered to investigate "un-American" and "subversive" propaganda activities, but its findings blurred the distinction between such activities and the New Deal program. The crisis of the thirties, the Dies Committee suggested, was the responsibility of a communist conspiracy; its reports implied that the New Deal had served as a tool of international communism. Congressman Jerry Voorhis, a Democratic member of the committee, bluntly accused it of having become "a political instrument of definite conservative bias."[7]

Congressional investigating committees during the New Deal years invariably assumed that one person, or a tiny but omnipotent interest group, had devised a diabolical plot to do evil. The Pecora investigation exposed the "money changer." The Nye Committee focused on the "merchant of death." The Black Committee denounced the utilities magnate. The La Follette Committee jousted with the "economic royalist" and his hired hoodlums. And the Dies Committee was preoccupied with the communist masquerading as New Dealer. Each committee discovered a conspiracy; each, perhaps, needed to find one in order to justify its existence and to command the attention of a large audience. The useful functions that congressional committees can perform—supervising, informing, and assisting Congress to legislate—all too often yielded to conspiracy theories of history.[8]

Most congressional investigations seem to pivot around the committee chairman. He is probably more familiar with the subject matter of the investigation than any other member of the committee. He determines the scope and procedure of his investigation; key staff members will be chosen by him; and he stands to gain or lose the most from the success or failure of the investigation. In a word, he is responsible. Whether he

[6] Arthur M. Schlesinger, Jr., *The Politics of Upheaval*, p. 322.

[7] August Raymond Ogden, *The Dies Committee*, pp. 43, 105, 295; Leuchtenburg, *Franklin D. Roosevelt and the New Deal*, pp. 280–281.

[8] McGeary, *Developments of Congressional Investigative Power*, p. 83. I am grateful to Professor Alan F. Westin for directing my attention to this point. The more recent McCarthy and Kefauver investigations indicate that congressional committees have remained preoccupied with conspiracy theories.

chooses to retain that responsibility or to delegate it, his conception of the chairman's role is crucial. For example, Robert M. La Follette, Jr., and Duncan U. Fletcher both chaired Senate investigating committees, but one is remembered as the La Follette Committee and the other has been known only as the Pecora investigation. Committee nomenclature may not be conclusive, but, at the very least, it is indicative.

Senator La Follette, veteran of a decade in the upper house when his investigation began, was the type of senator who has been labeled a "professional politician."[9] He came to the Senate with considerable political experience, provided by years in his father's service. When La Follette aspired to the Senate, after his father's death in 1925, Louis D. Brandeis declared that the La Follette boys, Bob and Phil, "have had more experience in politics than any boys since the days of the Roman Senators."[10] But to be a La Follette was to be a political maverick. Like his father, Bob, Jr., was a Senate nonconformist who defined his role not merely as a representative of his state but also as a national leader.

Shortly after his election on the Republican ticket La Follette announced to his Senate colleagues that he intended to pursue "the independent course which I have marked out for myself."[11] He easily fulfilled his pledge. In the spring of 1927 he introduced a resolution opposing a third term for Republican president Calvin Coolidge; a year later he skillfully guided it through a Republican-controlled Senate. Convinced that the Hoover Congress would not take the necessary steps to alleviate the impact of the Depression, La Follette and several other senators of his persuasion urged a conference of Progressives to formulate constructive legislative proposals. Solutions might be found, the group suggested, by persons "who are aligned with different political parties."[12] In 1934 La Follette joined Wisconsin's Progressive Republicans when they launched a separate party, and he campaigned successfully for re-election as a Progressive.

[9] Donald R. Matthews, *U.S. Senators and Their World*, pp. 61–65. Matthews identifies four types: (1) the patrician politician, with high social status and considerable political accomplishment prior to becoming a senator; (2) the amateur politician, with a far lower degree of prior political involvement and achievement; (3) the professional politician, with political experience but without the "old family" background of the patrician; and (4) the agitator, often of low social origins, who jumps quickly into the Senate from a minor position. Recent examples of each type would be Henry Cabot Lodge, Jr. (Mass.), Homer Capehart (Ind.), Alben Barkley (Ky.), and Joseph R. McCarthy (Wis.).
[10] Belle Case La Follette and Fola La Follette, *Robert M. La Follette*, I, 295.
[11] Quoted in Edward N. Doan, *The La Follettes and the Wisconsin Idea*, p. 148.
[12] *Ibid.*, p. 165.

In La Follette's case, political nonconformity was a blessing rather than a handicap. In a decade of ample Democratic majorities, it freed him from dependence upon a Republican minority. Although La Follette found New Deal measures "inadequate and often piecemeal," he rendered valuable assistance to the administration. His positions on the Finance and Education and Labor Committees thrust him into the midst of important Depression battles. He could articulate his major concerns—unemployment and labor relations—with the expectation of a sympathetic hearing in the White House. La Follette and Roosevelt each found in the other a useful ally.[13]

Nothing in La Follette's career better illustrates his commitment to labor organization and collective bargaining than his service as chairman of the subcommittee that bears his name. Not long after his election to the Senate La Follette had demonstrated his interest in labor relations by demanding an investigation of alleged police brutality in the Passaic textile strike. He had also been a leader in the fight to enact the Norris-La Guardia anti-injunction bill. The National Labor Relations Act, cornerstone of New Deal collective-bargaining policy, won his enthusiastic endorsement. When enforcement of its provisions foundered, La Follette came to the act's defense. He sponsored the resolution authorizing an investigation of interference with labor's right to organize, and for four years he chaired the committee that conducted the inquiry.

La Follette's interest in the problems investigated by his committee rarely flagged, but his commitment to the investigation itself often did. In fact, the name "La Follette Committee" obscures the extent to which the committee and the investigation were not La Follette's at all. It also distorts the role that La Follette played, or chose not to play, as chairman.

The available evidence suggests that the chairman's importance to such investigations has often been overstressed. At the very least, a committee's public hearings, where the chairman easily leaves his mark, must be distinguished from the far more crucial prehearing investigations and preparations, in which the chairman may occupy an entirely subordinate position. Application of this distinction to the La Follette investigation is instructive. To judge solely by the committee's well-publicized hearings, La Follette was the key figure in the investigation. He (and less frequently his partner, Senator Elbert D. Thomas) questioned witnesses. He received the plaudits or barbs of the committee's admirers and detractors. His picture often appeared in newspapers and national magazines,

[13] *Ibid.,* p. 154; James M. Burns, *Roosevelt: The Lion and the Fox,* p. 201.

and he was the most frequently quoted committee member. Much of the correspondence elicited by the investigation was addressed to him. From this perspective, "La Follette Committee" seems an apt designation.

The committee's public hearings, however, only confirmed what staff members already knew. Hearings rarely revealed unexpected information. On the contrary, they invariably yielded the "correct" answers—those answers that the committee secretary and counsel had furnished La Follette, with a list of questions, the night before. The rush of events during 1936–1937, diligent field work by committee investigators, and skillful synthesis by staff members shaped the investigation far more than did any actions of the chairman. La Follette was not a figurehead; he wielded authority when the occasion warranted, and staff underlings never doubted his command. But La Follette trusted his staff and gave its members wide discretion. A committee chairman who is a national political figure can hardly spare the time required to supervise the minutiae of an extensive inquiry. His reputation as chairman is often for others to determine. "La Follette Committee" is a convenient label, but the designation conceals more than it reveals.[14]

The committee, as La Follette's enabling resolution indicated, focused on infringements of civil liberties that interfered with the right of workers to organize and to bargain collectively. The right to organize was not itself a civil liberty by any traditional definition of the term. But this right, guaranteed in the Wagner Act, was inseparable from specific civil liberties, particularly the freedoms of speech and assembly. If union organizers could not speak to workers or distribute union literature, or if workers could not hold meetings in which union preferences were freely expressed, then the "right" to organize was meaningless. The *raison d'être* of the La Follette investigation was the guarantee, on paper, of the right to organize, in conjunction with the denial, in practice, of the civil liberties on which that right depended.

Prior to the Wagner Act the legal rights of workers had been extremely precarious. In 1922 Chief Justice William Howard Taft, the "labor law architect" of the New Era, told his brother that organized labor was a faction "we have to hit every little while. . . ."[15] For the most part the

14 Wiltz has reached similar conclusions about the Nye Committee. Its secretary, Stephen Raushenbush, became "a key figure in the investigation," and the field work, which he directed, determined the investigation's course. "So important was the secretary's role that one might contend the name Nye Committee was a misnomer" (Wiltz, *In Search of Peace*, p. 49).

15 Irving Bernstein, *The Lean Years*, p. 190; William Howard Taft to Horace Taft, May 7, 1922, quoted in Henry F. Pringle, *The Life and Times of William Howard Taft*, II, 967.

Supreme Court did just that. "All that the employees had," wrote William Leiserson, "was a right to try to organize if they could get away with it. . . ." [16] Workers defended this right with strikes, picket lines, and boycotts, but adverse court decisions repeatedly hindered their efforts.[17]

Workers could organize into unions as long as their purpose was not criminal syndicalism. ("Revolutionary" unions, such as the I.W.W., did not have even the right to exist; state antisyndicalism statutes declared mere membership a punishable offense.) Workers could strike, but only if the purposes of the strike were lawful. Strikes to raise wages or shorten hours were legal; the status of sympathetic strikes and strikes for the closed shop was dubious; strikes to abrogate a yellow-dog contract were illegal. Courts circumscribed the conduct of strikes as well as their purposes. Nonpeaceful picketing was illegal; in the *Tri-City* case (1921) the Supreme Court severely restricted peaceful picketing, with Chief Justice Taft declaring that the word "picket" was "sinister." Lower courts were hopelessly divided. Many jurisdictions permitted peaceful picketing, but a California decision in 1909 had held picketing per se a tort, and a federal court in 1905 found the term "peaceful picketing" as inconceivable as "chaste vulgarity" or "lawful lynching."

If the courts blunted workers' weapons, they sharpened those of management. "In the administration of justice between employer and employee," wrote Felix Frankfurter and Nathan Greene, the injunction "has become the central lever. . . ." [18] Courts sanctioned injunctions to prohibit intimidation, to limit the number of pickets or to prevent picketing altogether, and even to forbid a strike or a union meeting. In the *Hitchman* decision (1917) the Supreme Court upheld the use of an injunction to enforce yellow-dog contracts. Employers could, of course, attack unions directly by bringing damage suits and criminal prosecutions against them and their members. Furthermore, most hostile acts of employers were legal. No federal legislation prohibited espionage or strikebreaking or regulated the purchase of munitions for use in industrial controversies. Many states banned the importation of armed guards, but arms and men

[16] Leiserson, *Right and Wrong in Labor Relations*, p. 27.

[17] This section is based on the following sources, which will not be individually cited except for direct quotation: Bernstein, *Lean Years*, pp. 190–215; Leiserson, *Right and Wrong in Labor Relations*; Charles O. Gregory, *Labor and the Law*, chaps. 4–10; Edwin Stacey Oakes, *The Law of Organized Labor and Industrial Conflicts*; Felix Frankfurter and Nathan Greene, *The Labor Injunction*; Edwin E. Witte, *The Government in Labor Disputes*; Francis Bowes Sayre, "Labor and the Courts," *Yale Law Journal*, XXXIX (March 1930), 682–705.

[18] *The Labor Injunction*, pp. 52–53.

could be brought in separately. The conduct of private police was virtually ignored by state and federal law.

While employers managed to find loopholes in the Sherman and Clayton Acts, the Supreme Court stringently applied these statutes to restrict union activities. The Clayton Act, the court held, did not exempt a union from antitrust prosecution. The court struck down a collective bargaining agreement under the Sherman Act. In a notorious example of judicial legerdemain, Judge John J. Parker of the Fourth Circuit ruled that a union which struck to organize the unorganized segment of an industry had violated the Sherman Act. In the twenties courts sowed the winds of a constitutional crisis; in the thirties they would reap a whirlwind.

During both decades many American workers undoubtedly did not want to join unions. But the framers of the Wagner Act and the members of the La Follette Committee were concerned with those who did. "Labor," in the context of the La Follette investigation, meant those workers who wished to become union members. Their major grievance, in the absence of laws directly restraining union activity, was the exercise of unchecked private power by employers. Workers seeking to curb this power demanded legal redress for the harassment they suffered while attempting to organize. Prior to the Wagner Act antilabor practices had presented ethical rather than legal problems. After 1935, however, these practices were no longer merely unethical but also illegal. Workers had long sought countervailing power; with boosts from the Wagner Act and the La Follette Committee they achieved it.

Although the La Follette Committee investigated only employer interference with the right of workers to organize, it was referred to as a *civil liberties* committee. This designation suggests an unexplored dimension of the New Deal years: the close association between civil liberties and workers' liberties. "Civil liberties" generally refers to those individual rights secured by the Constitution against abridgment by state or federal governments. These rights are enumerated in the first eight amendments, in the Fourteenth Amendment, and in other, scattered constitutional provisions. Before 1925 the Bill of Rights inhibited only the federal government. But in a series of decisions since that time the Supreme Court has expanded the meaning of "liberty" in the due-process clause of the Fourteenth Amendment to transform the First Amendment, and other provisions of the Bill of Rights, into curbs on state power as well.

Yet judicial interpretation only partially explains changing concepts of civil liberty during the New Deal. Of paramount importance was the fact that labor's militancy prompted civil libertarians to shed cherished dogma. They had inherited from the eighteenth and nineteenth centuries a deep distrust of centralized power; yet many of them had an equally strong, if not stronger, commitment to labor organization, a commitment that proved more enduring. Libertarians accepted, reluctantly at first, the exercise of federal power to guarantee the right to organize, and this acceptance forced them to revise their traditional notions about the exercise of governmental power. Federal responsibility for enforcing the safeguards of the First Amendment became, in fact, the new libertarian credo.[19]

The American Civil Liberties Union exemplified the transformation. This articulate and effective organization, led by Roger Baldwin, protested loudly, if ambivalently, against New Deal centralizing tendencies. The ACLU tolerated federal intervention that did not affect labor organization, but its opposition was aroused even by New Deal measures that *protected* the right of workers to organize, including, for a time, the Wagner bill. Such legislation touched a raw nerve, for federal and state intervention in labor-management relations had, in the past, usually meant siding with employers against workers. Such intervention periodically reinforced fears that government power *ipso facto* menaced liberty. Some ACLU leaders were slow to perceive that government power might also secure liberty. Not until 1935 did they finally do so.

Yet, while ACLU reports and the statements of its officers are often revealing, they require cautious use, for the ACLU has always been an organization with sharp internal divisions. Such discord was particularly characteristic of the thirties, when concern for a principled defense of civil liberties clashed with, and frequently yielded to, a commitment to workers' rights at the expense of employers' civil liberties. Some civil libertarians used civil liberties as instruments for social change, as means rather than as ends. These libertarian "instrumentalists" defended civil liberties because they wanted to hasten the arrival of a new social order. Other ACLU members, who might be called libertarian "idealists," did not face the conflict of divided loyalties; for them the Bill of Rights was

[19] Historians still tend to regard the nineteenth century, with its laissez-faire values, as the time of maximum liberty. One has written, "Throughout the nineteenth century the American people had almost unlimited freedom of expression" (Donald Johnson, *The Challenge to American Freedoms*, pp. vii–viii). It has also been said that the character of nineteenth-century America was "open, mobile, diverse, heterogeneous, fostering dissent, and welcoming ethnic variety" (William Preston, Jr., *Aliens and Dissenters: Federal Suppression of Radicals, 1903–1933*, pp. 3–4). For a challenging interpretation to the contrary, see the various writings of John P. Roche cited in the Bibliography.

a shield for all Americans, not a partisan weapon. These differences profoundly affected ACLU policy on a number of issues. The clarity of an annual report or public declaration often concealed internal discord. The board of directors and the membership at large spoke occasionally with one voice, but never with one mind.

It must also be stressed that the ACLU, as a defense and educational organization and as a pressure group, attempted to solve specific problems, not to expound a doctrinaire theory of liberty. ACLU rhetoric should not be taken for libertarian dogma. The ACLU's willingness to sacrifice a revered libertarian tenet to concrete legislative gains indicated that the ACLU was not imprisoned by abstractions. But just as internal division does not invalidate all references to an ACLU "position," so a series of ad hoc statements does not preclude all discussion of a libertarian "creed."

Examination of ACLU archival material reveals that civil-liberties problems in labor relations were particularly acute during the thirties. Yet the New Deal has rarely been credited with exceptional sensitivity to civil liberties. In a depression decade, when the Roosevelt administration confronted monumental economic problems, the President had neither the time nor the inclination to reflect upon abstract concepts of liberty. Congress, too, grappled with specific issues and could hardly be expected to debate the meaning and relevance of the Bill of Rights in the twentieth century. The Democratic Party, at its 1936 and 1940 conventions, adopted platform planks pledging support of the First Amendment but took no steps to implement them.[20] The Roosevelt administration, in sum, hardly seemed preoccupied with civil liberties. Expanding the application of the Bill of Rights never became an articulated part of the New Deal program.

The New Deal's civil liberties record was, however, considerably brighter than this evidence suggests. In fact, the Roosevelt administration registered important, if hitherto neglected, libertarian achievements, the key to which was the recognition that the state could protect, as well as destroy, liberty. "The crisis of the depression," William E. Leuchtenburg has written, "dissipated the distrust of the state inherited from the eighteenth century. . . ."[21] Americans began to perceive the menace to liberty from agglomerations of power in private hands. Libertarians found themselves clamoring for increased federal intervention once they realized that state and local authorities, and private corporations, had become agents of

[20] For the Democratic platforms, see *New York Times*, June 26, 1936, July 18, 1940.
[21] *Franklin D. Roosevelt and the New Deal*, p. 333.

repression more active than any instrumentality of the federal government. Problems of labor organization hastened this awakening; at the beginning of the Depression no group of Americans was further beyond the pale of the Bill of Rights than industrial workers. Once the Roosevelt administration deemed protection of their right to organize essential to its recovery program, a civil liberties breakthrough was bound to follow.

The La Follette Civil Liberties Committee offers a vantage point for analyzing each of these facets of the New Deal's civil liberties record. Its investigation indicates that the exercise of federal power need not mean the destruction of civil liberties. Its findings demonstrate that civil liberties were impaired, in industrial relations at least, when private economic power remained unchecked. And its focus reflects the pre-eminence of the American industrial worker, not only in libertarian aspirations, but in the expansion and protection of the Bill of Rights in twentieth-century America.

Labor, Libertarians, and Liberty:
World War I to the Wagner Act

THE provisions of the Constitution," wrote Justice Oliver Wendell Holmes, Jr., "are not mathematical formulas having their essence in their form; they are organic, living institutions. . . ."[1] Holmes's dictum has particular relevance to the Bill of Rights, for Americans have not permitted James Madison and the First Congress to speak the final word on these constitutional amendments. "The meaning of the First Amendment," Zechariah Chafee, Jr., observed, "did not crystallize in 1791."[2] As the United States evolved into a heterogeneous urban nation, each generation had to redefine its liberties and win them anew. The First Amendment required new dimensions in an industrial age. But industrial life in the United States, often exploitative and frequently violent, left Americans unsure of the limits of liberty. Such names as Homestead, Coeur d'Alene, Ludlow, Centralia, and Gastonia represented a nation's failure to expand the meaning of civil liberties sufficiently to keep pace with its industrial growth.[3]

Industrial workers in the United States fought many lonely and abortive battles to enjoy the blessings of liberty, although First Amendment freedoms were rarely uppermost in their minds. Higher wages, shorter working days, improved conditions, union recognition, and collective bargaining took precedence. To be sure, the rhetoric of labor demands rested implicitly upon the Bill of Rights. The right to organize, for example, depended upon the freedoms of speech, press, and assembly. As long as workers were denied these freedoms, they could not easily join a union.

[1] *Gompers* v. *United States*, 233 U.S. 604, 610 (1914).
[2] Chafee, *Free Speech in the United States*, p. 29.
[3] For a perceptive analysis of rural and urban traditions of liberty see John P. Roche, "American Liberty: An Examination of the 'Tradition' of Freedom," in Milton R. Konvitz and Clinton Rossiter, eds., *Aspects of Liberty*, pp. 129–162.

By the eve of World War I it had become apparent that many industrial laborers who wished to become union members could not exercise traditional freedoms of expression.

The United States Commission on Industrial Relations, authorized by Congress in 1912 to inquire into labor conditions in principal industries, exposed the abysmal state of civil liberties in industrial communities and revealed the violence that underlay American labor relations.[4] During the life of the commission the strike of nine thousand coal miners in southern Colorado, culminating in the Ludlow massacre, graphically illustrated the incompatibility of industrial autocracy and political democracy. The commission, concerned with the relation of economic power to individual liberty, devoted more attention to this labor controversy than to any other.

Systematic suppression of the freedoms of speech, press, and assembly by the Colorado Fuel and Iron Company had preceded the strike. Union organizers could not enter the mining camps or address meetings, and union periodicals were censored. The coal operators used their power of summary discharge to squelch political activity deemed inimical to their interests.[5] Within days after the strike began, guerrilla warfare erupted between strikers and armed guards. The miners' demand for a voice in determining working conditions was replaced by a desperate struggle for physical survival.

The temper of Colorado officials during the strike may best be gauged by the experiences of Mother Jones, the workers' indomitable eighty-year-old ally, who told the Commission on Industrial Relations: "I reside wherever there is a good fight against wrong—all over the country." [6] Mother Jones arrived in Trinidad, Colorado, on the morning of January 4, 1914. National Guardsmen met her at the station and deported her to Denver. On January 12 she returned; she was arrested, held incommunicado in a hospital for nine weeks, and returned to Denver. Upon her arrival there Mother Jones boarded another train for Trinidad. National

[4] Because the principle of civil liberty received no organized group defense in this country before World War I, my background analysis of labor and civil liberties begins at that point. Cf. John P. Roche, *The Quest for the Dream*, pp. 22–23; Johnson, *Challenge to American Freedoms*, pp. 196–197. For a study of the Commission on Industrial Relations, see Graham Adams, Jr., "Age of Industrial Violence" (unpublished doctoral dissertation).

[5] George P. West, *Report on the Colorado Strike*, pp. 5–8, 16, 53–54.

[6] *Final Report and Testimony Submitted to Congress by the Commission on Industrial Relations*, XI, 10618.

Guardsmen removed her from the train and placed her in a cell where, for twenty-six days, she fought sewer rats with a beer bottle. The governor of Colorado justified her arrest and imprisonment on the ground that her speeches—which she had yet to deliver—incited to violence.[7]

The Ludlow incidents, to which Mother Jones's experiences were only a prelude, convinced the Commission on Industrial Relations that American workers, lacking economic power, often had to resort to violence in order to secure their political rights and civil liberties.[8] Its superb research staff, directed by Basil Manly, framed the fundamental issue: "Whether the workers shall have an effective means of adjusting their grievances, improving their condition, and securing their liberty, through negotiation with their employers, or whether they shall be driven by necessity and oppression to the extreme of revolt." [9]

The commission deplored the aggregate of private corporate power which, in industrial communities owned or controlled by a single company, "present[ed] every aspect of a state of feudalism except the recognition of specific duties on the part of the employer." [10] The rights of free speech and assembly were seriously abridged in these communities. "Every reasonable opportunity," the commission urged, "should be afforded for the expression of ideas and the public criticism of social institutions." [11]

In a lengthy series of hearings on labor and the law the commission heard a succession of witnesses describe the sacrifice of workers' rights to corporate power. In labor cases, Clarence Darrow told the commission, "constitutional provisions have been absolutely nullified." He concluded, "I don't think we live in a free country or enjoy civil liberties." Samuel Gompers predicted that civil liberties would not be won until workers could organize and exercise economic power.[12]

In its final report, the commission sharply reminded the federal government of its responsibilities to American workers—responsibilities that the government persistently evaded. Appalled by national unconcern for workers' rights, the commission recommended ratification of a constitutional amendment "providing in specific terms for the protection of the

[7] West, *Colorado Strike*, p. 122; *Final Report and Testimony*, XI, 10632–45; Adams, "Age of Industrial Violence," pp. 232–275; Mary Field Parton, ed., *Autobiography of Mother Jones*, pp. 178–194.
[8] West, *Colorado Strike*, p. 8.
[9] *Final Report of the Commission on Industrial Relations*, p. 66.
[10] *Ibid.*, pp. 78–79.
[11] *Ibid.*, p. 99.
[12] *Final Report and Testimony*, XI, 10775, 10777, 10786, 10861, 10639.

personal rights of every person in the United States from encroachment by the Federal and State Governments and by private individuals, associations, and corporations." [13] It criticized the uncertain legal status of nearly every act committed by a union in a labor dispute. Whereas courts generally restricted union activities, the commission noted, "the weapons of employers, namely, the power of arbitrary discharge, of blacklisting, and of bringing in strike breakers, have been maintained, and legislative attempts to restrict the employers' powers have generally been declared unconstitutional. . . ." [14] The commission's report, which was far in advance of its time, passed into the limbo reserved for rebukes to the industrial order.

Despite the hue and cry raised by the industrial relations commission, the civil liberties of workers remained precarious. Only the Industrial Workers of the World, those menacing radicals who seemed to portend revolution, explicitly staked out claims to a share of the First Amendment. A series of free-speech fights, from New Castle to Missoula to San Diego, measured the gap between constitutional promise and community practice. The free-speech campaign disrupted numerous communities. When local authorities arrested I.W.W. organizers for preaching revolution, Wobblies crowded the jails until municipal officials capitulated. For their pains the Wobblies earned nationwide opprobrium; they were, wrote one newspaper editor, "the waste material of creation and should be drained off into the sewer of oblivion there to rot in cold obstruction like any other excrement." [15]

The Wobblies' most famous fight for free speech occurred in San Diego. In January 1912 the Common Council passed an ordinance prohibiting any person from addressing a gathering in an area seven blocks square in downtown San Diego. A California Free Speech League organized in protest; the I.W.W. invited to the city everyone who believed in freedom of speech. Hundreds of Wobblies came, were arrested, and were shipped by San Diego authorities to jails in surrounding counties. The Common Council responded with an antipicketing ordinance; an armed guard patrolled the county line to repel invaders; hawkers of the San Francisco *Bulletin*, which supported the free speakers, were arrested. Emma Goldman was not permitted to speak in the Socialist Hall. Con-

---

[13] *Final Report*, p. 61.

[14] *Ibid.*, p. 90.

[15] San Diego *Tribune*, March 4, 1912, quoted in Paul F. Brissenden, *The I.W.W.: A Study of American Syndicalism*, p. 266.

stables forced one hundred Wobblies to kneel and kiss the American flag. The chief of police refused to sanction public meetings without a permit, and I.W.W. speakers were not granted permits. "If the sword of our own law is turned against us," the San Diego *Evening Tribune* cautioned the Wobblies, "we claim the right, under the unwritten law, to resort to the law of nature." [16]

In April, Governor Hiram Johnson appointed a commissioner to investigate the San Diego disturbances. His report contained curious inconsistencies. The right of free speech, he stated, "should be inviolable. . . ." Every man possessed the right "to speak his mind freely in unforbidden places." Nonetheless, municipalities might enact regulatory measures "whenever necessary." And the police must arrest "those who violate these regulative measures, or who, in the exercise of free speech in unforbidden places, violate the law by the use of improper, unfit or incendiary language." [17] What the commissioner gave with one hand he took with the other. Wobblies might speak freely, but not too freely.

Yet the I.W.W. campaigns prompted some editors and a few troubled citizens to attempt a definition of free speech. An editorial in the San Francisco *Evening Post* stated: "The right of free speech means the right of any man to publicly condemn anything he may choose to condemn." A contributor to the Portland, Oregon, *Journal* insisted: "Our Constitution says a man shall be allowed to freely speak his thoughts, being held responsible for his words, as, for example, if they be libelous or inciting to riot." [18] Theodore Schroeder, a New York attorney and the outstanding advocate of a broad interpretation of free speech in the Progressive era, argued in a series of articles that the freedoms of speech and press precluded punishment not only prior to utterance but also subsequent to utterance, unless actual injury resulted.

Free speech, Schroeder insisted, "means that no man should be punished for any expression of opinion on any subject so long as the consequences of the speech [are] nothing but the creation of a state of mind in someone else." If a speech produces violence, the speaker is culpable "for his participation in the violence, but not for the speech as such." But many

---

[16] Theodore Schroeder, "History of the San Diego Free Speech Fight," *Free Speech for Radicals*, pp. 116–190; Brissenden, *The I.W.W.*, pp. 262–266; Ralph Chaplin, *Wobbly*, pp. 149–151; Leon Whipple, *The Story of Civil Liberty in the United States*, pp. 224–225.

[17] Harris Weinstock, *Disturbances in the City of San Diego and the County of San Diego, California* (Report), p. 11 and *passim*.

[18] Quoted in Schroeder, "San Diego Free Speech Fight," pp. 155, 162.

American courts, Schroeder complained, "have blindly followed Blackstone and have upheld something [seditious libel] that the Constitution . . . was intended to destroy." [19] Few people, however, grasped the issues that agitated Schroeder. Discussions of seditious libel seemed to belong to the eighteenth century; Schroeder alone acknowledged their contemporary relevance.

World War I transformed occasional speculation about seditious libel into a pressing national problem. The Espionage and Sedition Acts and postal censorship threatened critics of American policy, thereby stimulating efforts to define and expand the concept of free expression.[20] Issues of civil liberty in labor disputes receded. Until the armistice the most pressing libertarian problems arose from the clash between free expression and the government's commitment to waging total war.

Federal policy during the war produced and molded the first organized civil liberties movement in the United States. The National Civil Liberties Bureau, predecessor of the American Civil Liberties Union, rallied pacifists, conscientious objectors, and others of assorted political persuasions who opposed the Espionage and Selective Service Acts and wished to assist the victims of this legislation. Defending conscientious objectors became indistinguishable from defending civil liberty itself. From their inception the Civil Liberties Bureau and the organized civil liberties movement had a radical tinge. Their leaders opposed the war, or capitalism, or both.[21] Opposition to the war entailed opposition to the government that manipulated patriotism to justify curtailing the Bill of Rights.

The armistice brought no rapprochement between civil libertarians and the federal government. Although the Justice Department abandoned many of its prosecutions under the Espionage Act, it continued to persecute the Industrial Workers of the World. This trend disturbed Roger Baldwin, director of the Civil Liberties Bureau. Baldwin appreciated the need to defend labor's right to share in the First Amendment; he hoped to assist unions to secure the civil liberties of their members. The I.W.W., he said, "blazed the trail . . . for free speech which the entire American working class must in some fashion follow." [22] In December 1919 the National Civil Liberties Bureau was reorganized and named the American Civil Liberties Union. Defense of the First Amendment would continue

[19] Theodore Schroeder, "The Meaning of Unabridged 'Freedom of Speech,' " *Free Speech for Radicals*, p. 41; *Final Report and Testimony*, XI, 10841–43, 10884, 10894. As to whether the First Amendment was in fact intended to abolish the common law doctrine of seditious libel, see Leonard W. Levy, *Legacy of Suppression*.

[20] Whipple, *The Story of Civil Liberty*, p. v.

[21] Johnson, *Challenge to American Freedoms*, Preface, pp. 194, 196, 197–198.

[22] Quoted in Chaplin, *Wobbly*, p. 151.

unabated, but "a dramatic campaign of service to labor" would be inaugurated.[23] Linking a civil liberty to conscientious objection no longer sufficed in the postwar era. An attack on industrial capitalism became the new corollary of protecting First Amendment freedoms.

"We are not concerned," the American Civil Liberties Union insisted, "to promote any radical program or the cause of any class. But the circumstances of industrial conflict today force us chiefly to champion the rights of labor to organize, strike, meet and picket, because labor is the class whose rights are most attacked."[24] The ACLU, believing that American libertarian traditions had expired during World War I, prepared to resuscitate them by linking liberty to the cause of industrial unionization.[25] Its dedicated coterie of civil libertarians, scarred but not subdued by wartime repression, selected the American worker as the beneficiary of their next great crusade.

During the ensuing two decades the ACLU was to fight tenaciously for the civil liberties of those industrial laborers who found in unions the solution to their bargaining weakness as individuals. Many American workers—probably a majority—did not perceive unionism as the answer to their problems; for these men the ACLU manifested slight concern. But some civil libertarians, impelled by strong feelings of class consciousness, believed that powerful unions could remake American society. Civil liberties—particularly the freedoms of expression necessary to spread the gospel of unionism—became weapons in this struggle. The question of the liberties of nonunionists or employers did not excite the ACLU, for these liberties were not threatened and campaigns to preserve them were unlikely to accelerate the arrival of a new industrial order. The "circumstances of industrial conflict," reinforced by the class consciousness of civil libertarians, shaped the major civil liberties struggles between the two world wars.

While the ACLU revamped its organization after World War I, and formulated its program, labor militancy erupted. The "heritage of conflict" in American labor relations, often obscured by power or by paternalism, again became apparent.[26] In September 1919, steel workers, incensed at Judge Gary's refusal to meet their demands, issued a strike call.[27] The great steel strike, which lasted from September until January,

[23] Johnson, *Challenge to American Freedoms*, pp. 101, 107, 145–147.
[24] American Civil Liberties Union, *A Year's Fight for Free Speech*, Foreword.
[25] *Ibid.*, p. 7.
[26] For an excellent study of this heritage in the nonferrous metals industry, see Vernon H. Jensen, *Heritage of Conflict*.
[27] William E. Leuchtenburg, *The Perils of Prosperity, 1914–32*, pp. 71–75.

involved more workers than any strike preceding it in American history. Coinciding with the hysteria of the postwar Red scare, and following on the heels of the Boston police strike, it elicited impassioned denunciations from the business community, the press, and the frightened middle class. With labor organization linked to bolshevism, civil liberties were dismissed as irrelevant impediments to national security. The mayor of one steel town declared, "Jesus Christ himself couldn't speak in Duquesne for the A.F. of L." [28]

Before the strike was a month old, the Interchurch World Movement had authorized a Commission of Inquiry, chaired by Bishop Francis J. McConnell, to investigate industrial unrest, in particular the causes of the steel strike. For five months field investigators combed the steel towns of Pennsylvania and Ohio, confronting workers with two questions: Why did you strike? What do you want? Supervising the investigation was a thirty-five-year-old newspaperman, Heber Blankenhorn. During the war Blankenhorn had originated the idea of dropping propaganda leaflets from airplanes behind German lines to demoralize the enemy. Writing to his wife from General Pershing's headquarters, where he was a captain in the division of Army intelligence, he revealed his tenacity: ". . . We shall fight our way through the red tape yet, and do." [29] Blankenhorn eagerly applied this credo to the Interchurch investigation.

The Interchurch findings, issued in two volumes in 1920 and 1921, reaffirmed the conclusions reached by the Commission on Industrial Relations. The Interchurch investigation is best remembered for its condemnation of the twelve-hour day in the steel industry ("a barbarism without valid excuse"). Its criticism of civil liberties violations attracted less attention. The Commission of Inquiry concluded that public opinion approved "the degradation . . . of civil liberties in behalf of private concerns' industrial practices." [30] Consequently, thousands of workers had concluded that American institutions were either undemocratic or undemocratically administered. World War I, the commission believed, had inured the nation to the abrogation, in the name of a worthy cause, of free speech and assembly. [31]

Commission investigators discovered pervasive anti-unionism, the com-

---

[28] Quoted in J. Raymond Walsh, *C.I.O.*, pp. 51–52. Cf. Robert K. Murray, *Red Scare*, pp. 135–152; David Brody, *Labor in Crisis: The Steel Strike of 1919*.

[29] Interchurch World Movement, *Report on the Steel Strike of 1919*, p. iii; Heber Blankenhorn, *Adventures in Propaganda*, pp. v, 49; *New York Times*, January 2, 1956.

[30] *Report on the Steel Strike of 1919*, pp. 84, 238, 239.

[31] *Ibid.*, p. 235.

ponent parts of which were blacklists, discharges for union affiliation, labor detectives, and persistent attempts to influence the local press, pulpit, and police. When steel company officials in Pittsburgh produced secret service reports of "radical" activities to justify such practices, the commission stumbled upon evidence of a vast network of industrial espionage. Its investigators knew of the existence of espionage, but they doubted its importance. When they inquired about company procedure to ascertain workers' needs, they were shown "labor files" filled with detailed accounts of workers' activities.[32] These secret reports ranged "from the illiterate scribblings of professional parasites to the most accurate transcriptions of union locals' secret meetings." [33] The commission itself was spied upon; from a company spy Judge Gary received a picturesque description of "Pink Tea Socialists and Parlor Reds" in the Interchurch movement.[34] Although legal, espionage sharply curtailed the freedom of workers to associate and to speak; dismissal was not an unusual consequence of attendance at union meetings.

The findings of the Commission of Inquiry raised alarming questions about the state of civil liberty in industrial communities and about institutional barriers to full enjoyment of First Amendment freedoms. In company towns, anti-unionism inevitably entailed abrogation of the right of assembly, suppression of speech, and violations of other personal rights. Maintenance of law and order, as defined by the company, not infrequently required the presence of state militia or federal troops. By implication, management insisted that the preservation of civil peace depended upon the denial of civil liberty.[35] The commission discovered no power in American society equal to that exerted by industrial corporations. "Among American democratic institutions," it reported, the worker "found none to fit his need, no Federal body or machinery for acting on his case nor even any governmental institution of inquiry, which . . . was reaching out to learn his grievances." [36] The worker had but one recourse: to await the next strike. "Can our democratic society," the commission inquired, "be moved to do industrial justice without the pressure of crisis itself?" [37]

[32] *Ibid.*, pp. 14–15, 27.
[33] *Ibid.*, p. 227.
[34] *Ibid.*, pp. 233–234.
[35] *Ibid.*, p. 197; Interchurch World Movement, *Public Opinion and the Steel Strike*, p. 164.
[36] *Report on the Steel Strike of 1919*, p. 244.
[37] *Ibid.*, p. 245. The Interchurch investigation is discussed briefly in David Brody, *Steelworkers in America: The Nonunion Era*, p. 271; Donald B. Meyer, *The Protes-*

These warnings and questions stirred few responsive chords. Dr. Richard C. Cabot, professor of social ethics at Harvard, was struck by the espionage findings of the Commission of Inquiry; in 1920 he financed an investigation of its nature and scope. Portions of the study appeared in *The New Republic* and in a short volume, *The Labor Spy*, published in 1924. Industrial espionage, the authors observed, "is, indeed, a curious substitute for industrial relations." [38] Virtually nobody cared.

Throughout the twenties, industrial employers developed new tactics or refined old ones to deter labor organization and to avoid genuine collective bargaining. These tactics ranged from the so-called American Plan, which entailed the use of every hostile technique of anti-unionism, to the paternalism of welfare capitalism. In the first case, belligerent techniques such as espionage, stockpiling of munitions, employment of private police and strikebreakers, and yellow-dog contracts came to the fore. In the second, the employee-representation plan, or company union, launched by John D. Rockefeller, Jr., after the Ludlow massacre, manifested a more benevolent approach. Whether belligerent or benevolent, employers gained strikingly similar results: In the country's major mass-production industries, the open shop—in reality a nonunion shop—prevailed.[39] In those industrial communities where civil liberties seemed incompatible with management policy, civil liberties invariably yielded.

Two union campaigns in the 1920's—one at the beginning of the decade, one at the end—measured the impotence of civil libertarians in postwar labor relations. In 1920 the United Mine Workers sent organizers into the coal fields of Mingo and Logan counties in West Virginia. The ACLU took an active interest in this organizing drive; in April, it dispatched a representative to Logan County, where miners could not invite organizers into their homes, or even live in them if they went out on strike. The ACLU agent discovered a total absence of legal procedure and a very real danger of civil war. After the battle of Matewan, in which seven detec-

---

tant *Search for Political Realism, 1919–1941*, pp. 58–62; Paul A. Carter, *The Decline and Revival of the Social Gospel*, p. 21; Robert Moats Miller, *American Protestantism and Social Issues, 1919–1939*, pp. 211–215; Murray, *Red Scare*, pp. 151–152. A contemporary critique of the investigation is Marshall Olds, *Analysis of the Interchurch World Movement Report on the Steel Strike*.

[38] Sidney Howard, *The Labor Spy*, p. 16. Cf. "The Cabot Investigation of Espionage in American Industry," U.S. Senate, Subcommittee of the Committee on Education and Labor, *Hearings on S. Res. 266*, 74th Cong., 2d Sess., 1936, pp. 337–344.

[39] Irving Bernstein, *The Lean Years*, chaps. 3, 4; Arthur M. Schlesinger, Jr., *The Crisis of the Old Order, 1919–1933*, chap. 14.

tives, three miners, and the mayor were killed in a blazing gun duel, the agent went to Washington to plead for a congressional investigation, to no avail. An injunction was issued that, in effect, restrained organizers from soliciting new members. Sporadic violence persisted, the state militia prohibited union meetings, and the UMW newspaper was suppressed. The Senate finally authorized an inquiry, but nothing came of its hearings or report.[40]

On April 1, 1929, the Communist-controlled National Textile Workers Union struck the Loray mill in Gastonia, North Carolina, in response to the discharge of five union members. The NTWU initially pursued trade-union objectives: a minimum weekly wage of twenty dollars, abolition of the stretch-out, elimination of piecework, and recognition of the union. But in Gastonia, where workers were treated "as mere instruments of economic production," such demands did not even receive a hearing.[41] The city council passed an ordinance prohibiting parades; picketing, equated with parading, was banned. Strike leaders were arrested on the slightest pretext. Special deputies dispersed gatherings of strikers. Civic clubs, but not Communists, were permitted to stage mass meetings. One evening police officers visited union headquarters inside the strikers' tent colony (the mill had evicted strikers and their families from company houses). The officers were challenged to show a warrant; shooting broke out; the police chief was badly wounded and died the next day.

Sixteen organizers and strikers were indicted and tried for conspiracy to murder, but the court declared a mistrial when a juror went insane. That night a mob, singing "Praise God From Whom All Blessings Flow," kidnaped three NTWU organizers and beat them severely. Throughout the second trial the prosecutor injected testimony relating to the political and religious beliefs of the defendants and their witnesses. Praying before the jury, he branded the defendants "foreign Communists, fiends incarnate, who came sweeping like a cyclone . . . to sink their fangs into the heart and life blood of my community." In every case in which strikers were tried, convictions were secured; in no case involving Gastonia's anti-unionists, including those who murdered union balladeer Ella May Wiggins in broad daylight, was there a conviction. No one knew whether the convictions were attributable to the defendants' guilt or to their radi-

[40] Donald Johnson, "The American Civil Liberties Union: Origins, 1914–1924" (unpublished doctoral dissertation), pp. 302–329.

[41] Bernstein, *Lean Years*, pp. 20–22; Liston Pope, *Millhands and Preachers*, pp. 214–223, 233.

calism. But Fred Beal, NTWU organizer, knew that "in so far as the Bill of Rights was concerned, [Gastonia] was not part of America."[42]

Gastonia was an extreme example of a typical pattern. Throughout the New Era civil libertarians derived slight satisfaction from their forays into industrial controversies. Furthermore, the anachronistic restraints imposed by their own ideology blunted the cutting edge of their libertarian weapons.

Civil libertarians remained inveterate worshipers at the shrine of Thomas Jefferson and adhered to a tradition that measured individual liberty by government abstinence. "Congress shall make no law . . ." read the First Amendment; and in *This Land of Liberty* Ernest Sutherland Bates wrote that "as long as the American people remained of the same mind as they were in 1791, there could be no danger."[43] Roger Baldwin and other ACLU leaders retained a deep distrust of centralized power. Baldwin had gone to prison in 1918 for violating the Selective Service Act, and it would take years to dissipate his antipathy to state authority. Civil libertarians did not easily overcome the trauma induced by war legislation. Arthur Garfield Hays argued that "a new theory of government based on . . . [the] need of legal restraint, is displacing liberty." The Constitution, he reiterated, restrained government only. "This was thought necessary to preserve liberty," wrote Hays, who, quite clearly, still thought so. "Those who believe in old American ideals," he added, "are to-day regarded as dangerous innovators. In fact, they are quite conservative and old-fashioned."[44]

Such conservatism did more than confine civil libertarians to a rigid theoretical framework; it also produced a definition of civil liberties that closely resembled eighteenth-century concepts. In 1930 Robert E. Cushman, writing on "Civil Liberties" for the *Encyclopaedia of the Social Sciences,* stated that the freedom denoted by the concept of civil liberty was "a right of the individual as against the authoritarian state." Cushman perceived a "clear tendency" since World War I to relax interest in civil liberties; he also mourned the loss of many specific rights. Given civil libertarian premises, his conclusion was irrefutable: "The increasing governmental control necessitated by the complexities of modern social and

[42] Pope, *Millhands and Preachers,* pp. 250–302; "The Gastonia Strikers' Case," *Harvard Law Review,* XLIV (May 1931), 1118–24; Tom Tippett, *When Southern Labor Stirs,* pp. 77–78; Fred E. Beal, *Proletarian Journey,* p. 146.

[43] Ernest Sutherland Bates, *This Land of Liberty,* p. 147.

[44] Hays, *Let Freedom Ring,* pp. xvi, xix, xxii.

industrial life results in continuous encroachments upon rights fundamental to the older philosophy of individualism." [45]

The Depression eroded the "older philosophy of individualism," but neither it nor the coming of the New Deal undermined the civil libertarian creed. The New Deal, in fact, posed a dilemma for the ACLU. On the one hand its leaders, predisposed against capitalism, welcomed the departure of the Hoover regime. On the other hand the emergency powers requested by President Roosevelt, and the tremendous burst of government activity in Washington, seemed to presage federal intrusion on civil liberties more severe than during World War I. The ACLU could not easily shed its suspicion of strong central government. Consequently, for more than two years it balanced fear of the Roosevelt administration with hope for the constructive exercise of federal power. This ambivalence was reflected in the sharp contrast between the actions and the attitudes of civil libertarians. The ACLU repeatedly prodded the federal government to protect the rights of labor; at the same time its public pronouncements warned of threats to liberty from federal action. Janus-faced, the ACLU looked reverently to Jefferson while it attempted to harmonize the Bill of Rights with modern industrialism.[46]

Midway through Roosevelt's first term the ACLU evaluated the New Deal's civil liberties record:

"The enormous increase of the power of the federal government under New Deal policies carries with it inevitable fears of inroads on the right of agitation. Alarms are widely expressed over alleged dictatorship by the President, the abrogation of states' rights and the vast economic powers of the federal government, reaching out to every home and business in the land." [47]

The New Deal, the ACLU admitted, had not yet found it necessary to restrict the rights of any group. But the absence of wholesale suppression offered slight cause for rejoicing, *"because there is as yet no significant opposition to suppress."* The power to do ill, although not used, still

[45] Robert E. Cushman, "Civil Liberties," *Encyclopaedia of the Social Sciences,* III, 509, 511.

[46] Ironically, the nation's wartime experiences, which furnished a serviceable model for the centralized economic direction of the early New Deal, also provided a framework within which anti-New Deal attitudes developed. See Leuchtenburg, *Franklin D. Roosevelt and the New Deal,* p. 33.

[47] American Civil Liberties Union, *Liberty Under the New Deal: The Record for 1933–1934,* p. 3.

existed. "Yet unless that power is changed," the ACLU declared, warning of potential federal censorship, *the danger is always present*." [48]

If the New Deal appeared ominous to libertarians, other potential sources of repression also bore watching. "Despite the *unparalleled power* of the federal government," the ACLU observed, "effective control over the exercise of civil liberties in the United States rests where it has always been,—*with the masters of property*." [49] Industrial conflict during the first year of the New Deal had no recent equal. "Not in many years," declared the union, "have the issues of civil liberty in the industrial struggle been so sharp, so widespread, so bitterly fought as they have during the year of the New Deal's attempt to bring order out of industrial conflict." The battle between capital and labor, announced the American Civil Liberties Union, is "the central struggle involving civil liberties. . . ." [50]

In this battle the ACLU never hesitated to take sides. Many of its leaders advocated mass unionization and approved of sweeping social reforms, quite apart from the civil liberties aspects of these problems. To the ACLU—and to Roger Baldwin, its indefatigable spokesman—no civil liberties issues seemed as compelling as those arising from labor-management relations. As late as 1938, in one of the Godkin Lectures at Harvard University, Baldwin stated the problem as vividly as anyone did during the New Deal:

"However important or significant may be the struggle for the political rights of fifteen million Negroes; however important or significant the defense of religious liberties; of academic freedom; of freedom from censorship of the press, radio, or motion pictures, these are on the whole trifling in national effect compared with the fight for the rights of labor to organize." [51]

[48] *Ibid.*, p. 9.

[49] *Ibid.*, p. 10. The ACLU was fully aware of nonfederal sources of repression. Warning of dangers from Washington, it also declared that the "chief instruments of repression are still local . . ." (*ibid*).

[50] *Ibid.*, pp. 3, 4–5, 9. There is an element of danger in equating the American Civil Liberties Union with a "civil libertarian" creed. Nevertheless, of all civil libertarian organizations the ACLU was the most articulate, the largest, the most widely known, and perhaps the most respected. It enjoyed this status despite (or because of) the radical political views of its leaders, particularly of Roger Baldwin. This point is not without significance for an understanding of the civil libertarian "creed" as it developed between the two world wars. In large measure the creed was articulated and implemented by men who did not swim in the mainstream of American political life.

[51] Roger N. Baldwin and Clarence B. Randall, *Civil Liberties and Industrial Conflict*, p. 17.

As workers responded to early New Deal encouragement of labor organization—most notably in section 7(a) of the National Industrial Recovery Act—their spokesmen and allies used the constitutional guarantee of civil liberties as an instrument to forge a powerful labor movement. First Amendment abstractions were honed into serviceable weapons for an assault on those citadels of anti-unionism, the mass-production industries. Once unionization came to be equated with freedom, the Left saw in every antilabor gesture the precursor of domestic fascism. Ella Winter, describing labor relations on the West Coast, warned: "Few persons realize the astonishing rapidity with which the United States is following in the footsteps of Hitler's Germany. . . ." [52] J. B. Matthews, then in an early stage of his odyssey as a fellow traveler, concluded from observations of civil liberties trends "that the discernible drift is at present in the direction of fascism. . . ." [53] Antifascism, in the guise of a civil libertarian crusade, appealed to the Left, which often manipulated the Bill of Rights and labor organization for ends having little to do with civil liberties.

The swift pace of labor developments after Roosevelt's election exhilarated civil libertarians but also threw the ACLU into a quandary. As early as the first hundred days of the Roosevelt administration, ACLU files were already overflowing with clippings, reports, and correspondence bearing on the rights of workers attempting to organize. Each piece of New Deal labor legislation brought a flood of complaints alleging that workers desiring to join a union had encountered persistent intimidation and harassment. But the ACLU vacillated in its approach to the exercise of federal power in labor-management relations. It organized a Committee on Workers' and Farmers' Rights to prod Roosevelt on civil liberties infringements in labor disputes. Yet the National Labor Relations bill, with its guarantees of the rights to organization and collective bargaining, disquieted some ACLU libertarians. The specter of federal power still haunted these ACLU leaders. Roger Baldwin, for example, opposed the Wagner labor relations bill "on the ground that no such federal agency [as the NLRB] intervening in the conflicts between employers and employees can be expected to fairly determine the issues of labor's rights." [54]

---

[52] Ella Winter, "Fascism on the West Coast," *Nation*, CXXXVIII (February 28, 1934), 241.

[53] J. B. Matthews and R. E. Shallcross, "Must America Go Fascist?," *Harper's Magazine*, CLXIX (June 1934), 10–11, 15.

[54] Baldwin to Robert F. Wagner, April 1, 1935, American Civil Liberties Union Papers (cited hereafter as ACLU), Vol. 780.

Significantly, a storm of protest from within the union forced Baldwin to rescind his statement. Arthur Garfield Hays admitted that "we have heretofore taken the position that governmental interference or power ordinarily results in a denial of rights to the workers; that labor can advance only through its own power, not through legislation." But, Hays argued, nothing in the Wagner bill denied civil liberties to any individual or to any union; "it actually gives further opportunity to protect these rights." Attorney Morris Ernst knew of no better procedure than that contained in the Wagner bill "by which labor can be aided in its battle for organization in order to develop a strength which may possibly defeat fascistic movements." Under such pressure, Baldwin notified Senator Wagner that the union would take no official position on his bill.[55] The needs of the moment dictated that an immediate goal—labor organization—take precedence over an article of faith deeply ingrained in libertarian dogma.

The ACLU's *volte-face* on the Wagner bill ended the negative phase of American civil libertarian thought. It had the same symbolic significance as did the decision of the American Federation of Labor, at its 1932 convention in Cincinnati, to endorse government-sponsored unemployment insurance.[56] As the federation turned its back on voluntarism, so the American Civil Liberties Union relaxed its hostility toward the state. When the federal government held out the promise of protecting liberty, traditional libertarian antipathy toward federal power melted away.

The ACLU and labor co-operated on several fronts. In January 1934 Mike Tighe, president of the Amalgamated Association of Iron, Steel, and Tin Workers, apprised Roger Baldwin of conditions in Homestead, Aliquippa, and other Pennsylvania company towns where corporations staunchly resisted unionization. The steel companies, Tighe wrote, "have such a hold on their employees that they are virtually slaves and are afraid to own their very souls. . . . Fear among the workers is the one great problem we have to face in trying to organize the men."[57] In the best Wobbly free-speech campaign tradition, but without the ebullient legions of the I.W.W. as support, the ACLU planned a three-month drive to open up five towns where union meetings were prohibited: Farrell, Am-

55 Arthur Garfield Hays to ACLU, May 7, 1935, Morris L. Ernst to Baldwin, May 10, 1935, Baldwin to John W. Edelman, May 23, 1935, ACLU, Vol. 780.

56 Bernstein, *Lean Years*, pp. 347–354.

57 Mike F. Tighe to Baldwin, January 2, 1934, ACLU, Vol. 754.

bridge, Homestead, Clairton, and Aliquippa.[58] Baldwin outlined tactics for the Pittsburgh Civil Liberties Union to pursue: first, meetings would be held under ACLU auspices; joint union-ACLU meetings would follow; finally, the civil libertarians would support union efforts to hold independent meetings.[59]

The free-speech drive began with high hopes but soon lagged when the Amalgamated Association conducted a tepid organizing campaign. In July an ACLU field worker reported, "In Ambridge and Aliquippa there are no civil rights whatsoever. Homestead is equally shut tight. . . ." [60] Four months later Mrs. Gifford Pinchot, wife of the Pennsylvania governor, informed Baldwin that an Aliquippa worker had been railroaded into an insane asylum for his union activities. Mrs. Pinchot had planned to kidnap him from the asylum "in a very dramatic way . . . to draw the attention of the country to the fact that the machinery of justice was being used against the workers." Governor Pinchot "knocked [her] plan galley west," however, when he discovered a loophole in the Welfare Code permitting him to release the man.[61]

Toward the end of the year the ACLU sponsored a Conference on Civil Liberties in Washington, D.C. "As speaker after speaker told his or her story," reported Jonathan Mitchell in the *New Republic*, "it was clear that there is no form of Nazi suppression that has not, at least in scattered instances, been practiced here." [62] Many of the issues discussed at the conference touched on workers' rights. The ACLU sent a copy of the labor resolutions to President Roosevelt; the conference condemned company unions, asked that employers be required to bargain with representatives of a majority of their workers, and advocated the extension of collective bargaining to farm workers. Its most significant recommenda-

[58] In Homestead in mid-1933, Secretary of Labor Perkins spoke to steel workers in the post-office building after the local burgess, insisting that the men were "undesirable Reds," had refused to permit her to address them from the steps of the Hall of Burgesses or in a public park (Frances Perkins, *The Roosevelt I Knew*, pp. 218–220).

[59] Baldwin to Pittsburgh Civil Liberties Union, February 15, 1934, ACLU, Vol. 754.

[60] Baldwin to Harvey O'Connor, November 6, 1934, ACLU, Vol. 754; Herbert Abrons to ACLU, July 27, 1934, ACLU, Vol. 677.

[61] Mrs. Gifford Pinchot to Baldwin, November 16, 1934, ACLU, Vol. 754. For a fuller discussion of this incident, see Richard C. Cortner, *The Wagner Act Cases*, p. 59.

[62] Jonathan Mitchell, "Civil Liberties Under Roosevelt," *New Republic*, LXXXI (December 26, 1934), 186.

tion, however, appeared almost as an afterthought. The conference urged "an investigation by a Committee of the Senate of the so-called vigilantes and other lawless elements which have attacked strikers, raided their quarters, destroyed their property, without rebuke or proceedings against them by local or federal officials." [63]

The plea for a congressional investigation of infringements of workers' civil liberties was hardly novel. Sporadic union demands and occasional congressional resolutions invariably came to nothing, however. Two months before Roosevelt's inauguration, for example, Roger Baldwin inquired whether Senator Bronson Cutting would scrutinize the "desperate" conditions in Harlan County, Kentucky, long a center of violent intimidation and repression. Cutting advised Baldwin that the time was not propitious for such an investigation.[64] In 1934 A. L. Wirin, an ACLU attorney, reported that he had sounded out Rexford Tugwell, Assistant Secretary of Agriculture, and Lloyd K. Garrison, chairman of the National Labor Relations Board, on an investigation of vigilantism and mob violence in strikes. Garrison and Wirin decided to press for a presidential commission; the NLRB chairman agreed to speak to Secretary of Labor Perkins about the matter. Tugwell, also receptive, promised to do what he could. Although these efforts proved fruitless, libertarians refused to stop trying. Government action, despite its presumed dangers for libertarians, occasionally seemed preferable to unrelenting repression of labor. In January 1935 Roger Baldwin exhorted Senator Burton K. Wheeler to introduce a resolution authorizing the Senate to investigate the activities of labor detective agencies and vigilante groups. Wheeler, citing the pressure of Senate business, declined.[65]

[63] Harry F. Ward, *et al.*, to FDR, December 26, 1934, Franklin D. Roosevelt Papers (cited below as FDRL), OF 2111. In the Roosevelt Papers there is a memo signed by Wilma Meredith, secretary to Stephen Early, reporting a discussion with J. Edgar Hoover regarding the propriety of a Presidential statement to the Conference on Civil Liberties. Hoover, she reported, "would not dignify [the ACLU] by a Presidential message. . . ." ACLU members, according to Hoover, "carry on vigorous and vicious campaigns for what they call 'civil liberties.' . . ." Hoover believed that a message "might offend many who hold to conservatism and law enforcement and would only lend dignity to an undeserving group" (Wilma Meredith memo, December 5, 1934, *ibid.*).

[64] Baldwin to Bronson Cutting, January 5, 1933, Cutting to Baldwin, January 6, 1933, ACLU, Vol. 659. The clipping files in the Legislative Reference Library, Madison, Wisconsin, date such requests as far back as 1923.

[65] A. L. Wirin to Baldwin, August 3, 1934, ACLU, Vol. 735; Baldwin to Burton K. Wheeler, January 24, 1935, Wheeler to Baldwin, January 26, 1935, ACLU, Vol. 789.

But in 1935, for the first time, the American Civil Liberties Union received substantial assistance from other organizations concerned with labor and civil liberty and anxious for Congress to investigate. Paramount among them was the Federal Council of the Churches of Christ in America. Organized in 1908, the Federal Council had branded capitalism anti-Christian and had adopted a "Social Creed" pledging member churches to stand "for equal rights and complete justice for all men in all stations of life." At its 1908 meeting the Reverend Frank Mason North, chairman of the Committee on the Church and Modern Industry, called on the church to diligently promote the rights of labor. The council sent a representative to every convention of the American Federation of Labor after 1909; it campaigned for a six-day week and for abolition of the twelve-hour day in the steel industry; and it conducted a series of investigations following major strikes. After World War I it developed a comprehensive program for promoting industrial democracy, including minimum wage and social security legislation, public works projects, experimentation with profit-sharing and co-operative ownership, and abolition of child labor.[66]

During the 1920's James Myers, a Presbyterian minister, joined the council staff as Industrial Secretary. He traveled throughout the country, preaching the doctrine that "labor unionism is after all the basic expression of the self-respect of American workers who demand democracy in industrial relations. . . ." The "Social Creed" was revised in 1932 to incorporate a plea for the right of employers and employees alike to organize for collective bargaining purposes.[67] "From the perspective of Christianity," the council insisted, "it is intolerable that masses of men, women and children should be denied the opportunities which comfortable people regard as necessities. God did not create wage-earners to be mere instruments for the making of money for others. . . ." [68] Myers carried the social gospel to factory towns, coal fields, textile villages, and cotton plantations. To join a union, he told textile workers at the funeral of strikers killed during the 1934 Honea Path strike in South Carolina, "seems to me to be

[66] John A. Hutchison, *We Are Not Divided*, pp. 25, 34–53; Miller, *American Protestantism*, pp. 88–89, 220–223; Henry Steele Commager, *The American Mind*, pp. 173–177; Walter C. Hurd, "The Labor and Industrial Program of the Federal Council of Churches 1932–1940" (unpublished master's essay), pp. 1–30.

[67] Hurd, pp. 44, 59-A; Hutchison, *We Are Not Divided*, pp. 104, 106–125.

[68] Federal Council of Churches *Information Service*, September 4, 1937.

a religious duty. . . . By that act [workers] exhibit an unselfish devotion to improve the lot of *all* the workers in industry." [69]

In May 1935, 250 prominent clergymen—including Myers, Monsignor John A. Ryan, the Reverend Harry Emerson Fosdick, Bishop Francis J. McConnell, Dr. Stephen S. Wise, and Rabbi Sidney Goldstein—petitioned the Senate Judiciary Committee to investigate nationwide infringements of civil liberties. President Roosevelt received a copy of the statement, which warned of organizations desiring "to repress demands for economic change on the part of labor and to maintain the special privileges and power which they now enjoy." [70] A month later the Social Justice Commission of the Central Conference of American Rabbis echoed this appeal to the Judiciary Committee, citing threats to First Amendment guarantees from federal and state legislation and from reactionary groups which "in the name of patriotism are engaged in unpatriotic efforts to limit our liberties." [71]

Advocates of a congressional inquiry needed only a striking issue to mobilize congressional liberals. In 1935–1936 many signs pointed toward northeastern Arkansas, where a courageous band of sharecroppers and their sympathizers had been struggling since 1934 to sustain a tenant farmers' union.

[69] Copy of Myers speech, September 9, 1934, Federal Council of Churches Industrial Department Papers, Federal Council Archives; cf. *Labor Journal* (Va.), October 10, 1935, in the same archives.

[70] James Myers, *et al.*, to Marvin McIntyre, May 15, 1935, FDRL, OF 1581; Federal Council *Information Service*, May 18, 1935. In later years James Myers and Roger Baldwin tended to overestimate the influence of this petition on the establishment of the La Follette Committee. Cf. Baldwin and Randall, *Civil Liberties and Industrial Conflict*, p. 59; Baldwin to Samuel McCrea Cavert, January 17, 1939, ACLU, Vol. 2081; James Myers and Harry W. Laidler, *What Do You Know About Labor?*, p. 250.

[71] *Hearings on S. Res. 266*, pp. 243–244.

⤳ II ⤳

"... All We Want Is Justice"

Southern sharecroppers constituted "a kingdom of neglect and want."[1] No group of Americans suffered more during the Depression; none received less assistance from the government during the early years of the New Deal. Sharecroppers tilled the cotton fields "from can to can't," but entire families rarely received as much as two hundred dollars for a year's work. Their diet consisted of cornbread, molasses, and fatback, and their hovels could hardly be called homes. Many croppers, it was said, "could study astronomy through the openings in the roof and geology through holes in the floor. . . ."[2] Scantily clothed children attended school primarily to keep warm; malaria and pellagra took a constant toll. Sharecroppers owned nothing but their own labor. An archaic credit system, which left them without cash and at their planter's mercy, also contributed to an impoverished and degrading rural society.[3]

The legal relationship between landlord and sharecropper reflected their disproportionate power. Croppers had no legal claims in regard to improvements they made in their homes or on their land. Lengthy tenure did not confer the right to remain on a landlord's property. Landlords could terminate tenancy at will; the cropper, whose status was not unlike that of a resident in a company town, might be charged with trespassing the moment a landlord decided to dismiss him. Sharecroppers retained but slight choice in the selection of crops or in methods of cultivation, harvesting, and marketing. They shared the hazards of plantation life, but they never shared control.[4]

[1] Arthur F. Raper and Ira De A. Reid, *Sharecroppers All*, p. 20.
[2] Charles S. Johnson, Edwin R. Embree, and Will W. Alexander, *The Collapse of Cotton Tenancy*, p. 12; Howard Kester, *Revolt Among the Sharecroppers*, pp. 39–41; Herman C. Nixon, *Forty Acres and Steel Mules*, p. 23.
[3] Kester, *Revolt*, pp. 42–43; Johnson, *et al.*, *Collapse of Cotton Tenancy*, p. 8; Rupert B. Vance, *Farmers Without Land*, p. 1; Gunnar Myrdal, *An American Dilemma*, pp. 246–251.
[4] Vance, *Farmers Without Land*, pp. 1, 11; Raper and Reid, *Sharecroppers All*, p. vi. Legal distinctions between sharecroppers and tenant farmers were based on the equipment and livestock that they contributed, which in turn determined the percentage of their crop paid to the landlord. Tenant farmers furnished their own

Lacking secure tenure, without incentive to improve their land or buildings, and devoid of status in their communities, sharecroppers discovered that the rungs of the agricultural ladder had become bars to their advancement.[5] Squalor and injustice constantly tormented them. "You no i am tirde wearing cotton sack, flour sack," wrote Glennie French of Arkansas; "i am in kneed, children in kneed, house in kneed." Said another: "it is worser now than it was slavery. . . ." Lula Parchman: ". . . We are Starveing, being driven from place to place, and pressed down by The unjust laws of man." Ansley Garrett: "we are working men, and till the soil, and all we want is Justice." [6]

The Agricultural Adjustment Act of 1933, the New Deal's initial response to the rural ravages of the Depression, only exacerbated the sharecroppers' distress. Congress paid scant attention to the croppers when it considered this legislation. They were not parties to AAA contracts between landlords and the Secretary of Agriculture. Nor did they participate in local administration of the act; county committees were invariably dominated by planters. AAA provisions for acreage reduction often meant tenant displacement. From the sharecroppers' perspective, however, the act's most deplorable feature was the allocation of proportionally larger benefit payments to landlords because of their greater equity in the crops produced. Initially, payments went directly to landlords, and croppers complained that they rarely received their share. Subsequently, when payments to croppers were required, landlords altered their status to that of wage hands in order to disqualify them. AAA policy thus tended to drive sharecroppers and tenant farmers from the land, to lower their status still further, or to reinforce their subservience to their landlords. The purpose of the act, AAA director Chester Davis reminded his district agents, was to meet the agricultural emergency, not to solve a "deep-seated social problem." [7]

---

equipment and animals and paid between one-fourth and one-third of the crop; sharecroppers, receiving animals and tools along with the land, usually paid one-half of their crop. Approximately one-third of all southern tenant farmers in the midthirties were sharecroppers. The Southern Tenant Farmers Union included both.

[5] Report of the President's Committee, *Farm Tenancy*, p. 5.

[6] Workers Defense League, *The Disinherited Speak* (Report), pp. 4, 7, 19, 27.

[7] Edwin G. Nourse, Joseph S. Davis, and John D. Black, *Three Years of the Agricultural Adjustment Administration*, pp. 255–256, 342–348; Henry I. Richards, *Cotton Under the Agricultural Adjustment Act*, pp. 17–19, 135–146; Myrdal, *American Dilemma*, pp. 255–256; Harold Hoffsommer, "The AAA and the Cropper," *Social Forces*, XIII (May 1935), 494–502; David Eugene Conrad, "The Forgotten Farmers: The AAA and the Southern Tenants, 1933–36" (unpublished doctoral dissertation), pp. 56, 78–80, 101.

The "social problem" was particularly acute in northeastern Arkansas, across the Mississippi River from Memphis. In the Delta, friction between landlords and tenants, fanned by AAA, threatened to ignite a social conflagration. Rich bottom lands, which thirty years earlier had supported a prosperous lumbering industry, no longer seemed capable of sustaining their inhabitants. Delta plantations—new, large, and highly commercialized—attracted thousands of tenants, whose distress absentee planters rarely recognized. Displacement resulting from government policies, coinciding with rapidly increasing mechanization, confronted Arkansas sharecroppers with a dismal future.[8] Disenchanted with the New Deal, and disgruntled over their squalid existence, they grew receptive to alternatives. The Socialist Party, which spawned vigorous local organizations in the Delta, eagerly became the catalyst for their discontent.

Some years earlier, in 1927, Harry L. Mitchell, the son of a Tennessee tenant farmer, had moved to Tyronza, a tiny Arkansas town thirty-five miles west of Memphis. In his youth Mitchell had become acquainted with the South's severest problems: poverty and race relations. When he was eight years old, he picked cotton and received fifty cents for ten hours work. At ten, he witnessed his first lynching. After graduation from high school Mitchell raised crops in Tennessee and in Mississippi, before moving to Tyronza in search of work that would sustain him and his wife. Local sharecroppers fared so poorly, however, that he decided to enter the dry-cleaning business instead.

The Depression provided Mitchell with unexpected leisure; he used it to read the works of Upton Sinclair and to follow the progress of Huey Long's Share Our Wealth program. One day he wandered into the gas station operated by his neighbor, Henry Clay East. After listening to East expound his political theories, Mitchell told him that he sounded like a socialist. Before long, both men were exploring socialist solutions to capitalism's mounting ills. During the 1932 presidential campaign they drove to Memphis to hear Norman Thomas, the Socialist Party's nominee. Thomas' speech struck a responsive chord; Mitchell and East decided, "We should organize."[9] Mitchell became state secretary of the Socialist Party. He and East organized Socialist locals and led spirited protests against planter control of administration of New Deal relief and public

[8] Stuart Jamieson, *Labor Unionism in American Agriculture*, pp. 303–306.

[9] Harry L. Mitchell, "Biographical Sketch," Southern Tenant Farmers Union Papers (cited hereafter as STFU), Box 80; Harry L. Mitchell, Oral History Collection, Columbia University (cited hereafter as COHC), pp. 2–9; Donald H. Grubbs, "The Southern Tenant Farmers Union and the New Deal" (unpublished doctoral dissertation), pp. 81–83.

works programs. Increasingly, however, their attention turned to the desperate plight of sharecroppers and tenant farmers.

Mitchell learned about Delta plantation problems from customers of his dry-cleaning establishment. Planters admired him as a rising entrepreneur and spoke freely about their labor difficulties. White and Negro sharecroppers found a sympathetic listener, and they, too, confided their grievances. Mitchell came to believe that Upton Sinclair and other Socialists offered more promising solutions to agrarian and industrial distress than did the President or the Congress of the United States.[10] Soon he and East were being praised as "natural-born Socialists. . . ." Party members in Arkansas were encouraged by their energy and dedication. "Here is a chance," a Socialist organizer told Norman Thomas late in 1933, "to grip them tightly." In Arkansas, Thomas' correspondent continued, "you will find the true proletariat . . . moving irresistibly toward revolution and no less." But, Thomas was warned, "the Communists, if they ever learn to use Southern leaders would sweep these bottom-lands like wildfire"; therefore, "We MUST have a Socialist program for sharecroppers."[11] Heartened by the news that Mitchell had "pepped up things" in the Delta, Thomas decided to personally encourage his Southern disciples.[12]

In mid-February 1934 Thomas visited Tyronza and addressed gatherings of Socialists and sharecroppers. During lunch at Clay East's house Mitchell and East related their recent futile attempt to run for office on the Socialist Party ticket. Thomas conceded that political activity was a risky venture for Arkansas Socialists; but, he suggested, why not organize a sharecroppers' union?[13] The idea appealed to Mitchell and East, both of whom pledged their co-operation.[14] Thomas' visit "stirred up a hornets nest" in eastern Arkansas; the publicity it received infuriated Tyronza residents. Under cover of darkness, however, Mitchell managed to organize a Socialist Party local in Tyronza.[15] Within six weeks he was predicting that nearly every local sharecropper would join a union; in fact,

[10] Mitchell, "Biographical Sketch," STFU, Box 80; Mitchell, COHC, p. 8.

[11] Martha B. Johnson to Norman Thomas, November 7, 1933, Norman Thomas Papers, Box 6.

[12] Clarence Senior to Thomas, November 22, 23, 1933, *ibid*.

[13] Mitchell, COHC, pp. 19–20B; Norman Thomas, COHC, pp. 92–93; Mitchell to Thomas, March 11, 1934, Thomas Papers, Box 9.

[14] Mitchell to Thomas, February 21, 1934, *ibid*., Box 8.

[15] Mitchell to Thomas, February 21, 1934, *ibid*.; William R. Amberson to Roger Baldwin, March 10, 1934, ACLU, Vol. 733; Mitchell to Thomas, April 12, 1934, Thomas Papers, Box 10.

he told Thomas, with ample time and sufficient funds all the croppers might be brought into the Socialist Party as well. "No other organization or persons," Mitchell observed, "have dared to challenge the landlords supremacy." [16]

While Mitchell and East extended their network of Socialist locals, Thomas launched a vigorous verbal assault on the New Deal's agricultural program. "Never in America," he told Secretary of Agriculture Henry Wallace, "have I seen more hopeless poverty" than among the Arkansas sharecroppers. "My criticism is not of a section," he insisted, "but of a nation and of an economic program." [17] The political overtones of Thomas' and Mitchell's activities did not escape notice. Tyronza's town council passed a resolution deploring the Socialist Party's "frenzied efforts to organize and send forth propaganda intended to discredit the Democratic party. . . ." And the chief of AAA's cotton section noted the development of "a well-defined and very widespread political attack upon our entire agricultural adjustment program. . . ." [18]

Mitchell's efforts soon brought impressive results. By July he could count on three full-time organizers and more than a dozen communities with party locals. He even hoped to swallow up Huey Long's Share Our Wealth clubs. ". . . We can fix things," he told Thomas, "so that it won't look as tho' these things are direct party activities." [19] Mitchell was particularly successful in the Tyronza area, where, two years earlier, absentee landlord Hiram Norcross had earned the sharecroppers' enmity by evicting fifty of them from his plantation. Subsequently, his sharecroppers alleged, Norcross cheated them out of their AAA benefit payments. During the spring of 1934 Mitchell organized Norcross' croppers into a branch of the Socialist Party local at Tyronza. When Norcross insisted that they sign a contract which they considered highly unjust, they verged on rebellion.[20] Mitchell parlayed their discontent into the sharecroppers' union suggested by Thomas.

On a sultry July evening a small group of white and Negro croppers,

[16] Mitchell to Thomas, March 25, 1934, *ibid.*, Box 9.

[17] Thomas to Henry Wallace, February 22, 1934, *ibid.*, Box 8; Thomas to Editor, Memphis *Commercial Appeal*, March 3, 1934, *ibid.*, Box 9.

[18] Resolution, Town Council of Tyronza, March 17, 1934, and Cully Cobb to Paul Appleby, March 28, 1934, both in Agricultural Adjustment Administration Papers, RG 145.

[19] Mitchell to Thomas, June 18, 1934, Thomas Papers, Box 11; Mitchell to Thomas, July 4, 1934, *ibid.*, Box 12.

[20] Mitchell, COHC, p. 13; Mitchell to Thomas, April 12, 1934, Thomas Papers, Box 10; Mitchell to Thomas, July 28, 1934, Workers Defense League Papers.

encouraged by Mitchell and East, gathered in a rickety schoolhouse on the Norcross plantation to organize the first local of the Southern Tenant Farmers Union. Several had been members of a Negro union wiped out in the Elaine massacre fifteen years earlier; some of the whites were former Ku Klux Klan members. For the moment, however, they put aside racial animosities and elected a white sharecropper chairman and a Negro minister vice-chairman. Mitchell and East arrived during a heated debate on the merits of the union's becoming a legal organization; they supported the proposition. On July 26 the union was incorporated. Its declaration of principles spoke of two agricultural classes: exploiters and "actual tillers of the soil who have been ground down to dire poverty. . . ." The union dedicated itself to the abolition of tenancy. "We seek," it stated, "to establish a co-operative order of society by legal and peaceable methods." [21]

The very existence of the union posed a direct and radical challenge to the established order in Arkansas. Militantly class conscious and avowedly interracial, it ran roughshod over local prejudices. Borrowing some of the tactics of trade unions and the fervor of religious revivals, it quickly became the sharecroppers' advocate, teacher, preacher, and lobbyist. But the salient characteristic of the Southern Tenant Farmers Union was its role as Socialist critic of New Deal agricultural policy. Its organizing drive illustrated its character as agitator; the attendant nationwide publicity never ceased to be a Socialist thorn in the New Deal's side. In no other area, perhaps, did Socialists mount such an effective counterthrust to the program of the Roosevelt administration.[22]

The union took its radical cues from Mitchell, its indefatigable leader and spokesman. Mitchell's primary hope was to build a strong radical movement; the union, he thought, could lay the foundation for such a movement in the South. "I felt that it was necessary to have some support," he explained, and "we had none whatever until we aligned ourselves with Thomas and his crowd." [23]

Mitchell tried to camouflage the union's Socialist ties. ". . . We have got to be as wise as owls," he once said, "and appear as gentle as lambs." [24] In private, however, Mitchell showed less restraint. "If we can build the Union," he told a close friend, "we will take over all the damn planta-

[21] Mitchell, COHC, pp. 22–25; documents in STFU, Box 80; Kester, *Revolt*, pp. 55–57; STFU Constitution, copy in Workers Defense League Papers.

[22] For an account that exaggerates STFU independence from the Socialist Party, see Grubbs, "Southern Tenant Farmers Union," pp. 89–91.

[23] Mitchell to Gardner Jackson, September 3, 1936, STFU, Box 4.

[24] Mitchell to J. R. Butler, February 2, 1936 (unsigned), STFU, Box 1.

tions. . . ." He anticipated the time when, as he expressed it, "the whole South can come under the Collectivist Farm system." [25]

Although he looked to the future, Mitchell did not ignore the present. He and Clay East became the union's best organizers; every night they drove to an outlying church or schoolhouse to rally the croppers. (East, who was Tyronza's sheriff, showed a fine grasp of local *Realpolitik;* on these nightly ventures he displayed his star and pistol prominently.) Mitchell instructed his organizers: "Never promise the workers that the Union is going to do something for them. Let them join the Union and do something themselves." [26] He won pledges of support from county preachers, Negro and white, and from some local businessmen who faced financial ruin from competition with the planters' commissaries. Early in August he assured Norman Thomas that "the share-croppers black and white are going to go down the line with us. . . . The union is growing." [27]

As it spread to adjacent counties, the Southern Tenant Farmers Union attracted fervent supporters. Howard Kester, a Methodist minister and a member of the Socialist Party's executive council, learned of union activities through party contacts and offered his services. Kester, who described AAA as the "bastard child of a decadent capitalism and a youthful Fascism," became Mitchell's devoted assistant. Other young radical ministers flocked to Arkansas to join the battle. The Socialist Party's Workers Defense League sent a representative to handle publicity, and the League for Industrial Democracy made financial contributions. Protestant denominations lent spiritual support, and the American Civil Liberties Union furnished legal aid. Students from Commonwealth College in Mena traveled across the state to help with assorted tasks; for a brief time the president of their student association was a young Arkansan named Orval E. Faubus. "If it had not been for outside support," H. L. Mitchell admitted, ". . . we never would have been able to continue. . . ." [28]

Sharecroppers responded to their union—which they occasionally confused with a religion—with devotion and courage. Gathering in abandoned

[25] Mitchell to Howard Kester, March 22, 1936, Mitchell to Clyde Johnson, April 20, 1936, STFU, Box 2.

[26] Kester, *Revolt*, p. 58; Mitchell, COHC, p. 24; "Instructions to Organizers," No. 1, STFU, Box 1.

[27] Mitchell to Thomas, August 2, 1934, Mitchell to Thomas, August 9, 1934, Workers Defense League Papers.

[28] Kester, *Revolt*, p. 26; Oren Stephens, "Revolt on the Delta," *Harper's Magazine*, CLXXXIII (November 1941), 656–664; Grubbs, "Southern Tenant Farmers Union," pp. 268, 304–308; Mitchell, COHC, pp. 68–69; Arthur M. Schlesinger, Jr., *The Coming of the New Deal*, p. 377.

warehouses or in the cotton fields, always late in the evening after a full day of backbreaking work, they sang "We Shall Not Be Moved" and recited the Lord's Prayer before attending to union business. "I do not mind giving my life for the union," one of them told Mitchell. "We ant goner quit if for eney thing," promised the president of one local, "for we are in the Union to live or Die." Another sharecropper wanted "to help in The Fight for Rightiousness" because he had been "ignored and rejected. . . ." The planters, Mitchell was told, "are far worse than Fairrow was in his day." [29]

Planters translated their political and economic power into persistent anti-union violence. They padlocked church doors and packed school-houses with bales of hay to prevent union rallies. Their riding bosses flogged croppers sympathetic to the union and drove them from their plantations. The Harahan bridge, spanning the Mississippi at Memphis, became the gateway to safety for union organizers. [30] Two days after the formation of a local in Crittenden County its organizer, a Negro minister, was beaten and jailed. His arrest posed a serious challenge to the union: failure to defend a Negro member might split it asunder. Mitchell and East sought assistance from a Memphis attorney, but he told them, "I'm one Jew who isn't going over to Crittenden County to get a Nigra out of jail because he is charged with organizing a union." The lawyer claimed to have left his courage in the Argonne Forest and ushered them out of his office with a copy of *Progress and Poverty* as a gift. But an attorney from Marked Tree, accompanied by fifty white sharecroppers, marched to the local jail and secured the organizer's release. [31]

During the winter of 1934–1935 the union, confronted by unremitting violence, turned to Washington for redress. When the Department of Agriculture failed to respond with sufficient vigor, union demands upon the Roosevelt administration grew more strident and criticism of the New Deal increasingly vitriolic. The union despaired of obtaining government action yet never tired of seeking federal assistance. Alleged federal indifference served as a perpetual rallying cry for the union; its leaders vented their frustrations, caused by local conditions, in attacks on a re-

[29] Thomas, COHC, pp. 96–97; Naomi Mitchison, "White House and Marked Tree," *New Statesman and Nation*, IX (April 27, 1935), 586; Workers Defense League, *The Disinherited Speak*, pp. 16, 17, 19, 27, 29.

[30] Kester, *Revolt*, pp. 61–62, 78.

[31] *Ibid.*, pp. 60–61; Mitchell, COHC, pp. 29–30; Mitchell to A. L. Wirin, August 13, 1934, ACLU, Vol. 733.

mote target that, unlike the planters, would not retaliate.[32] Furthermore, union publicity was useful to the Socialist Party. As one party official wrote, during a well-publicized union fracas, "This is our chance to make a real splash in the country, because we are right there in the heart of the business." [33]

Early in 1935 two incidents focused national attention on the union, winning it new converts and underscoring the New Deal's failure to alleviate the distress of sharecroppers. In Marked Tree, at a union rally called to celebrate the return of a delegation from Washington, Methodist preacher Ward Rodgers told the assembled sharecroppers that if necessary, in the absence of relief, he "would lead a group that would lynch every planter in Poinsett County. . . ." Rodgers was arrested as he left the speakers' platform and charged with anarchy, blasphemy, and attempted overthrow of the government. A jury of planters, meeting in an impromptu court session held in a local store, convicted him of anarchy. Shortly thereafter Marked Tree adopted an ordinance prohibiting speeches in public without the prior consent of town officials.[34]

The Rodgers incident had predictable consequences. It enraged the planters, some of whom had heard Rodgers' remarks; it attracted hundreds of new union members, who responded to Rodgers' foolhardy courage; and it made the union a pawn in efforts by Socialists and Communists to capitalize on the incident. Socialists in New York worked diligently to thwart attempts by the International Labor Defense, legal arm of the Communist Party, to assume responsibility for Rodgers' defense. A trusted Socialist was sent to work with the union, and Norman Thomas decided to return to Arkansas.[35]

In mid-March Thomas arrived in the Delta. Union leaders hoped that his visit would expedite the transfer of their following into the Socialist Party. Rodgers expected Thomas' appearance to spur "a terrific organizational campaign for the Socialist Party of Arkansas. . . ." Mitchell told the party's executive secretary that Thomas' trip "would mean that the

[32] For AAA confusion over union attacks and entreaties, see Paul A. Porter to William R. Amberson, April 2, 1935, Thomas Papers, Box 17.

[33] Clarence Senior to Edward Levinson, February 6, 1935, Socialist Party Papers.

[34] Ward Rodgers to Thomas, January 24, 1935, Thomas Papers, Box 16; Mitchell, COHC, pp. 34–36; *New York Times*, April 16, 1935.

[35] On union gains see Amberson to Lucille B. Milner, January 25, 1935, ACLU, Vol. 827. On Socialist-Communist rivalry, see Thomas to Mitchell, January 26, 1935, and Senior to Mitchell, January 29, 1935, both in Socialist Party Papers.

entire section would go for us." [36] Thomas' visit, however, was abruptly interrupted. While speaking in Birdsong he was surrounded by a crowd of angry planters and deputies. Demanding to know by whose authority he was being restrained from speaking, Thomas was told that no "Gawd-Damn Yankee Bastard" was welcome in Arkansas.[37] He was escorted from the platform and driven to the county line; after his return to New York he described a "reign of terror" to a nationwide radio audience. Eastern Arkansas, Thomas told a friend, "is more cruel and barbarous than any place I've ever seen." [38]

The Rodgers and Thomas debacles marked the onset of a critical period for the Southern Tenant Farmers Union. Arkansas planters and officials, observed a *New York Times* correspondent, had become convinced that only drastic steps would forestall the overthrow of "white supremacy, Christianity, the American flag and the sanctity of home and family ties. . . ." [39] They banned union meetings and arrested members on the slightest pretext. Sharecroppers were evicted, their churches were burned, and vigilantes patrolled the highways. Mitchell and other union officers fled to Memphis to establish new headquarters. Night riders tried to assassinate the union attorney and vice-president; Clay East was escorted out of Mississippi County; the body of a union member was found floating in the Coldwater River. Planters in Marked Tree sponsored a company union, placed a loyal minister in charge, and tried to lure STFU members with promises of immediate employment. "We are on the edge of bloodshed," Mitchell told the Department of Agriculture. "When that blood flows it will drip down over your Department, from the Secretary at the top to [the] Cotton section at the bottom." [40]

Norman Thomas deluged friends in Washington with vivid accounts of the Arkansas situation. He insisted, according to one of them, "that anything else the liberals do, while remaining inactive with respect to

[36] Rodgers to Senior, March 10, 1935, and Mitchell to Senior, February 10, 1935, *ibid.*

[37] H. L. Mitchell, "Norman Thomas Visits the Cotton Fields," copy in Thomas Papers.

[38] Thomas, COHC, pp. 82–84; Kester, *Revolt*, pp. 80–85; Thomas to Brooks Hays, March 30, 1935, Thomas Papers, Box 16.

[39] *New York Times*, April 15, 1935.

[40] Kester, *Revolt*, pp. 82–84; Mitchell to Jack Herling, March 22, 1935, and Mitchell to Thomas, March 26, 27, 1935, both in Thomas Papers, Box 16; Harold E. Fey, "Sharecroppers Organize," *Fellowship* (April 1935), clipping in ACLU, Vol. 786; Mitchell to Paul A. Porter, March 27, 1935, AAA Papers, RG 145.

[the sharecroppers], is merely petifogging." [41] His words registered. On April 30 Representative Tom Amlie (Prog.-Wis.) introduced H. R. 270, a resolution drafted by former AAA attorney Lee Pressman denouncing "wholesale violations of the ordinary civil rights of these agricultural producers when they seek to exercise their prerogatives as American citizens to protest against their conditions and to organize for their mutual benefit and protection." Amlie's resolution authorized the appointment of a committee to investigate the living and working conditions of sharecroppers, tenant farmers, and farm laborers. [42]

Prominent religious leaders explored the idea of a church-sponsored investigation, Dr. Reinhold Niebuhr sounded out officials of the Federal Council of Churches: "Some of the men most active in the [Arkansas] situation," he noted, "believe that a Church committee could do more to mitigate the terrific social struggle down there than anyone else, since the State is solidly religious." Niebuhr believed that "a good Committee of liberal Southern churchmen will help to stiffen the backs of the parsons in Arkansas, who are trying to resist the hysterical mood of the planters." [43] James Myers of the Federal Council paid a visit to Arkansas, where members of the local clergy persuaded him that for the moment, at least, outside ministers should not attempt to intervene. [44]

When the Southern Tenant Farmers Union refused to halt its organizing campaign during the winter of 1935–1936, evictions of sharecroppers reached their peak. Hundreds of families lined the Arkansas highways, huddling together in the snow for warmth, without food, adequate clothing, shelter, or firewood. On January 16, 1936, the deputy sheriff of Earle disbanded a union meeting called to protest evictions from a Cross County cotton plantation; union members scattered amid a hail of bullets, and two received shotgun wounds in the back. When news of the incident reached union headquarters in Memphis—the only place where STFU

[41] Frederick A. Ballard to Baldwin, April 5, 1935, ACLU, Vol. 827.

[42] Gardner Jackson to Baldwin, April 24, 1935, ACLU, Vol. 779; copy of H.R. 270 in ACLU, Vol. 781. Jackson had earlier urged investigations by the AAA, the National Labor Relations Board, and the Labor Department, or by a Senate committee. Concerning the latter, Jackson admitted, "the out about that is that it would necessitate a special appropriation" (Jackson to Mary Hillyer, March 29, 1935, Thomas Papers, Box 16).

[43] Reinhold Niebuhr to Rev. Samuel McCrea Cavert and Rev. James Myers, April 2, 1935, and Niebuhr to Cavert, April 8, 1935, Federal Council of Churches Industrial Department Papers.

[44] James Myers to Bishop William Scarlett, May 8, 1935, *ibid.*

organizers, known as the "exiles," could meet in safety—the union called another protest rally for the following day. Three union workers decided to attend: Howard Kester; Evelyn Smith, a girl from New Orleans, just out of high school and a dedicated socialist, who worked as union secretary; and Herman Goldberger, a Memphis attorney who came to the union by way of the International Labor Defense.[45]

Early in the afternoon of a bleak January day, Kester, Goldberger, and Miss Smith arrived at St. Peter's Baptist Church (Negro), near Earle. First Goldberger spoke to the sharecroppers, who packed the small building. Kester, who followed him to the lectern, was interrupted by the entry of a group of armed planters and deputies. Two of the intruders, kicking and slapping, pulled Kester from the building. Others used ax handles to empty the church of sharecroppers and their wives and children. Goldberger also was roughly treated. The two union men and Miss Smith were shoved into Kester's automobile; armed deputies, with guns drawn, stood on each running board. They directed Kester through Earle to a prearranged spot several miles from town, where he and his passengers were ordered from the car. "It was my feeling at the time," Kester later recalled, "that the mob actually planned to lynch us or beat us severely but the presence of Miss Smith . . . moved them to milder considerations." Warned of continued violence "if the damn union wasn't dissolved," Kester was advised to stay out of Arkansas or risk death.[46] From union headquarters Kester wired an account of the incident to Norman Thomas. "We should," he insisted, "work for a congressional investigation immediately. It would do the Committee good to see all of these poor, hapless families sitting on the roadside in snow tonight." Mitchell reiterated Kester's plea: "Now is the time," he urged Thomas, "to push that Resolution of Amlie's for a Congressional investigation."[47]

In Washington, several people shared Kester's and Mitchell's determination to publicize the sharecroppers' distress by means of a congressional inquiry. One, Gardner Jackson, retained a deep concern for exploited

[45] Mitchell to Thomas [January 1936], Thomas Papers, Box 20; Howard Kester to Jerold S. Auerbach, May 4, 1963; Conrad, "Forgotten Farmers," p. 133; Mitchell, COHC, p. 62; William R. Amberson to Thomas, November 1, 1935, Thomas Papers, Box 18.

[46] Kester to Auerbach, May 4, 1963; Mitchell to Thomas [January 1936], Thomas Papers, Box 20; Socialist Call, January 25, 1936; Progressive, February 1, 1936.

[47] Kester to Thomas, January 18, 1936, and Mitchell to Thomas [January 1936], Thomas Papers, Box 20.

farm workers from his student days at Amherst College when, during weekend visits to Northampton, he had become friendly with Polish workers in tobacco and onion fields. ("I felt they had a raw deal," Jackson reminisced many years afterward.[48]) After college Jackson channeled his effusive energy into assisting those who had encountered "a raw deal." Swept up in the turmoil of the Sacco-Vanzetti case ("It just shook thunder out of me," Jackson remembered), he dedicated himself to finding "the right opportunity for crusading." The Depression brought a plethora of opportunities. As a free-lance journalist Jackson covered the dissolution of the Bonus Army by climbing aboard one of the tanks headed toward Anacostia Flats to dispel the dispirited veterans. Rexford Tugwell and Jerome Frank brought him into the Department of Agriculture, where he worked in the office of the Consumers' Counsel. When the office was abolished in 1935, as a result of the sharp internecine battle between Frank and Chester Davis over remedying the sharecroppers' miseries, Jackson, soon to be known as the "Champion of Lost Causes," organized the National Committee on Rural and Social Planning.[49]

For months the National Committee represented farm workers before various government agencies, but with scant success. Howard Kester's tribulations galvanized Jackson once again. He consulted with Senator Edward P. Costigan (D-Colo.) and Senator Lewis B. Schwellenbach (D-Wash.) about a Senate investigation. He wired Kester funds to enable him to come to Washington in order to recount his experiences. He alerted the People's Lobby, of which he was vice-president, to prepare for Kester's visit.[50]

The People's Lobby was an unpretentious organization that reflected the progressivism of Benjamin C. Marsh, its dynamic leader. Marsh, a "tall stooping loose-jointed Westerner, with white hair, an aquiline Yankee beak and a genial and mobile bright black eye," worked as the liberals' favorite Washington lobbyist.[51] He tried always to measure up to the creed of his mentor, Dr. Simon Patten: "Faith is unimpeded tendency to activity."[52] Marsh quickly translated his faith in the justice of the sharecroppers' cause into activity directed toward relieving their distress.

[48] Gardner Jackson, COHC, p. 697.

[49] *Ibid.*, pp. 223–224, 385, 422, 651–652; Mitchell, COHC, p. 76.

[50] Jackson to Thomas, February 25, 1936, Kester to Thomas, January 18, 1936, Jackson to Mary Fox, January 20, 1936, Mitchell to Thomas [January 1936], all in Thomas Papers, Box 20; Socialist *Call*, February 1, 1936.

[51] Edmund Wilson, "Two Protests," *The American Earthquake*, p. 303.

[52] Marsh, *Lobbyist for the People*, p. 6.

Marsh and Jackson conferred with Kester early in February. Kester brought affidavits collected by the Southern Tenant Farmers Union during a year of futile effort to make the sharecroppers' existence more tolerable. At this meeting plans were made for a dinner, with senators and congressmen in attendance, at which the groundwork for a congressional inquiry would be laid. One of the most avid supporters of the People's Lobby, Mrs. Ethel Clyde of New York, agreed to underwrite the dinner at Washington's Cosmos Club. She commissioned Jackson to assemble an appropriate gathering.[53]

Jackson sent a letter to officials of church organizations, to labor leaders, educators, and government personnel, urging their presence at the dinner. A group of senators and representatives, he noted, "believing the drive against civil liberties in various regions of the country during the past year or more merits the earnest concern of all American citizens," had agreed to sponsor "a private, informal dinner" on February 21 to consider suggestions for remedial measures. It included Senators Edward P. Costigan (D-Colo.), Robert M. La Follette, Jr. (Prog.-Wis.), Lewis B. Schwellenbach (D-Wash.), and Burton K. Wheeler (D-Mont.), and Representatives Caroline O'Day (D-N.Y.), Maury Maverick (D-Tex.), and George J. Schneider (Prog.-Wis.). The purpose of the dinner, Jackson wrote, "will be specifically to assess the widespread violations of our Constitutional Bill of Rights . . . and to determine whether any Congressional action looking toward the thorough investigation and subsequent remedy is possible." [54]

A number of concerned people responded to Jackson's call. Officials of the National Grange, the Farm Bureau, and the National Farmers Union attended. John L. Lewis led the labor delegation. Representatives of the Federal Council of Churches, the National Catholic Welfare Conference, and the Central Conference of American Rabbis were present. In addition to the sponsors, Congress was represented by Senators Lynn Frazier (R-N.D.) and Henrik Shipstead (FL-Minn.), and Representatives Marion Zioncheck (D-Wash.), Fred Sisson (D-N.Y.), and John Sparkman (D-Ala.). Howard Kester came from Memphis, bringing a sharecropper who

[53] John Herling to Thomas, February 9, 1936, Thomas Papers, Box 20. Mrs. Clyde, granddaughter of the founder of the Clyde steamship line, had met Ben Marsh in 1931. Her interest in the work of the People's Lobby had prompted her to cover its deficit and finance the promotion campaign for its *Bulletin* (Marsh, *Lobbyist*, p. 91).

[54] Jackson to Mrs. Ethel Clyde, February 11, 1936, letter in possession of Mrs. Clyde; Jackson to Baldwin, February 18, 1936, ACLU, Vol. 890.

had been beaten and was still bandaged—the "prize exhibit" for Jackson, who presided.[55]

Although Kester delivered the main address, a recapitulation of two years of terror in Arkansas, the remarks of John L. Lewis left the deepest impression, at least on Gardner Jackson. Lewis spoke knowingly, and with characteristic grandiloquence, of the chaotic situation in Arkansas. But he treated Jackson as "a very nice, young, immature, unrealistic boy, who had all the right instincts and yearnings but just didn't realize . . . how things in Congress really worked." Lewis thought that the idea of a congressional investigation of civil liberties infractions was "fanciful." "Not until there [is] blood flowing in the streets of our cities," he intoned, would Congress authorize such an inquiry.[56]

Jackson heard Lewis with dismay, for all except one of the congressmen and senators present had already expressed doubts. Finally, "with real sinking in my heart," Jackson turned to Bob La Follette. Quietly but firmly, the intense Wisconsin Progressive, just forty years old but with a decade in the Senate behind him, expressed his conviction that the Senate would authorize the inquiry that Jackson, Marsh, and Kester hoped for. "Pat," he told Jackson, "if you'll set up a committee of [the] people here . . . and we get a resolution, I will undertake to introduce it and we will try to get it passed."[57] One month later La Follette fulfilled his pledge.

[55] Marsh, *Lobbyist*, pp. 211–212; Jackson, COHC, pp. 665–666; Kester to Auerbach, May 4, 1963.

[56] Kester to Auerbach, May 4, 1963; Jackson, COHC, pp. 663, 666–667; interview with Gardner Jackson, December 3, 1963.

[57] Jackson, COHC, pp. 665–667; interview with Jackson, December 3, 1963; Jackson to La Follette, read at Workers Defense League dinner, May 9, 1941, in Workers Defense League, *Labor, Defense and Democracy* (Report), p. 31; interview with Mrs. Clyde, May 16, 1963. In addition to the Kester incident, the flogging, tarring, and feathering of Joseph Shoemaker on the evening of November 30, 1935, contributed to the sense of urgency that generated the Cosmos Club dinner. Shoemaker, a socialist who hoped to capture the Democratic Party in Florida, as Upton Sinclair had done in California, was meeting with friends to organize the "Modern Democrats" when he was arrested. After his release from the Tampa police station he was "taken for a ride," apparently with the collusion of police officers. Left unconscious after a merciless beating, Shoemaker eventually made his way to a hospital, where he died on December 10. Norman Thomas and the ACLU publicized the incident throughout the country (Committee for the Defense of Civil Rights in Tampa, *Tampa—Tar and Terror* [Report]; Federal Council *Information Service*, May 9, 1936; John Davids to Mary Fox, December 6, 1935, James Myers to John Davids, December 10, 1935, Thomas Papers, Box 19; *Labor, Defense and Democracy*, p. 3).

〜〜〜 III 〜〜〜

A Committee to Drain
the Industrial Swamp

THE plight of Arkansas sharecroppers did not alone account for Senator La Follette's promise at the Cosmos Club dinner. The Southern Tenant Farmers Union was not politically strong enough to overcome traditional congressional apathy, or hostility, toward an investigation of alleged infringements of civil liberties. Although Congress had manifested concern for civil rights under the duress of civil war, it had rarely admitted responsibility for the defense of civil liberties.[1] New Deal politics also were an impediment: Senator Joseph T. Robinson of Arkansas, one of Roosevelt's stalwart congressional leaders, objected to an investigation of conditions in his home state.[2] Furthermore, many advocates of a civil liberties inquiry believed that organization of labor in industry, rather than in a southern plantation region, presented the most pressing civil liberties issues. The sharecropper story might constitute a chapter in a larger study of insensitivity to the Bill of Rights, but it could hardly stand as the entire volume. In 1935–1936, however, other chapters were being written.

In December 1935 Edward Levinson, labor editor of the New York *Post*, published *I Break Strikes!*, a bitter indictment of professional strikebreakers and their self-proclaimed "king," Pearl L. Bergoff.[3] Levinson's

[1] By "civil rights" are meant those constitutional guarantees, particularly in the Fourteenth and Fifteenth Amendments, that require equality of treatment for all American citizens. By "civil liberties" are meant those constitutional guarantees, particularly in the First Amendment, that touch on the freedom of expression and belief. (The procedural guarantees in the Second–Eighth Amendments are also "civil liberties" guarantees.) Cf. Andrew Hacker, "The Indifferent Majority," *New Leader*, XLVI (March 18, 1963), 18–22.

[2] Joseph T. Robinson to Norman Thomas, April 3, 1935, Norman Thomas Papers, Box 17.

[3] In an introduction to Levinson's subsequent book, *Labor on the March*, Walter Reuther wrote: "Almost singlehandedly, and certainly more than any other single

book, an expanded version of two *Post* articles written in 1934, stripped
the veneer of respectability from strikebreaking and exposed it as a thoroughly sordid business.[4] In fact, Levinson nearly did for strikebreaking
what Upton Sinclair had done for the meat-packing industry by publishing *The Jungle* thirty years earlier.

In the best muckraking style Levinson traced the strikebreaking business back to Allan Pinkerton, who launched the practice of hiring spies
and armed guards to corporations after the Civil War. Bergoff, a worthy
successor, added twentieth-century refinements to the art of strikebreaking. After 1909, when Bergoff's men broke the Rapid Transit Company
strike in Philadelphia, industrialists paid dearly for his services. His
"prison-pedigreed" minions precipitated riots, clashed with strikers, and
gassed civilians. Levinson studied their police records and concluded:
"Pimp and pickpocket, . . . swindler and slugger, fence and fugitive, briber
and usurer, blackmailer and extortionist, wire tapper and abductionist,
gambler and gunman, . . . they have all placed their left hands on their
hearts, raised their right hands in oath and been sent forth to uphold law
and order." Bergoff, a burly man nearing sixty, boasted, "There's not a
city I haven't broken a strike in." [5]

Levinson, a member of the Socialist Party, condemned the system more
than he did the men who embodied its worst aspects. Private industrial
armies, he believed, had a certain "immutability" under capitalism. Big
business blessed strikebreaking; government ignored it. "Violence by
labor," Levinson wrote, "has . . . been a drop in the bucket compared
with the force used by capital." [6] He convinced at least one reviewer, who
declared, "No one reading this cool, precise, and completely documented
record of strikebreaking in the United States can doubt, after it, that there
is a class war, whatever capitalists and their apologists may call it, and
that, in this war, the government does take sides, and the side it stands on

---

person, Eddie Levinson was responsible for the creation of the La Follette Senate
Civil Liberties Committee. The committee was established as a result of his exposure
of the pernicious system of labor espionage in American industry" (p. xiv). Frank
Winn, UAW Public Relations Director, confirmed this statement on Mr. Reuther's
behalf (Frank Winn to Jerold S. Auerbach, February 9, 1961). This statement exaggerates Levinson's importance, however; in fact, he said little about labor espionage.
  [4] *New York Post*, October 24, 25, 1934. Bergoff had told Levinson, "I have come
to look upon the services rendered by my organization . . . as basically similar to
those of the physician to the ailing individual."
  [5] Levinson, *I Break Strikes!*, pp. 10, 50, 76, 105, 118, 227.
  [6] *Ibid.*, pp. 145, 182, 186, 197.

is that of the property holders." [7] The impact of *I Break Strikes!* was felt throughout labor circles; in its 1935 convention the American Federation of Labor demanded an "immediate and thorough" investigation of agencies supplying strikebreakers, guards, and labor spies. [8]

No exposé of strikebreaking agencies, however, could even begin to encompass the range of anti-union practices that stifled organization and collective bargaining. The simplest and most direct weapon remained the power to discharge a man, or discriminate against him, for union activity. Section 7(a) of the National Industrial Recovery Act had the unanticipated consequence of encouraging use of a second weapon, the company union. [9] Company unions occupied the middle ground between individual bargaining and genuine collective bargaining; they usually indicated an employer's willingness to comply with the letter of a collective-bargaining statute, yet evade its spirit. [10] Prodded by company unions, employers, observed one worker, "would fix the floors, they would fix the lighting, they would give us a large milk bottle, but that was practically the extent of the company union's usefulness." [11] Management's favorite unions were those which, in Mr. Dooley's words, had "no strikes, no rules, no contracts, no scales, hardly iny wages, an' dam' few mimbers." [12]

Resistance to unionization prompted unprecedented government intervention in labor-management relations. New Deal labor policy involved the government in the very process of collective bargaining. [13] As the stakes of victory rose, labor and management militancy increased. The result, according to *Fortune*, was "the irrepressible conflict of the twentieth century." [14] The Roosevelt administration hoped to institutionalize

[7] Review by "I. S.," *Saturday Review of Literature*, XIII (December 28, 1935), 19–20.

[8] American Federation of Labor, *Report of Proceedings of the Fifty-Fifth Annual Convention* (1935), p. 610; Socialist *Call*, March 21, 1936.

[9] "Employer Interference with Lawful Union Activity," *Columbia Law Review*, XXXVII (May 1937), 817–827.

[10] Alfred L. Bernheim and Dorothy Van Doren, eds., *Labor and the Government*, p. 78.

[11] U.S. Senate, Subcommittee of the Committee on Education and Labor, *Hearings Pursuant to S. Res. 266, Violations of Free Speech and Rights of Labor*, 74th–76th Congs., 1936–1940, Pt. 4, p. 1269 (cited hereafter as *Hearings*).

[12] Quoted in "The Coming Open-Shop War," *Literary Digest*, LXVII (November 27, 1920), 19.

[13] Irving Bernstein, *The New Deal Collective Bargaining Policy*, p. 39; Philip Taft, "Organized Labor and the New Deal," in Harry A. Millis, ed., *How Collective Bargaining Works*, pp. 4–5.

[14] "It Happened in Steel," *Fortune*, XV (May 1937), 91.

and localize this conflict in a succession of labor boards, but its early efforts failed dismally. Neither the National Labor Board, established to quell conflict and clarify Section 7(a) of the National Industrial Recovery Act, nor the first National Labor Relations Board, created under Public Resolution No. 44, resolved the issues. Francis Biddle, the NLRB's second chairman, found "the diverging conflict between labor and industry . . . at white heat." [15] By the spring of 1935 the NLRB "seemed to have come to the end of its tether." Its jurisdiction was restricted; it could rarely secure compliance; it exercised limited powers of subpoena; and it could not enforce its decisions. Its frustrations, and the sweeping midterm victory for the New Deal in the 1934 elections, prompted Senator Robert F. Wagner (D-N.Y.) to introduce new and, he hoped, permanent labor legislation.[16]

Wagner believed that "a free and self-disciplined labor movement . . . is essential to [the] democratic purpose of maintaining our system of free enterprise." [17] Consequently, Section 7 of his labor relations bill guaranteed to employees "the right to self-organization, to form, join, or assist labor organizations, to bargain collectively through representatives of their own choosing, and to engage in concerted activities, for the purpose of collective bargaining or other mutual aid or protection." Section 8 made it an unfair labor practice for an employer "to interfere with, restrain, or coerce" employees in the exercise of their rights. Clearly, this section was intended to proscribe such practices as espionage and blacklisting. [18]

Enactment of the Wagner bill, and its subsequent affirmation by the Supreme Court, marked a critical turning point for labor-management relations in the United States. "For the first time," David Brody has written, "workmen had the legal right to express through majority rule their desires on the question of union representation." [19] Before 1935 employers could oppose organization of their workers by almost any means they chose. Employees had no legal recourse against anti-union tactics;

[15] Francis Biddle, *In Brief Authority*, p. 8.

[16] Arthur M. Schlesinger, Jr., *The Coming of the New Deal*, p. 400; Bernstein, *New Deal Collective Bargaining Policy*, p. 88.

[17] Robert F. Wagner, Introduction to Louis G. Silverberg, ed., *The Wagner Act: After Ten Years*, p. 3.

[18] Bernstein, *New Deal Collective Bargaining Policy*, p. 94. Sections 7 and 8 of the bill are reproduced in Silverberg, *The Wagner Act*, p. 155.

[19] Brody, "The Emergence of Mass-Production Unionism," in John Braeman, Robert H. Bremner, and Everett Walters, eds., *Change and Continuity in Twentieth-Century America*, pp. 239, 243–244.

they did not, in fact, even have the legal right to organize a union. The Wagner Act gave workers this right; it constricted the sphere of legitimate management activity and expanded workers' freedom.

It was in the latter sense that the act was to be hailed as a momentous libertarian victory. First Amendment guarantees of freedom of speech and assembly now applied to the workers' side of labor-management relations. To be sure, the Wagner Act circumscribed the liberty of employers. Whereas employees could speak on behalf of unions, employers were no longer free to oppose them. Yet, on balance, the Wagner Act certainly enlarged the bounds of liberty. By 1935 absolute power of employer over employee could no longer be justified; the scales of liberty were readjusted accordingly.

Senator Wagner's bill authorized the creation of a new National Labor Relations Board to prevent employers from engaging in unfair labor practices affecting interstate commerce, and to investigate any controversy concerning the representation of employees in unions of their own choosing. But the NLRB, responsible for implementing the mandate of the Wagner Act, faced a series of ordeals. Within a short time, and at a critical juncture in American labor history, it became paralyzed by the very conflict it was established to resolve.[20] "It could not be expected that industry would welcome the act with open arms," the board admitted at the end of its first year. An employer, it observed, "must give up cherished habits of dictating terms of employment before he can expect his employees to take a reasonable and thoughtful attitude toward mutuality of interest in the enterprise in which they are both engaged."[21] Many employers, however, showed understandable reluctance to alter "cherished habits"; important segments of American industry ignored the Wagner Act and threatened to squeeze the life out of the NLRB. They launched a three-pronged campaign—verbal, legal, and clandestine—to maintain their hegemony. Within months a labor correspondent wrote, "The chief reason why there has been no news about the Board's achievements is that there have been no achievements. . . . The Board is . . . in a state bordering on suspended animation."[22]

On the day President Roosevelt signed the Wagner Act, the National Association of Manufacturers issued a bulletin advising its members that in most manufacturing industries unfair labor practices did not have a

[20] National Labor Relations Board, *First Annual Report*, p. 21.
[21] *Ibid.*, p. 67.
[22] William P. Mangold, "On the Labor Front," *New Republic*, CXXXIV (October 23, 1935), 297.

direct and substantial effect on interstate commerce. The legal department
of the NAM had already declared that the act did not apply to manufacturing—a statement that undoubtedly surprised the act's framers.[23] These
preliminary shots from management's propaganda arsenal presaged the
major verbal barrage on the Wagner Act that was to come two months
later. In September the National Lawyers' Committee of the American
Liberty League issued its report on the constitutionality—or unconstitu-
tionality—of the National Labor Relations Act.

"Times and our economy may have changed," conceded the Liberty
League lawyers, "but we have not changed our Constitution nor even
deemed it advisable so to do. It is our task to expound our constitutional
law as it is, apart from its economical or social consequences. . . ."[24] The
Lawyers' Committee scrutinized the Constitution, placed the Wagner Act
beside it, and found the latter wanting in several vital respects. First, the
act abridged freedom of contract, thereby denying due process of law.
If representatives selected by a majority of employees become the sole
bargaining agents for all, the prized freedom of a solitary worker to bargain with a corporation over the conditions of his employment would
vanish. Government might interfere with freedom of contract in order
to protect the health and safety of citizens; to do so on other pretexts
constituted "serious threats to our freedom of action, whether we stand
as employers or as employees."[25]

Not only did the Wagner Act annul freedom of contract; it also violated the Tenth Amendment. Labor relations and industrial controversies,
the Liberty League lawyers insisted, "are matters which are subject to the
powers reserved by the Constitution to the several States." The Railway
Labor Act of 1926 marked the maximum limit permissible in regulation of employer-employee relations. Such regulation "must be confined
to interstate carriers and . . . even in that field, congressional action will
be allowed only to the extent necessary to secure uninterrupted service."
The Wagner Act obviously put government on the wrong side of this
inviolable boundary; it transferred industrial relations from "the adjusting
processes of economic laws" to "the field of politics and . . . the artificial

[23] U.S. House of Representatives, *Hearings Before the Special Committee to Investigate the National Labor Relations Board*, XIII, 2578–80 (cited hereafter as
NLRB *Hearings*).

[24] American Liberty League, National Lawyers' Committee, *Report on the Constitutionality of the National Labor Relations Act*, p. x.

[25] *Ibid.*, pp. iii, iv, 117, 121.

processes of political machinery." [26] Furthermore, the Wagner Act would certainly "stimulate industrial strife and encourage the enmity of workers toward employers." [27] During his exegesis of the Wagner Act, Earl F. Reed, counsel to the Weirton Steel Company and chairman of the sub-committee responsible for drafting the Liberty League report, told re-porters: "When a lawyer tells a client that a law is unconstitutional it is then a nullity and he need no longer obey that law." [28] J. Warren Mad-den, chairman of the National Labor Relations Board, declared that "this kind of incitation to disobedience" made administration of the Wagner Act "impossible." [29]

With the Liberty League brief as their guide employers filed suit in District Courts to enjoin the National Labor Relations Board from fulfill-ing its statutory obligations. Charles Fahy, NLRB general counsel, de-clared that the board's task in meeting these suits "might have proved insuperable had it not been for one striking phenomenon. The suits dis-played a startling uniformity." [30] Thus the board's overworked staff could draft one rejoinder to cover virtually every complaint. Nevertheless, in-junction proceedings seriously hampered the board's work. By February 1936 District Courts had granted nearly forty temporary injunctions. Of eleven cases already decided the courts had ruled against the government in five. Some district judges enjoined the board even from holding hear-ings, the basic preliminary procedural step. During its first year the board encountered some eighty injunction proceedings; before the Supreme Court ruled on the constitutionality of the Wagner Act, the number would climb to nearly one hundred. Chairman Madden said, "District judges, who are directed by the statute not to disturb our cases, reach out with anxiety to get them," while judges of the Circuit Court of Appeals, "directed by the statute to handle our cases expeditiously, have great hesi-tation in doing anything with them." [31]

For twenty-one months, wrote Fahy ruefully, the Wagner Act existed

[26] *Ibid.*, pp. vi, 19, 65, 83.

[27] American Liberty League, *The Labor Relations Bill* (Report), p. 2.

[28] Quoted in George Wolfskill, *The Revolt of the Conservatives*, p. 72.

[29] NLRB *Hearings*, XIII, 2580; Charles Fahy, COHC, p. 164. NLRB member John Carmody called the Liberty League brief "almost subversive" and "a declaration of war" (John Carmody, COHC, p. 352).

[30] Charles Fahy, "The NLRB and the Courts," in Silverberg, *The Wagner Act*, p. 44.

[31] Mangold, "On the Labor Front," *New Republic*, CXXXVI (February 26, 1936), 74; NLRB, *First Annual Report*, p. 46; "Activities of National Labor Relations Board, 1936–37," *Monthly Labor Review*, XLVI (May 1938), 1144; Fahy, COHC, p. 164.

"as little more than a vehicle for protracted litigation. . . ." [32] The board was stymied by law suits. Its staff grew discouraged, and some able members departed for more promising positions elsewhere in the administration. The board tried to muster a counterattack: it accused the Liberty League lawyers of a "deliberate and concerted effort . . . to undermine public confidence in the [Wagner Act], to discourage compliance with it, to assist attorneys generally in attacks on the statute, and perhaps to influence the courts." [33] The charge had slight impact. Those friends of the labor movement who envisioned a "magna charta," noted *New York Times* labor correspondent Louis Stark, were finding the Wagner Act "a frail reed on which to lean." [34]

When the National Labor Relations Board held hearings, it encountered the very employer practices that the Wagner Act had prohibited. The board, anticipating continuous litigation, conducted a careful search for test cases, by which to measure the constitutional limits of its powers. It wanted one case in interstate transportation, another involving a large manufacturing company in a major industry, and, finally, one involving a smaller manufacturing company. The board encountered little difficulty finding cases that met its requirements. But the pervasive uniformity of antilabor practices in every type of case came as a distinct shock. Its very first case, involving the Greyhound bus company of Pennsylvania, furnished considerable evidence of industrial espionage. "Maintenance of open surveillance of the union meetings of employees," declared the board, "is a vicious form of restraint and coercion. . . ." [35]

But the board had only tapped the surface. In November 1935 all its members went to Detroit to hear evidence on the charge that the Fruehauf Trailer Company had interfered with its employees' efforts to unionize and had discharged several men for joining the United Automobile Workers. Detroit workers viewed the board skeptically. Dissatisfied with the administration of the Automobile Labor Board under the National

[32] Fahy, "The NLRB and the Courts," p. 46; Carmody, COHC, p. 359. It should be noted, however, that the board won numerous victories in the District and Circuit Courts. Even some defeats proved advantageous, for they enabled the board to select its strongest cases for appeal, thereby avoiding a defense of the Wagner Act based on weak cases not of its choosing. As the Schechter case indicated, the NRA had been less successful in this tactical maneuvering (Richard C. Cortner, *Wagner Act Cases*, pp. 98–99, 103–104).

[33] NLRB, *First Annual Report*, pp. 46–47.

[34] *New York Times*, March 8, 1936.

[35] Thomas I. Emerson, COHC, pp. 373–376; Case No. C–1, decided December 7, 1935, *Decisions and Orders of the National Labor Relations Board*, I, 22.

Recovery Administration and aware that spies honeycombed their unions, they now doubted the NLRB's ability to survive a Supreme Court test.[36] In fact, two weeks before hearings commenced board headquarters received a warning that the Fruehauf workers, upset by discriminatory discharges, were on the verge of striking. Frank Bowen, NLRB field agent in Detroit, had to assure the union organizer of immediate attention from the board in order to prevent a strike call, "which in this case would have indicated that the Union believed that they would have to resort to direct action and did not have much confidence in the ability of the Board to punish."[37]

Despite union suspicions the board had confidence in the strength of its case. Its regional attorney, evaluating the union complaint, concluded, "We are in a particularly good strategic position to 'crack down' on this Company."[38] Hearings began on November 6; a day later the NLRB attorney forced the vice-president of Fruehauf to admit that the company had hired a Pinkerton operative to spy on the union. The man had taken a job in the plant, but his essential task was to keep the company informed of union activities. Adept at his trade, he joined the union and became treasurer of the Fruehauf local. He reported to company officials at least once a week and passed union membership lists to the plant superintendent. With these lists in hand the company discharged nine men and threatened to discharge three others if they did not cease their union activities. The NLRB, ordering their reinstatement, stated that nothing "is more calculated to interfere with, restrain, and coerce employees in the exercise of their right to self-organization" than espionage.[39]

Later in November the board opened hearings in St. Louis on the charge that the Brown Shoe Company of Salem, Illinois, had engaged in unfair labor practices when it laid off four employees for their union activities. During the previous summer the president of the Boot and Shoe Workers Union wrote in desperation to Secretary of Labor Perkins to

[36] Louis G. Silverberg, "Detroit: The Battleground," in *The Wagner Act*, pp. 79–80.

[37] Frank H. Bowen to Benedict Wolf, October 23, 1935, NLRB Case No. C-2, National Labor Relations Board Case Files.

[38] G. L. Patterson to Charles Fahy, September 27, 1935, *ibid*.

[39] Frank H. Bowen to Benedict Wolf, November 7, 1935, *ibid.*; Case No. C-2, decided December 12, 1935, NLRB, *Decisions and Orders*, I, 68–76; NLRB, *First Annual Report*, p. 73; *New York Times*, November 8, 1935. The Fruehauf case, one of five to reach the Supreme Court in the test of the Wagner Act's constitutionality, is discussed at greater length in Cortner, *Wagner Act Cases*, pp. 50–51, 107–113.

request an investigation of the Brown Shoe Company's interference with labor organization. His letter recounted the classic experiences of union organizers:

"Many of our representatives have never been allowed to get further than the railroad station. They were met by large groups when they arrived and forced to leave on the next train, under threat of bodily injury. Several weeks ago, . . . our representatives had arranged to hold a meeting. . . . As fast as the different representatives reached the hotel they were threatened and ordered out of town. . . . The hall they had rented . . . was refused them, but this, of course, is a very common occurrence." [40]

The Labor Department forwarded the letter to the board, which shortly thereafter initiated proceedings against the company.

When NLRB staff members examined the evidence they realized that the Brown Shoe Company fought unionization with no holds barred. It hired the services of A. A. Ahner, manager of the largest labor detective agency in the Mississippi Valley; it encouraged the formation of citizens' committees, ostensibly neutral, but in fact dedicated to maintaining the company's anti-union policy; and, as a last resort, it relied upon direct intimidation of workers. Board officials wired news of their discoveries to Washington, where data indicating the nationwide extent of such practices were being processed.[41] Back from headquarters came a list of questions to be asked of Ahner at the hearings. They were intended to reveal the nature of his agency's services, the ties between his organization and a national detective agency, the Railway Audit and Inspection Company, and co-operative efforts on the part of Ahner and anti-union employers' associations and citizens' committees.[42]

Hearings confirmed the labor board's suspicions. Following settlement of a strike in 1934, the Brown Shoe Company had employed Ahner as its "industrial relations counselor." Ahner, a former district manager of the Railway Audit and Inspection Company, had previously hired himself out as a labor spy; he was, declared the board, "notorious in the St. Louis industrial area for successful terrorism in his chosen field." As the Brown

[40] John J. Mara to Frances Perkins, August 15, 1935, NLRB Case No. C–20, National Labor Relations Board Case Files.

[41] Robert Watts to NLRB, November 5, 6, 1935, and Watts to Charles Fahy, November 6, 1935, ibid.

[42] Heber Blankenhorn to J. Warren Madden, November 20, 1935, ibid.

Company's chief adviser in labor matters, Ahner planted a spy who toured the Salem factory with a candy wagon, picking up stray bits of information from the employees during their work breaks. After enactment of the Wagner bill, when the Boot and Shoe Workers Union stepped up its activities, the company threatened to close its Salem plant and move elsewhere if organizers persisted in their efforts. A citizens' committee appeared, and local vigilantes ran organizers out of town. Company officials assured Mayor McMakin of Salem that as long as the plant operated peacefully no shutdown would occur. When a strike was called, the mayor, eager to oblige, ordered his police force to disperse the picket lines. The mayor testified that although the picket lines were orderly, under Illinois law an assemblage of two or more persons could constitute a "mob." When an NLRB attorney inquired about the constitutional right of peaceful assembly, the mayor replied candidly, "That doesn't stand in the courts of Illinois." [43]

For one NLRB special investigator these tactics struck a familiar note. Heber Blankenhorn, supervisor of the Interchurch Investigation that followed the great steel strike of 1919, saw the Interchurch findings gather dust during the New Era. He lingered in various labor positions, hoping always to see an end to labor relations based on distrust, hostility, and violence. For five years Blankenhorn worked at the National Bureau of Industrial Research, a private organization in New York; in 1923 he prepared a study of the Somerset County (Pa.) coal strike of that year, which the bureau published. It revealed Blankenhorn's deeply rooted belief in labor unions as an index of the exercise of human rights in a democratic society.

Blankenhorn had learned, too, that "what civil rights were won depended perhaps more on incessant talking about them in the papers than on arguing in court." [44] Before World War I, Blankenhorn had moved from cub reporter to acting city editor of the New York *Evening Sun*, and now his propensity for exposure and publicity led him back to reporting. He became managing editor of the *New Leader*, overseas correspondent for *Labor*, the publication of the railway brotherhoods, and a devoted follower of international labor congresses.

In 1933 Blankenhorn went to Washington to work in the National

[43] Case No. C–20, decided May 29, 1936, NLRB, *Decisions and Orders*, I, 804–824; Official Report of Proceedings Before the National Labor Relations Board, Case No. XIV–C–2, November 16, 1935, NLRB Case Files, pp. 649ff., 741ff., 780ff., 822ff., 995ff.; St. Louis *Post-Dispatch*, November 13, 14, 15, 20, 21, 1935.

[44] Heber Blankenhorn, *The Strike for Union*, pp. 79, 81.

Recovery Administration; at Senator Wagner's behest he transferred to the National Labor Board and stayed on with succeeding boards.[45] He soon became a familiar figure in Washington liberal and labor circles. Wiry, balding, and bespectacled, he prowled through government buildings in a worn army trenchcoat, apparently always engaged in clandestine activities. Boris Shishkin, an economic researcher for the American Federation of Labor, remembered him as "a man of considerable parts. . . . By his choice and his gifts, he was really very much of an operator on a grandiose scale. He had big visions of things to be done. . . ."[46] Blankenhorn's goal—a strong labor movement—never receded; his technique—publicity—never changed.

In September 1935 the National Labor Relations Board approved a proposal to investigate industrial espionage, strikebreaking, deputy sheriff systems, factory arsenals, and labor detective agencies. The board, eager to learn whether such practices were hampering its operations and frustrating the objectives of the Wagner Act, assigned the task to Blankenhorn. His report revealed that labor detective agencies offered spies, armed strikebreakers, and munitions for sale. " 'Labor trouble' is not merely to their business advantage; it is practically their whole business. They inform clients of 'trouble,' they threaten it, and where it is not forthcoming they make it," he asserted.[47] It was to Blankenhorn that NLRB staff members in St. Louis referred their evidence in the Brown case. He dug into his files for information, prepared the questions in the examination of Ahner, and went to St. Louis to observe the proceedings. Blankenhorn expected the hearings to put on record so substantial an account of antilabor activities that the Brown case alone would substantiate a demand by the NLRB for a congressional inquiry.[48]

With one board case after another indicating that practices outlawed by the Wagner Act had become "a prime cause of strikes and other forms of industrial unrest," Blankenhorn conceived of a congressional investigation as the means by which the Wagner Act could be made effective.[49] By the winter of 1935–1936 he had sounded out board members J. Warren

45 NLRB *Hearings*, XX, 4252–53.

46 Boris Shishkin, COHC, pp. 665–666.

47 NLRB *Hearings*, XX, 4260; NLRB, *First Annual Report*, p. 32; George Soule, "Liberty League Liberty," *New Republic*, LXXXVI (September 9, 1936), 123.

48 Blankenhorn to Edwin S. Smith, November 15, 1935, NLRB Case No. C–20, NLRB Case Files.

49 NLRB, *First Annual Report*, p. 137.

Madden and John Carmody; assured of their support, he made overtures to friends in the Senate.[50]

In a confidential letter to Senator La Follette, Blankenhorn recalled his prediction that the Wagner Act would prompt undercover agencies to increase their anti-union activities; the board's experience had soon confirmed his expectations. Emphasizing that not in twenty years had the Senate, despite numerous demands, concerned itself with labor espionage and strikebreaking, Blankenhorn asked La Follette how an investigation could be launched. Although he declined to speak officially, he nonetheless expressed his belief that the board would request such an inquiry; would La Follette indicate those with whom Blankenhorn should confer in order to ease the request noiselessly through Congress? The overriding objective, Blankenhorn stressed, was to destroy espionage, strikebreaking, and industrial munitions companies and to expose their links to Liberty League lawyers.[51]

In a letter to Robert F. Wagner two weeks later, Blankenhorn discussed his proposal in more detail. Reiterating the points he had made to La Follette, he went on to propose that a special Senate committee hold hearings throughout the spring and summer, exposing the activities of undercover agencies, employers who hired them, and lawyers who defended such practices. A committee might hold up to public scrutiny the conduct of leading industrialists (Blankenhorn had in mind Ernest T. Weir, Tom Girdler, Eugene Grace, Alfred P. Sloan, and Henry Ford) and Liberty League lawyers (Blankenhorn named Earl Reed, John W. Davis, and Raoul Desvernine). Blankenhorn noted, furthermore, that several senators had already acquired evidence of antilabor practices. If released, this material would become a mighty weapon in the approaching presidential campaign. In view of the exposures that could be expected, how workers would vote in the 1936 election was obvious (and hardly displeasing to contemplate).

In a separate memorandum Blankenhorn anticipated the results of any thorough investigation. It would reveal nearly 100,000 labor spies (an estimate Blankenhorn subsequently lowered considerably) infiltrating American industry and millions of dollars being paid annually to strikebreaking agencies. Such an inquiry would function as a splendid administration

[50] Interview with Mrs. Ann Blankenhorn, September 12, 1963.
[51] Blankenhorn to Robert M. La Follette, Jr., December 5, 1935, copy in possession of Mrs. Ann Blankenhorn.

counterattack against the economic royalists. It would convince the rank
and file of labor that Congress had not passed the Wagner Act merely as
a sop to forestall legitimate labor demands. An investigating committee
could serve as the NLRB's alter ego while the board itself was tied up in
legal knots in the courts.[52] A committee that investigated industrial espionage, Blankenhorn later suggested, would ultimately expose the roots of
fascism in the United States.[53]

Blankenhorn's campaign to salvage the Wagner Act was inconspicuous
but persistent. After writing his letters, he buttonholed senators on the
Committee on Education and Labor: first Hugo Black, who demurred
because of his lobby investigation; then Wagner, who wished to remain
aloof from activities touching on the implementation of his act; and finally,
Robert M. La Follette, Jr.[54]

Plans for an investigation remained in flux during the early months of
1936. In mid-February, a week before the Cosmos Club dinner, Gardner
Jackson expected a resolution, drafted by NLRB lawyers, to be introduced in the House of Representatives. It authorized an investigation of
the use of the National Guard in labor disputes, but it also covered the
sharecroppers' difficulties. Representatives O'Day, Maverick, and Vito
Marcantonio (R-N.Y.) were prepared to introduce the measure; William
P. Connery, Jr., chairman of the Labor Committee, had given oral assent
to the appointment of a subcommittee.[55] But La Follette's promise at the
Cosmos Club dinner directed hopes toward the Senate. Jackson and
Blankenhorn led a small group in drafting a suitable resolution; by mid-
March they had finished the draft.[56] On March 12 Jackson reported to the
American Civil Liberties Union that La Follette "has in his hands a brief,
simple resolution drawn by the best government legal talent we've got
calling for a hearing or hearings . . . of the whole field of civil liberties—
academic, labor organization, espionage, etc. etc." [57]

On March 23, after he had spent some time tinkering with the wording

[52] Blankenhorn to Robert F. Wagner, December 23, 1935, Robert F. Wagner
Papers.
[53] Blankenhorn to Wagner, January 3, 1936, *ibid.*
[54] Interview with Mrs. Ann Blankenhorn, September 12, 1963. Professor J. Joseph
Huthmacher of Georgetown University, Wagner's biographer, suggested Wagner's
reluctance to involve himself in any political maneuvering over the implementation
of the Wagner Act.
[55] Gardner Jackson to Clifton Read, February 15, 1936, ACLU, Vol. 890.
[56] Interview with Gardner Jackson, December 3, 1963.
[57] Jackson to Clifton Read, March 12, 1936, ACLU, Vol. 887.

in order to keep the resolution from the Judiciary Committee, La Follette submitted Senate Resolution 266 to the second session of the seventy-fourth Congress. It authorized and directed the Committee on Education and Labor "to make an investigation of violations of the rights of free speech and assembly and undue interference with the right of labor to organize and bargain collectively." [58]

The wording of the resolution invited disagreement concerning the scope of the proposed inquiry. Jackson, on behalf of the sharecroppers, sought an investigation sufficiently broad to publicize their story. He expected, as his letter of March 12 indicates, that the Senate committee would explore "the whole field of civil liberties." Once news of the resolution had circulated, a number of Washington liberals, particularly those among the press corps, supported Jackson's position. Paul Y. Anderson, the crusading journalist for the St. Louis *Post-Dispatch*, told him that Senate Resolution 266 was "made to order. We can do all sorts of things with [it]." [59] The Washington *Daily News*, a Scripps-Howard paper, indicated that an investigating committee would have a wide variety of civil liberties violations to study: lynchings, political imprisonments, suppression of demonstrations by the unemployed, violence caused by strikebreakers, and restrictions of academic freedom. An editorial urged "a courageous, full-sized and nation-wide study" of the extent to which Americans "are being looted of the liberties" guaranteed in the Constitution. Recent events, the newspaper observed, indicated "a waning faith in our democratic processes." Congress, it reminded its readers, "has no greater duty before it than to guard the civil rights of the people." [60]

Paul W. Ward, who contributed a weekly column to the *Nation*, was perhaps the most outspoken advocate of a broad civil liberties investigation. Arkansas, he wrote, "would make an excellent starting place for the impending Senatorial investigation of all the more acute manifestations of incipient fascism in this country." While the National Labor Relations Board's copious evidence of labor espionage might receive top billing, "anti-Semitism, lynch law, Ku Kluxery, and the nicer forms of fascism practiced by the overlords of our universities and colleges against free-

[58] *Congressional Record*, 74th Cong., 2d Sess., 1936, Vol. 80, p. 4151.

[59] Interview with Gardner Jackson, December 3, 1963. Material relating to the tenant farmers was not introduced for fear of alienating southern Senators. Cf. Jackson to Mitchell, April 14, 17, 1936, and John Herling to Mitchell, April 20, 1936, Southern Tenant Farmers Union Papers, Box 2.

[60] Washington *Daily News*, March 26, April 8, 1936.

thinking students and faculty members are at last to have the sort of day in court that they deserve." New Deal agricultural policy would receive its just share of criticism for insensitivity to civil liberties. Ward expected spokesmen for sharecroppers, sugar-beet workers, Ohio onion-pickers, and New Jersey vegetable-workers to testify and to be followed by representatives of "all those other millions of agricultural laborers to whom the New Deal's farm-relief plans seem never to apply." [61]

For Heber Blankenhorn and the National Labor Relations Board, however, the civil liberties requiring immediate attention were those jeopardized by industrial conflict. Their goals were less utopian than those of the Jackson group: they sought to eliminate obstacles to enforcement of the Wagner Act, in order to stand the NLRB on its feet, and to realize the promise of labor organization and collective bargaining.[62] Clearly, their primary concern was "undue interference with the right of labor to organize and bargain collectively," rather than "violations of the rights of free speech and assembly." When, at the end of March, La Follette requested the board to submit data pertaining to espionage and related practices, the board knew that it had gained the inside track.[63] Nor did this approach displease civil libertarians. The American Civil Liberties Union concurred with the board's emphasis. "The Senate Committee can be most useful," Roger Baldwin wrote, "by confining itself largely to the attack on the rights of labor, particularly strikers. Despite a tremendous drive against democratic rights by the reactionaries, there are not many cases of actual interference or overt acts on which testimony can be hung." [64]

Initially, La Follette was committed neither to the Jackson nor to the Blankenhorn approach; in fact, he was barely committed to the investigation. On April 9, the day before hearings on Senate Resolution 266 began, Gardner Jackson analyzed the senator's position for Roger Baldwin. La Follette, Jackson revealed, was "not in the least sure how far he is going to be able to go. . . . He is going to have to feel his way every inch of the way. . . . And as far as he himself goes—says he to me—he hasn't got too much time to give to the matter. . . ." Several weeks earlier, La Follette had been even more equivocal. "The night of the Cosmos Club supper and immediately thereafter," Jackson continued, "he took the position that there was not a ghost of a show of getting a resolution through

[61] Paul W. Ward, "Washington Weekly," Nation, CXLII (April 8, 1936), 140–141.
[62] Interview with Mrs. Ann Blankenhorn, September 12, 1963.
[63] NLRB Hearings, XXV, 6752; Washington Daily News, April 1, 1936.
[64] Roger Baldwin to Rabbi Sidney Goldstein, March 27, 1936, ACLU, Vol. 887.

the Senate and that the best we could hope for was to string out a pre-liminary hearing as long as we could with good headline stuff. . . . Now, however, he is taking the position that with a comparatively few witnesses presenting as strong material as possible, his subcommittee will make a favorable report to the whole committee with a chance that . . . [it] will, in turn, report it out favorably and get action on it this session."

La Follette had requested Jackson to prompt the ACLU to deluge the Education and Labor Committee with messages demanding a favorable report for the resolution. In forwarding this advice, Jackson concluded, "Those of us who are worried about the question will have to show [La Follette] and the others that there is a real case. Otherwise this thing is likely to be a boomerang and make civil libertarians a laughing stock." [65] Not everyone echoed Jackson's pessimism, however; following a conver-sation with Heber Blankenhorn on the eve of the preliminary hearings, Morris Ernst predicted, "We ought to have a swell party." [66]

Hearings on Senate Resolution 266 began on April 10, 1936, before a subcommittee comprising Senators La Follette, Elbert Thomas (D-Utah), and Louis Murphy (D-Iowa). J. Warren Madden, National Labor Rela-tions Board chairman, was the first witness, and he sounded the keynote for the entire investigation, declaring, "The right of workmen to organize themselves into unions has become an important civil liberty." Workers, he maintained, could not organize without exercising the rights of free speech and assembly; these rights were denied them by employers who tolerated espionage and other anti-union practices. Madden told of the board's experience in the Fruehauf case and cited the destructive impact of industrial espionage on the efforts of workers to organize and on the implementation of the Wagner Act. "The mystery and deadly certainty with which [espionage] operated was so baffling to the men that they each suspected the others, were afraid to meet or to talk, and the union was completely broken." As for the Wagner Act, Madden stated that espionage "is rapidly becoming . . . the chief obstacle to the realization of the policy of our statute." The board's own study of industrial espio-nage—limited by "lack of funds and lack of power"—could not begin to cope with the problem.[67]

Heber Blankenhorn eagerly documented his chairman's generalizations.

[65] Gardner Jackson to Baldwin, April 9, 1936, *ibid.*
[66] Morris Ernst to Baldwin, April 9, 1936, *ibid.*
[67] *Hearings on S. Res. 266*, pp. 2, 3.

Encouraged to release the frustrations that had accumulated since the Interchurch investigation, he quickly became the star witness of the preliminary hearings. Blankenhorn insisted that at least forty thousand labor spies infested American industry, at an annual cost of eighty million dollars. He introduced as an exhibit his report to the labor board on the characteristics of labor detective agencies, charging industry with supporting "an extensive and lucrative business of labor espionage and strikebreaking. . . . It is a business of destroying labor unions or of demoralizing collective bargaining." Blankenhorn submitted a list of more than two hundred espionage and strikebreaking agencies whose activities had come to his attention. Citing examples from the Nye Munitions Committee hearings, he linked the activities of strikebreaking agencies and munitions companies. "Moral indignation," Blankenhorn pleaded, "is no good. Mere indignation has expressed itself for many years in resolutions laid before [the Senate]. . . . Investigation is urgently needed." [68]

Blankenhorn directed much of his fire toward the American Liberty League. Angrily he declared several prominent Liberty League lawyers guilty of association with companies engaged in antilabor practices. He noted, for example, that Roy G. Bostwick, a director of the Federal Laboratories munitions company, was a law partner of Earl F. Reed, a participant in the drafting of the Liberty League brief on the Wagner Act. Raoul Desvernine, chairman of the Liberty League lawyers' committee, received a retainer from the H. C. Frick Coal and Coke Company, which employed a number of industrial spies. Among the attorneys who appeared as counsel against unions in various government proceedings were Reed, Desvernine, Thomas F. Veach, E. A. H. Shepley, and Hal H. Smith—all Liberty League lawyers. "It seems to us," Blankenhorn declared, "that that connection between plant munitioning, professional espionage, and legal obstruction deserves very full investigation. . . . It seems to us that that connection is too close for comfort." [69]

In his summary Blankenhorn cited numerous reasons why the labor board's experience warranted a congressional inquiry. The board's powers, he noted, "are limited and not unchallenged." The size, profits, and power of labor detective agencies had never received careful documentation, despite demands dating back more than two decades. If the board could not deal adequately with the labor spy system, neither could labor unions.

[68] *Ibid.*, pp. 48–49, 60, 61, 72–76, 276–277.
[69] *Ibid.*, pp. 57, 272; Baltimore *Sun*, April 15, 1936; *New York Times*, April 15, 1936.

"Even a simple investigation, mere exposure," Blankenhorn insisted, "damages none so much as the spy." Finally, he argued that "an important phase of any inquiry should be the part that espionage and privately armed police agents play in the destruction of civil liberties. . . ." [70]

Other labor board officials supported Blankenhorn's plea. John Carmody declared, "At this time industry is shot through with fear. . . . There are no jobs for men who lose their jobs today." Edwin S. Smith argued that "the tactics of the antilabor employer are part of a larger movement for suppression of civil liberties that threatens to become epidemic." He urged exposure of "this conspiracy against democracy"; a congressional investigation, he predicted, would "do much to prick our slumbering national conscience." [71] Robert S. Watts, associate general counsel in charge of litigation, told the subcommittee how injunction proceedings reinforced anti-union tactics in frustrating the intent of the Wagner Act. Unions seeking relief from the board "have suddenly . . . found themselves stopped and unable to present their cases. . . . They have been in effect prevented from continuing their organizing and collective bargaining and . . . of necessity [are] relying upon the guerilla warfare of industrial disputes to protect their rights. . . ." [72]

Labor leaders and workers confirmed the testimony of NLRB witnesses. An employee of Wheeling Steel said, "We have . . . patiently submitted our cases to the Board—board after board, with all the necessary red tape accompanying such. . . ." These boards, he conceded, did their utmost despite management's unyielding opposition. But they could not do enough. "We find the employers fighting us with spies and arming their plants. This, in excess of the usual coercion, intimidation, and discrimination. Are we," asked this worker, "to continue going to the boards while [employers] trample on our rights, ignore the laws of the land, try to riddle us with spies, and prepare to gas us?" [73]

Representatives of the United Mine Workers told chilling stories of efforts to organize in the coal fields and company towns of Harlan County, Kentucky. Miners, reported a UMW district president, "are suppressed, they are isolated, they are attacked, they are victimized, they are evicted from their homes when they show any desire to join, or when they begin to talk about joining the mine workers' organization." T. C.

---

[70] *Hearings on S. Res. 266*, p. 277.
[71] *Ibid.*, pp. 30, 292, 293.
[72] *Ibid.*, p. 279.
[73] *Ibid.*, p. 32.

Townsend, counsel to the UMW, stated bluntly, "Free speech, free assembly, freedom of the ballot, the right of the mine workers of Harlan County, Ky., to organize do not exist in that county." Spokesmen for Pennsylvania hosiery workers, Minneapolis truckers, New Jersey dyers, and North Carolina textile workers echoed these statements. All concurred in the judgment of William Green, president of the American Federation of Labor, that workers simply did not enjoy the "rights" guaranteed in the Bill of Rights; their testimony reinforced his demand that "a thorough-going investigation should be made." [74]

Not until April 21, the seventh and penultimate day of hearings, did the subcommittee hear from witnesses not directly involved in labor organization. Three prominent religious leaders, who had signed the 1935 petition imploring the Senate to investigate civil liberties infractions, reiterated their plea and stressed the importance of a broad inquiry. Rabbi Sidney Goldstein, representing the Central Conference of American Rabbis, called on the Senate to affirm that the Bill of Rights, and labor's right to organize, comprised federal guarantees that local citizens and state governments could not abridge. "We believe that it is the duty of the Senate to investigate any local or State violation of a constitutional guarantee," he declared. The Reverend W. M. Tippy, of the Federal Council of Churches, warned of "a kind of fringe, a subterranean fringe, growing up among our people." Many organizations, he insisted, capitalized upon fear to destroy civil liberty; these modern Know-Nothings required the scrutiny of a congressional committee to restrain their activities. [75]

In a striking statement the Reverend R. A. McGowan, representing the National Catholic Welfare Conference, cut to the core of New Deal civil libertarianism. McGowan tied the issue of civil liberty to the broader goal of economic and social change. The fight for civil liberties, he told the subcommittee, centered "in the question of whether or not the United States is going to continue . . . predominantly a country dominated by a relatively small number of the population." Violations of civil liberties, he said, "are merely efforts to try to keep that power intact. . . . We want a distribution of power and we want a change in the distribution of wealth in the United States." [76] McGowan thus alluded to two central tenets of the civil libertarian creed in the United States as it unfolded

[74] *Ibid.*, pp. 142, 125, 115.
[75] *Ibid.*, pp. 247, 255–256.
[76] *Ibid.*, p. 252.

between the two world wars. He perceived the relation of economic and political power to the exercise of First Amendment freedoms, and he suggested that the Bill of Rights be used rather than merely revered. Implicit in the campaign for a civil liberties investigation was the assumption that it would give disadvantaged persons a strong push toward fuller participation in American life.

Four weeks after the hearings closed the Committee on Education and Labor approved its subcommittee's recommendation and reported Senate Resolution 266 favorably. It, too, forged a strong link between the needs of labor and the labor board and the demands of libertarians. Preliminary hearings, reported the committee, "supplied presumptive proof in abundance of violations of civil liberties secured by the Constitution, and of undue interference with the rights of labor" as defined in the Wagner Act. Workers trying to organize discovered that their rights to assemble peaceably, to speak freely, and to vote were imperiled. When the National Labor Relations Board tried to assist them, it encountered "obstructive legalistic maneuvers" designed both to frustrate its efforts and to justify espionage, the usurpation of police power by private groups, and the stockpiling of munitions for use in industrial disputes. In sum, the board "found itself in a field of labor relations dotted with old-rooted obstructions, newly reinforced." An effective national labor policy required a clear field. In recommending approval of the Senate resolution the Education and Labor Committee declared the purpose of the investigation to be the acquisition of knowledge "of the full extent to which the rights of labor to organize . . . [are] being denied and the extent to which civil liberties are interfered with." [77]

Senate approval of Senate Resolution 266 seemed likely. In the spring of 1936 the climate in Washington was congenial to political investigation and exposure. April, observed one correspondent, was the month of congressional investigations. Senator Nye's Munitions Committee brought its disclosures to a climax. Hugo Black's Lobbying Committee, established in 1935 to investigate lobbying in connection with the Public Utilities Holding Company Act, became an administration weapon against anti-New Deal organizations. Adding to the fireworks, the La Follette subcommittee lumped Liberty Leaguers, industrialists, and antilabor hoodlums into one noxious package. Never had there been "such a volume of exposures of

[77] U.S. Senate, Committee on Education and Labor, *Report No. 2046*, 74th Cong., 2d Sess., 1936, pp. 1–3.

the sinister activities of those who have controlled successive administrations through first fooling the people, then ruling them, and then robbing them, both within and without the law." [78]

But several observers had reservations about La Follette's handling of the hearings; they also minimized the subcommittee's potential even if the resolution were approved. La Follette, charged Paul W. Ward, displayed neither sympathy nor tenacity during the preliminary hearings; Thomas and Murphy, Ward continued, indicated by their questions that they believed a full investigation would be useless.[79] An editorial in the *Progressive Miner* predicted glumly that the La Follette investigation "will be just like all of the others; a lot of the taxpayers' money spent; a nice vacation lark for some senators; nothing accomplished." [80] La Follette was criticized for holding preliminary hearings; according to *Newsweek* the very success of the preliminary hearings might convince conservative senators that a further inquiry was neither necessary nor desirable. Nearly everyone agreed on the seriousness of one obstacle; the Committee to Audit and Control the Contingent Expenses of the Senate, chaired by James F. Byrnes and including Millard Tydings of Maryland and John G. Townsend, Jr., of Delaware, would not look kindly upon a request for funds to finance an investigation of civil liberties or the activities of big business.[81]

After May 19, when Senate Resolution 266 moved from the Education and Labor Committee to the Audit and Control Committee, the American Civil Liberties Union bent every effort to ensure its ultimate success. The union, and especially Roger Baldwin, no longer regarded the Wagner Act "as a dangerous, fascist intrusion of government into unions." [82] The ACLU board of directors had already declared its support of the resolution and urged its local affiliates and other interested organizations to communicate their own approval to the Senate. "Our board has agreed to

[78] Charles W. Ervin, "What's Going On in Washington?," *Advance*, XXII (May 1936), 21; Wolfskill, *Revolt of the Conservatives*, pp. 225–245.

[79] Paul W. Ward, "Washington Weekly," *Nation*, CXLII (April 22, 1936), 503. The *Daily Worker* of April 24, 1936, reiterated this charge, accusing La Follette of an "indifferent and condescending" manner and predicting that unless public opinion forced him to fight for S. Res. 266 he would "lay down." Most critics of La Follette's conduct were left-wingers.

[80] Quoted in *Progressive*, June 13, 1936.

[81] *Newsweek*, May 2, 1936; *Progressive*, April 25, 1936. For the opposite view see *American Guardian*, April 17, 1936; Paul W. Ward, "The State of Civil Liberties," *Nation*, CXLII (June 10, 1936), 731–732.

[82] Roger Baldwin, COHC, pp. 167–168.

go the limit" on the investigation, Baldwin told Gardner Jackson during the preliminary hearings.[83] Jackson served as the ACLU's liaison with the subcommittee; he reported La Follette's eagerness to close the hearings quickly ("There is no need of putting in [a] more persuasive case," he wrote) and suggested, "Our job is to get as powerful an influence as possible on Senators of [the] whole committee and [the] whole Senate. Immediate effort along this line necessary."[84]

While the ACLU applied what pressure it could, the National Labor Relations Board, and particularly the irrepressible Heber Blankenhorn, channeled its energies toward the establishment of the committee it had come to envision as its savior. The board, "pretty well pleased" with the impression it had made on the La Follette subcommittee, awaited Senate action on Resolution 266 with considerable anxiety.[85] Blankenhorn moved restlessly from one labor group to another, stirring up support for the resolution. From the convention of the Amalgamated Association of Iron, Steel and Tin Workers he proudly reported labor's favorable response to recent signs of government attention. Convention delegates, he told the NLRB, had told him, " 'Why the Government also is ready to help. Look at the swat the Labor Board gave [employers] and look at that La Follette committee.' " Blankenhorn began to view the imminent organizing drive in steel with greater optimism if the Wagner Act, the labor board, and "the possibility of a La Follette committee investigation as a club" could be manipulated to maximum advantage. To George Soule of the *New Republic* Blankenhorn predicted, "The investigation is likely to go through but [it] may need some pushing." He promised Soule "meaty material" for a series of articles on the La Follette committee "to help in putting it over."[86]

On May 18, two days after Blankenhorn had written to Soule, the labor board received a severe jolt from the Supreme Court, one that increased the urgency of "putting over" the La Follette investigation. The court's

[83] ACLU Board of Directors, Minutes, April 13, May 4, 1936, ACLU, Vol. 866; Roger Baldwin to Gardner Jackson, April 14, 1936, ACLU, Vol. 887.

[84] Gardner Jackson to Roger Baldwin, April 21, 1936, *ibid.* On April 22, La Follette told Baldwin, "In the interest of prompt action upon this resolution the subcommittee hesitates to prolong these preliminary hearings any more than absolutely necessary" (La Follette to Baldwin, April 22, 1936, *ibid.*).

[85] Heber Blankenhorn to L. W. Beman, April 25, 1936, La Follette Civil Liberties Committee Papers, National Archives, Box 4 (cited hereafter as LFC).

[86] Blankenhorn to Madden, Carmody, and Smith, May 6, 11, 1936, NLRB *Hearings*, XXI, 4413, 4415; Blankenhorn to Soule, May 16, 1936, *ibid.*, XX, 4293.

decision in *Carter* v. *Carter Coal Company*, holding unconstitutional the labor provisions of the Guffey Act, convinced the board that the Wagner Act would meet a similar fate. "The relation of employer and employee is a local relation," declared the court, with Mr. Justice Sutherland speaking for a 6–3 majority.[87] A flood of new injunction proceedings, released by the *Carter* decision, threatened to inundate the board. Circuit Courts in the Second, Fourth, Fifth, Sixth, and Eighth Circuits ruled that the Wagner Act could not constitutionally be applied to manufacturing; six District Courts held likewise. Board attorneys, overworked and disheartened, found it difficult to believe that the *Schechter* and *Carter* decisions had not also doomed the Wagner Act. After the Guffey Act decision, the NLRB functioned "under the shadow of the dead hand."[88]

Heber Blankenhorn still kept the faith. Authorization of the La Follette investigation might, he reasoned, provide the NLRB with an escape from its impasse. Blankenhorn briefed La Follette and Wagner on the board's impending paralysis. He insisted that if the La Follette committee were established, it could hear testimony in the very cases in which an injunction restrained the board. What would prevent the committee, Blankenhorn asked J. Warren Madden, from "summoning the enjoined Board and its witnesses to hearings, say in steel and auto cases, in Pittsburgh or Detroit? What is to prevent the Senate committee subpoena being laid on the heads of recalcitrant corporations in such cases?" Blankenhorn anticipated that "it ought not to take more than one or two such hearings to make companies hesitant about rushing to courts for injunctions, at least so far as hearings go." A friendly committee could, however, do more than function as a club; it could also educate the nation and mobilize support for New Deal labor policy. "The principal job of this Board and of the La Follette committee investigation," Blankenhorn insisted, "is to clarify the country's mind in regard to the constitutional crisis. The bottom of that crisis is Capital-Labor relations."[89]

While Senate Resolution 266 lingered in the Audit and Control Com-

---

[87] *Carter* v. *Carter Coal Company*, 298 U.S. 238, 308 (1936).

[88] American Association for Economic Freedom, *Problems of the National Labor Relations Board* (Washington, D.C., n.d.), p. 5; Silverberg, "Detroit: The Battleground," *The Wagner Act*, p. 80; Emerson, COHC, pp. 449, 456. According to Emerson, only general counsel Charles Fahy refused to admit that the *Schechter* and *Carter* decisions had decided the constitutionality of the Wagner Act (*Problems of the National Labor Relations Board*, p. 6).

[89] Heber Blankenhorn to Madden, May 22, 1936, NLRB *Hearings*, XX, 4317; Blankenhorn to Sidney Howard, June 6, 1936, *ibid.*, XXI, 4420.

mittee, various sources increased pressure for a favorable report. The Executive Council of the American Federation of Labor approved the resolution unanimously. ACLU officials, noting the delay, urged President Roosevelt to bring his influence to bear on Chairman Byrnes; at Gardner Jackson's suggestion they communicated with Byrnes directly. Heywood Broun, for the American Newspaper Guild, notified Roosevelt of his organization's support of the resolution. His appeal, the President's secretary assured him, "was sympathetically received." Blankenhorn suggested that La Follette inform Byrnes of the existence of considerable evidence "available for Byrnes' use to get his anti-strikebreaking bill . . . through the House in the next few weeks." [90]

Blankenhorn's log-rolling proposition, pressure from the President, or an influx of petitions may have moved Senator Byrnes. On June 5, for whatever reasons, Byrnes reported Senate Resolution 266 from the Audit and Control Committee without amendment. On June 6 the Senate approved the resolution,[91] thereby granting the broadest mandate for a civil liberties investigation in the history of the United States. That same day, before learning of the Senate's action, Blankenhorn reminded a friend to what extent the findings of the Interchurch investigation nearly two decades earlier were responsible for the genesis of the La Follette Committee. "If the La Follette investigation takes wings," Blankenhorn noted with pardonable pride, "it would be called the 17-year locust." [92] The byways and detours of these years had not dimmed his vision or changed his destination, and in June 1936 Heber Blankenhorn finally reached his goal.

[90] American Federation of Labor *Weekly News Service*, May 16, 1936; ACLU Board of Directors, Minutes, June 1, 1936, ACLU, Vol. 866; Jackson to Roger Baldwin, June 1, 1936, *ibid.*, Vol. 925; Broun to Roosevelt, May 29, 1936, FDRL, OF 1581; Stephen Early to Broun, June 6, 1936, *ibid.*; Blankenhorn to Madden, May 22, 1936, NLRB *Hearings*, XX, 4317. The Byrnes Act made it a felony to transport any person in interstate commerce with intent to employ him to obstruct peaceful picketing or the right of organization. It was passed in the 74th Congress on June 24, 1936.

[91] *Congressional Record*, 74th Cong., 2d Sess., 1936, Vol. 80, pp. 9113, 9186; Washington, D.C., *News*, March 25, 1936.

[92] Blankenhorn to Sidney Howard, June 6, 1936, NLRB *Hearings*, XXI, 4420.

IV

Planning an Investigation:
"The Logic of Events"

THE antecedents of the La Follette Committee pointed toward a civil liberties investigation with strong labor overtones. As one periodical declared early in 1936, "The crucial struggle for civil liberty today is among tenant farmers and industrial workers, fighting for economic emancipation and security."[1] The organizing drive of the Southern Tenant Farmers Union and the frustrations of the National Labor Relations Board set the committee's guidelines. But the persistence of a labor orientation depended upon the committee's members and staff, and upon their conception of the committee's task. It also depended upon the committee's sensitivity to developments in labor-management relations. As the committee emerged from its embryonic stages and developed an identity, its personnel and union militancy reinforced its inclination to concentrate on the relation between civil liberty and labor's drive to organize.

In June 1936 Hugo Black, newly appointed chairman of the Education and Labor Committee, named Robert M. La Follette, Jr., Elbert D. Thomas, and Louis Murphy to the subcommittee authorized under Senate Resolution 266.[2] In accordance with congressional custom, La Follette, as sponsor of the resolution, was named chairman of the subcommittee, which became known as the La Follette Civil Liberties Committee. La Follette, elder son of a towering figure in American history, had learned politics in his father's company. His earliest memories were of the governor's mansion in Madison; his earliest acquaintances were the progressive leaders—Albert Beveridge, Jonathan Dolliver, Gifford and Amos Pinchot—who came to Wisconsin after the turn of the century to confer with his father. After a critical bout with pneumonia interrupted his attendance at the University of Wisconsin, the young La Follette went to Washington

[1] "New Attacks Upon Liberties," *Social Action*, II (January 10, 1936), 19.
[2] Murphy died in an automobile accident during the summer of 1936; no replacement was appointed until 1939.

to serve as his father's secretary. In 1922 he became chairman of the Wisconsin State Republican Committee; two years later he managed his father's unsuccessful campaign for the presidency. In 1925, just seven months after the election, and with three years of his fourth Senate term unserved, the elder La Follette died of a heart attack. His wife refused to consider filling the vacancy; Philip, the youngest son, whom many considered the natural heir to the La Follette political mantle, was two years shy of the constitutional age requirement. Bob, Jr., became the only willing and eligible family member. Following a special election held only months after his thirtieth birthday, Robert M. La Follette, Jr., entered Congress as the youngest senator since Henry Clay.[3]

La Follette soon enjoyed a reputation as one of the "Sons of the Wild Jackass"—the derisive label pinned to Senate progressives that became a badge of honor. Early in his first term he demanded a congressional investigation of the circumstances surrounding the serious textile strike in Passaic, New Jersey; he assailed the Coolidge administration for its inadequate farm relief policies; and he petitioned on behalf of Sacco and Vanzetti. By 1928 La Follette was urging a more progressive income tax, unemployment relief, public ownership of utilities, curbing of inflationary stock market practices, and prohibition of injunctions against striking workers. His sharp thrusts at the Coolidge and Hoover administrations prompted critics to call him an "economic Jeremiah." [4]

When the Depression struck, La Follette confronted its desperate problems unencumbered by doctrinaire solutions or evasions. He used his influential position in the Senate as a national forum and made trenchant proposals for federal unemployment relief. He urged the adoption of a federal public-works program and was a leader in the fight to enact the Norris-La Guardia anti-injunction bill. Even the measures of the New Deal did not satisfy the Wisconsin senator. La Follette always advocated more than the Roosevelt administration offered: a government-owned central bank, public ownership of railroads, government ownership of munitions plants.[5]

It took years in the Senate for La Follette to emerge from the shadow of his father's reputation. When he finally succeeded he was repeatedly

[3] Edward N. Doan, *The La Follettes and the Wisconsin Idea*, pp. 7, 141, 145–146; Wallace S. Sayre, "Robert M. La Follette, Jr.," *The American Politician*, ed. John T. Salter, pp. 139–140; *Current Biography* (1944), pp. 368–372.

[4] *Current Biography* (1944), pp. 368–372.

[5] *Ibid*.; Sayre, "Robert M. La Follette, Jr.," pp. 144–147; Doan, *The La Follettes*, pp. 168–173.

measured against the erratic brilliance of his brother Philip, who was three times governor of Wisconsin. Phil, political writers observed, was scintillating; Bob, Jr., was substantial. Stocky, round-faced, with jet black hair, and always carefully groomed and dressed, the senator seemed to epitomize poise and caution verging always on grimness. He had, according to Elmer Davis, almost every characteristic of his father "except the divine fire." Frederick Barkley sensed in La Follette "a horror of appearing in a futile light." Even possessing his father's quick, nervous stride and swift gestures he seemed to lack the flair that the other male La Follettes displayed so prominently.[6] Yet those close to La Follette sensed qualities that others missed. The senator, wrote Oswald Garrison Villard, "burns within. . . . You cannot go to him for sympathy for starved miners or frantic share croppers or half-famished unemployed . . . and come away empty-handed." La Follette was "the least introverted, the least depressed man" Francis Biddle knew. Biddle once asked La Follette if he could call him "Bob." "Sure can," La Follette replied. "Everyone in Wisconsin calls me Bob, or that son of a bitch!"[7]

La Follette's national image reflected his multifaceted personality. Some people branded him as one of the country's dangerous men; others hailed him as the plumed knight of liberalism.[8] Among the latter were the leaders of the American Civil Liberties Union. They admired his plea for investigations of police brutality in labor disputes, and they praised his fight for the Norris-La Guardia Act. Roger Baldwin, seeking a speaker for a luncheon commemorating the ACLU's fifteenth anniversary, told La Follette, "We are all agreed that you are the one man who can best represent the spirit and purpose animating the Civil Liberties Union. . . . Your championship of the rights of labor and your opposition to any measure of repression mark you as the man to do that job."[9] Even before his committee launched its investigation, La Follette seemed to personify in politics both sides of the New Deal libertarian coin: defense of the Bill of Rights and advocacy of its particular relevance to the needs of the industrial worker.

[6] Walter Davenport, "Fighting Blood," *Collier's*, LXXXIX (April 23, 1932), 47; Elmer Davis, "The Wisconsin Brothers," *Harper's Magazine*, CLXXVIII (February 1939), 269; Ray Tucker and Frederick R. Barkley, *Sons of the Wild Jackass*, pp. 151–155; *Current Biography* (1944), pp. 368–372.

[7] Oswald Garrison Villard, "Pillars of Government: Robert M. La Follette, Jr.," *Forum*, XCVI (August 1936), 90; Francis Biddle, *In Brief Authority*, pp. 132–133.

[8] Francis Brown, "La Follette: Ten Years a Senator," *Current History*, XLII (August 1935), 475.

[9] Baldwin to La Follette, January 10, 1935, ACLU, Vol. 774.

In 1932 La Follette became a member of the Senate Education and Labor Committee. For the duration of his political career he articulated concern for the problems of American industrialism and for the rights of American workers. He believed that labor organization and collective bargaining were "the cornerstone of industrial democracy." The growth of labor unions must be welcomed, not feared, because "it is vital to the functioning of our industrial system. . . . It increases purchasing power and enlarges the market for the products of the farm and factory. It helps to advance the cause of all social legislation." Union growth depended upon the freedom to speak and to assemble: "The right of self-organization and collective bargaining is a complex whole, embracing . . . meetings, speeches, peaceful picketing, the printing and distribution of pamphlets, news, and argument. . . . [It] is fundamental, is basic, being one phase of the process of free association essential to the democratic way of life." [10]

La Follette carefully drew the boundaries of the investigation to include "the examination and reporting of instances of resistance to and subversion of the fundamental national labor policy favoring collective bargaining for interstate industries. . . ." In reporting Senate Resolution 266 favorably, the Committee on Education and Labor had declared the purpose of the investigation to be the acquisition of knowledge "of the full extent to which the rights of labor to organize . . . [are] being denied and the extent to which civil liberties are interfered with." The two purposes dovetailed neatly. As La Follette indicated, "The most spectacular violations of civil liberty . . . proved upon investigation to have their roots in economic conflicts of interest. . . . Association and self-organization are simply the result of the exercise of the fundamental rights of free speech and assembly." The committee steadfastly maintained "that any concerted and prolonged rejection of the principles of collective bargaining leads to the invasion of constitutional liberty." [11]

La Follette's partner on the Civil Liberties Committee shared his commitment to trade unions as guardians of democracy. Elbert D. Thomas, a native of Salt Lake City, pursued a meandering route on his journey to political progressivism. After graduation from the University of Utah in 1906 he departed for Japan to fulfill a mission for the Church of Jesus

[10] *Progressive*, May 30, 1936, September 10, 1938; *Congressional Record*, 77th Cong., 2d Sess., 1942, Vol. 88, p. 3311.

[11] *Congressional Record*, 77th Cong., 2d Sess., 1942, Vol. 88, p. 3311; U.S. Senate, Committee on Education and Labor, *Employer's Associations and Collective Bargaining in California*, Report No. 1150, Pt. 1, 77th Cong., 2d Sess., 1942, p. 3.

Christ of Latter-Day Saints. Thomas taught English to students of the Japanese War College and learned to read and write their language fluently. He wrote a Mormon tract in Japanese and found time to play on the Tokyo-American baseball team. Returning home after five years to begin an academic career, Thomas taught Latin and Greek at his alma mater before accepting a fellowship in political science at the University of California. Within two years he had earned his doctorate, and in 1927 his dissertation, *Chinese Political Thought*, was published.[12]

Thomas won his Senate seat in 1932, defeating the venerable Republican conservative, Reed Smoot. He co-authored the bill establishing the Civilian Conservation Corps, and by the end of Roosevelt's first hundred days he had become a loyal administration supporter. Thomas hoped to have the CCC established on a permanent basis so that the unemployed would never again be forced to drift from city to city, from bread line to soup kitchen. He proposed a cabinet department of education and public welfare and consistently supported bills for education, health, and hospitals. Equally competent on the Senate floor or expounding the doctrines of Aquinas, Thomas epitomized the scholar in politics. A self-proclaimed disciple of Thomas Jefferson, he believed that democracy was "the one philosophy which makes the individual's life politically full."[13]

"Of what value is government," Thomas once inquired, "if it does not help its people?" Government could best do this by making certain that democratic procedures never yielded to undemocratic expedients. Freedom of speech, for Thomas, was basic: "[It] has been a tremendous healing balm to a lot of difficulties that the world has had. I wonder," he mused, "if it would work in industrial relations."[14] Collective bargaining must be based upon the mutual trust of the bargaining parties. Such words as "trust," "confidence," and "responsibility" recurred constantly in Thomas' speeches; the values that they represented were those that Thomas was determined to apply to labor-management relations.

La Follette and Thomas could not have been more dissimilar in background, appearance, and demeanor, yet as partners they complemented each other perfectly. Thomas reminded one observer of "a nice old

[12] *Current Biography* (1942), pp. 830–831; "Biography," Elbert D. Thomas Papers, Franklin D. Roosevelt Library.

[13] "Biography," Thomas Papers, FDRL; *Current Biography* (1942), pp. 830–831; Elbert D. Thomas, *Thomas Jefferson*, p. vii.

[14] *Congressional Record*, 76th Cong., 2d Sess., 1940, Vol. 85, p. 299; *Hearings*, Pt. 6, p. 2051.

country lawyer"; his manner, invariably genial, and his questions, always quietly asked, encouraged witnesses to unbend. While Thomas probed for attitudes rather than for factual details, La Follette grilled witnesses "sharply, steadily and coldly, working with the . . . precision and power of a steel-riveter." Thomas led witnesses into a bog of contradictory statements; La Follette's sharp thrusts, his tone incisive and his voice commanding, made them walk the plank of factual inaccuracies. La Follette projected restlessness and shrewdness. Thomas seemed endlessly patient, searching always for meanings, stating and restating the moral dilemmas uncovered by his questions.[15]

La Follette bore the brunt of cross-examination. He permitted a witness to spin his own web of half-truths and evasions. Then he pounced. Using documents from the witness' own files, La Follette would force him to renege, to contradict, and ultimately to destroy the plausibility of his own testimony. Thomas, constantly probing for some remnant of human values, set the witness up; La Follette, thoroughly grounded in facts, knocked him down. La Follette's manner of interrogation, and the witness' resistance to it, generated the suspense of the hearings. He rephrased each question until, as one observer commented, "the eel-like witness [could] no longer wriggle through it." [16] Equipped with a complete list of questions for every witness, with the correct answers carefully noted, La Follette did not tolerate equivocation. He persisted until he received the answer he wanted; only then did he move on to the next question; he left little in his investigation to chance.

As members of a "civil liberties" committee, however, La Follette and Thomas were acutely aware that the absence of procedural safeguards had damaged the credibility of many congressional committees. Investigating committees are not courts; they are bound neither by a common law of traditional practices nor by a formal set of rules. The atmosphere of an investigation emerges from the sensitivity of its members to means as well as to ends, from their sense of obligation to respect the rights of witnesses, and from their awareness of the need for self-restraint in a situation that tempts all but the most wary. La Follette appreciated that the rules of evidence did not (and perhaps should not) govern congressional investigations. Like many others, he found in grand

---

[15] Washington *Post*, April 25, 1937; Dwight Macdonald, "Espionage, Inc.," *Nation*, CXLIV (February 27, 1937), 238–239; Philadelphia *Record*, February 25, 1937; Clinch Calkins, *Spy Overhead*, p. 20; Meyer Levin, *Citizens*, pp. 413–414.

[16] *Spy Overhead*, p. 20.

jury proceedings the closest analogy to the proper exercise of congressional investigative power. Where they could, both senators improvised means by which to extend maximum protection to witnesses' rights. Every witness was granted the right to be accompanied by counsel. Lawyers were free at all times to advise their clients, and occasionally a temporary recess was called expressly for this purpose. Counsel could comment upon his client's testimony if he chose. Witnesses were permitted, and frequently encouraged, to submit statements of their own.

Although neither a witness nor his lawyer had the privilege of cross-examination, the committee developed a novel procedure to yield the same results yet expedite the hearings. When witnesses differed sharply in their interpretations, all of them—sometimes as many as a dozen—were placed on the stand simultaneously. Questioned in turn, they were invited to challenge as best they could the statements of those who contradicted them. This technique proved effective, if trying. La Follette occasionally had to caution excited witnesses that the committee desired testimony about events, not a re-enactment of them. Throughout most of its investigation the committee adhered to the principle that "the best evidence comes not from the accusers but from the accused." [17]

Sensitivity to procedural safeguards did not prevent the hearings from becoming, in the words of one sympathetic onlooker, "good theater." To justify appropriations beyond its initial allocation of $15,000 and to arouse concern for the conditions that it exposed, the committee, of necessity and by choice, put on a good show. Hearings generally ran for two hours in the morning and two in the afternoon. Every day, wrote one interested spectator, "the same people appear like faithful attendants upon a movie serial, happy when the witness speaks out bold and clear, heads strained forward to catch the faint tone of the reluctant man under catechism." [18]

La Follette and Thomas sat at the curve of a horseshoe-shaped desk raised three steps from the floor; they were flanked by their staff and the press. To one side, "like the donor in a painting," was Heber Blankenhorn. In the well, between the heels of the horseshoe, sat the witnesses. "Day after day," wrote Dwight Macdonald, "the strikebreaking gentry are butchered to make a Democratic holiday." Clinch Calkins discovered

[17] *Hearings*, Pt. 12, p. 4328 ; *New York Times*, February 12, 1937; *Hearings*, Pt. 26, p. 11035; U.S. Senate, Subcommittee of the Committee on Education and Labor, *Hearings on S. 1970*, 76th Cong., 1st Sess., 1939, p. 13.

[18] Calkins, *Spy Overhead*, p. 17.

"not the illusion of conflict, but its reality . . . people against property in its most intelligible terms of dollars, purchased violence and betrayal." [19]

La Follette and Thomas determined the scope and procedure of their investigation, but the committee staff generated the fervor underlying the inquiry and provided the committee with its point of view. The La Follette Committee was manna from the political gods for many bright young New Dealers with a passion for service. It placed them in the front lines of crucial New Deal domestic battles; it invited them to attack the old order of industrial management. At every stage the specific tasks of staff members shaped the investigation: observing the confrontation between strikers and a company, deciding whom to interview, collating information, recommending witnesses and proposing questions, and drafting committee reports. Value judgments were implicit in each of these tasks; the sum of the judgments gave the La Follette Committee its identity.

The committee drew its staff from assorted government agencies, using the standard New Deal technique—a blend of haphazard selection and premeditated choice. The staff's pivotal member was Robert Wohlforth, the secretary. Wohlforth, a slender, articulate young man with a bristly mustache, came to the committee with impressive, and apparently contradictory, credentials. A registered Republican from Connecticut, he had served in the administration sporadically since 1933. A former West Pointer, he had written a lively antimilitary novel, *Tin Soldiers*, about cadet life. After the Senate authorized the Nye munitions investigation in 1934, Wohlforth, whose views on the military brought him to the attention of Senators Nye, Borah, and Vandenberg, joined the Nye Committee staff as second in command to Stephen Raushenbush. His diligent work for Nye caught Heber Blankenhorn's eye; Blankenhorn introduced him to La Follette, and when the Nye investigation ended Wohlforth seized the opportunity to supervise the La Follette inquiry.[20]

Wohlforth relished the idea of occupying "the catbird's seat." "In the Munitions Committee," he explained, "I was only Number Two. And here I had my own committee. . . ." He and La Follette found immediate rapport. "I couldn't fudge a thing," Wohlforth recalled. La Follette "knew what he wanted, he knew what he wanted of me and what I had to do for him, and I had to deliver on the nail. He was a very tough task-

[19] Washington *Post*, April 25, 1937; Macdonald, "Espionage, Inc.," p. 239; *Spy Overhead*, pp. 18–19.

[20] "Scraps of Paper," *Literary Digest*, CXXII (September 5, 1936), 9; interview with Robert Wohlforth, November 6, 1963, copy in COHC, pp. 2–4.

master. . . . He was ideal to work for." The pressure and excitement of an impending hearing, the endless supervisory details, a shoestring budget, the incessant telephone calls and frequent trips to the Senate floor, the sheer joy of being in charge—all intoxicated Wohlforth. "You became caught up," he reminisced, "emotionally involved, committed. . . . You've got to deliver to the Senator; he's flying back from Wisconsin, and you've got to have the hearing. . . ." [21]

Once the outlines of a particular phase of the investigation had been drawn, Wohlforth acted on his own. He rarely consulted La Follette again until the eve of the hearings, when he and the committee counsel presented La Follette with a brief containing every question and documents furnishing every answer. Each hearing provided Wohlforth with a moment of fulfillment: "We scored on these things. We got something like 48,000 words out of Washington on AP every night, and La Follette was so bright: he'd save this stuff for 11 o'clock . . . so that it would hit the afternoon papers, . . . and then wait until 3 o'clock . . . to get the morning papers." A former newspaperman, Wohlforth appreciated La Follette's artistry.[22]

His experience with the Nye Committee had made Wohlforth highly sensitive to the need of every congressional investigation for extensive publicity. He recalled: "We took the most likely things . . . the things that were easiest to get hold of, the things that were most striking to command public attention, and to give the Committee . . . a 'Madison Avenue' posture or image. . . . I always felt that unless one of these investigating committees . . . could get enough attention and recognition, legislation wouldn't have much of a chance." A congressional committee can influence opinion—one of its primary objectives—only if its findings receive wide attention. Yet the need for publicity invariably impinges upon a committee's freedom of selection. To retain its audience it must dwell on the sensational, and often on the extreme. Similarly, in a successful investigation the commitment required from its staff will frequently encourage the sacrifice of procedure to results. La Follette, Wohlforth recalled, "gave me such complete confidence . . . that you just felt that you had to put out for him." But "putting out" occasionally meant erasing subpoenas and writing in new names, or drafting subpoenas without a senator's approval, or using the prospect of hearings as a means of pres-

[21] Interview with Robert Wohlforth, November 6, 1963, copy in COHC, pp. 13, 18, 54, 73.

[22] *Ibid.*, p. 15; interview with John J. Abt, March 22, 1963, copy in COHC, pp. 6–8.

suring corporation attorneys into relinquishing desired documents.[23] In a
memo to himself written shortly after he joined the La Follette Committee, Wohlforth asked, "Can you investigate an unethical system by ethical
means?"[24] The answer varied. When the committee's very existence
seemed to hang in the balance, Wohlforth believed that he had to make
concessions in order to protect the committee's ultimate objectives.

Wohlforth's right-hand man was John J. Abt, counsel to the committee until the middle of 1937. Abt, a brilliant lawyer, came from a comfortable German-Jewish family in Chicago. By his twenty-second year he
had graduated from the University of Chicago and from its law school;
for the next six years he practiced in Jerome Frank's Chicago law office,
specializing in corporate and real-estate law. In 1933, Abt followed Frank
to Washington, entered the Agricultural Adjustment Administration, and
became chief of its litigation section. His incisive mind and his reputation
as one of Frank's disciples served him well; he held responsible positions
with WPA and the Securities and Exchange Commission before Gardner
Jackson, acting on the suggestion of Jerome Frank and Lee Pressman,
recommended him to La Follette for the post of chief counsel.[25]

With Wohlforth, Abt sifted through every document and report in
order to prepare the questions for public hearings. La Follette's insistence
that the chairman play the major public role made Abt's task enormously
difficult. He had to anticipate all conceivable answers to a question; each
such answer entailed additional questions, all drafted in advance, to bring
the witness to the destination to which the evidence pointed. Abt never
examined witnesses during a hearing. His job, like Wohlforth's, was to
clear the senators' path, not to replace them on the journey.[26]

Other staff positions were filled from a variety of sources. The Harvard
Law School provided its quota of superior legal talent. Daniel F. Margolies, Phi Beta Kappa and a Corey Traveling Fellow at Harvard College,
came to the committee a year after earning his LL.B. David Demarest
Lloyd, who had graduated *summa cum laude* from Harvard before spend-

23 Wohlforth, COHC, pp. 53, 59, 73.

24 "List of Questions to Guide R.W.," Robert Wohlforth Papers, in possession of
Mr. Wohlforth.

25 Gardner Jackson, COHC, p. 742; Abt, COHC, pp. 1–2; U.S. House of Representatives, Committee on Un-American Activities, *Hearings Regarding Communism
in the United States Government*, Vol. IV, 81st Cong., 2d Sess., 1950, p. 2952. The
question of the alleged Communist affiliations of Abt and other committee staff members is discussed below in Chapter Seven.

26 Abt, COHC, pp. 6–8.

ing a year at Cambridge, left the Resettlement Administration to join the La Follette Committee. Margolies and Lloyd, who shared Abt's duties after mid-1937, remained with the committee until its investigations ended. At Abt's suggestion Charles Kramer, who had worked in the Office of the Consumers' Counsel at AAA, joined the staff as an investigator; his assignment to Detroit placed him in one of the committee's pivotal positions. Luke Wilson, a Justice Department Investigator, walked into Wohlforth's office and asked him for a job. Wohlforth replied, "There's a desk over there, go to work." [27]

The committee acquired most of its staff by the simple expedient of borrowing from the National Labor Relations Board. With the board crippled by injunctions, its attorneys, Wohlforth observed, "were absolutely in a condition of stasis." [28] Many of them eagerly contributed their time and energy to the La Follette Committee investigations, for the success of the committee, they realized, might ensure the NLRB's survival. During the period before April 21, 1937, the day on which the Supreme Court handed down the *Jones & Laughlin* decision, most of the board's Detroit staff received instructions to analyze the records of detective agencies, aid in the identification of labor spies, and serve Senate subpoenas. During its first year of activity the La Follette Committee borrowed three dozen people from the NLRB staff. The board's regional offices willingly furnished the committee with information from their own investigations. Committee investigators used NLRB offices as their own headquarters while they were in the field. Thus the committee and the board, sharing objectives, cemented their alliance.[29]

An *esprit de corps* pervaded the staff from the beginning of the investi-

[27] Jackson, COHC, p. 743; interview with Luke Wilson, September 12, 1963, copy in COHC, p. 2. Those who applied for staff positions by mail apparently underwent a more rigorous screening. In 1936 D. Lawrence Anderson, whose background "any self-respecting Liberal would shudder to own," tried to join the staff; he admitted to having been a National Guardsman, a special investigator for the Civil Works Administration, and a relief inspector, "all of which add up to one word—TORY." Wohlforth told him, "There is a marked division of opinion in your case. . . . [Perhaps] after a time we may be of a different mind" (Anderson to Wohlforth, August 3, 1936; Wohlforth to Anderson, August 3, 1936, LFC, Box 4).

[28] Wohlforth, COHC, p. 8.

[29] Silverberg, "Detroit: The Battleground," *The Wagner Act*, p. 80; NLRB *Hearings*, XXIV (Pt. 2), 5788; Robert H. Cowdrill to Wohlforth, March 16, 1937, LFC, Box 5; Charles Kramer to Dr. William Haber, October 30, 1936, LFC, Box 112. Other New Deal agencies, particularly WPA, assisted the La Follette Committee; Harry Hopkins loaned fourteen people to it from his staff (Washington *Star*, January 27, 1937).

gation. As the C.I.O. launched its organizing drives, committee investigators exhibited the zeal of missionaries. They darted from factory to union meeting to company office, grabbed meals on the run, wrote reports in the early morning hours, and spent their own money when appropriations were exhausted. "I am slowly but surely wearing out on this job," one investigator told Wohlforth. "I am running around at a tremendous rate of speed . . . I am a subpoena server and investigator and what not at the same time." [30] La Follette deemed it prudent to caution staff members that "we can not always follow our sympathies into action. . . . Our function is to get information and we do not go in for conversion, redemption or salvation." Under no circumstances, for example, were staff members permitted to address union meetings. But Detroit investigators drafted an article on the hearings for the UAW newspaper; occasional leaks to the press indicated that overzealous agents would evade the spirit, if not the letter, of their instructions.[31]

It would be difficult to overestimate the impact on staff members of participation in the committee's work. Few, if any, escaped total involvement. As seen by its personnel, the committee educated, fulfilled, and purified those who served it. "Thank you very much for what you have let me do," wrote a part-time investigator upon leaving the committee staff. "It has been more than fun for me—it has almost been my religion," he said. Nothing in Charles Kramer's experience "quite equals this last years work both in terms of expanding horizons . . . and in what at least temporarily seems to be the value of the work performed. I think it is more of a 'liberal' education than any other work I can conceive of. . . ." Another investigator, pleading with Representative Tom Amlie to assist the committee, declared "I really believe that today we are the most powerful agency in this country against Fascism." [32]

With the outlines of the investigation drawn and a staff assembled, committee members pored over evidence of a variety of civil liberties

[30] Benjamin Allen to Wohlforth, December 7, 1936, LFC, Box 4; Wohlforth to Allen, December 29, 1936, LFC, Box 113.

[31] La Follette to Harold Cranefield, March 9, 1937, LFC, Box 5; Charles Kramer to Wohlforth, November 8, 1936, LFC, Box 4; Benjamin Allen to Charles Rigby, December 17, 1936, LFC, Box 124; Wohlforth, COHC, p. 23.

[32] H. Eichenberg to Wohlforth, December 11, 1936, LFC, Box 4; Charles Kramer to Gerald Barnes, July 30, 1937, LFC, Box 87; Felix J. Frazer to Thomas Amlie, February 3, 1937, LFC, Box 5. The staff's impact can be gauged from the fact that in deciding which companies to examine in public hearings, Wohlforth and the senators depended almost entirely on the judgment of field investigators (unsigned memo, n.d., LFC, Box 124).

infractions. When Robert Wohlforth reviewed the committee's files, he discovered voluminous correspondence, assembled by Gardner Jackson, relating to sharecroppers, migrant workers, and violations of voting rights in southern states. He assured Jackson, in July, that "undoubtedly one of the phases of our study will include the sharecropper situation." Would Jackson, Wohlforth inquired, send a list of people to contact and whatever data Jackson possessed on sharecropper intimidation? [33] Wohlforth also planned to inquire into infringements of academic freedom and into the terror spread throughout the Midwest by the Black Legion, the notorious fascistic organization.[34]

For several months an investigation of academic freedom seemed likely. La Follette assigned a volunteer from the American Civil Liberties Union to gather information; as late as November 1936 Wohlforth told Roger Baldwin that a hearing on "teachers' rights" was contemplated; Wohlforth asked the ACLU to nominate "a general contact man . . . to line up a two hour hearing on this subject," and suggested that Robert M. Hutchins and James B. Conant "will make excellent first string witnesses. . . ." Baldwin was delighted with the prospect, but it never materialized. Wohlforth, the ACLU volunteer told Baldwin, "seemed, quite rightly perhaps, dominantly interested in violations of the Wagner Act, and likes to deal in stuff that will make the headlines." [35]

The Black Legion investigation suffered a similar fate. The ACLU strongly urged La Follette not to ignore the terroristic activities of this group, but La Follette apparently was "somewhat hesitant about taking up . . . any matter not already canvassed by the committee in its preliminary hearings." [36] Baldwin's enthusiasm for a broad investigation now far

[33] La Follette to Elbert D. Thomas, June 22, 1936, Thomas Papers, Box 19; Wohlforth, COHC, p. 6; Wohlforth to Gardner Jackson, July 10, 1936, LFC, Box 4. The STFU prepared a statement for the preliminary hearings, but La Follette, H. L. Mitchell wrote, "as a matter of strategy asked that we withhold our material until the Resolution could be passed." The STFU still hoped to be heard during the winter of 1936–1937. (Mitchell to Harry A. Poth, September 9, 1936, ACLU, Vol. 887). Mitchell, Jackson, and Kester spoke to La Follette periodically about the Arkansas situation, to no avail (Mitchell to Auerbach, April 26, 1963).

[34] Memo, n.d., in Wohlforth Papers.

[35] Charles K. Cummings, Jr. to Roger Baldwin, July 1, 1936, and Wohlforth to Baldwin, November 23, 1936, ACLU, Vol. 887; Wohlforth to Baldwin, December 9, 1936, and Baldwin to Wohlforth, December 12, 1936, ACLU, Vol. 872; Charles K. Cummings, Jr. to Baldwin, November 15, 1936, ACLU, Vol. 887.

[36] Roger Baldwin to Avrahm G. Mezerik, June 30, 1936, ACLU, Vol. 887. Late in the summer of 1936 Senator James Couzens urged the committee to investigate the Black Legion. The Conference for the Protection of Civil Rights, in Detroit, "un-

outran that of the La Follette Committee. He asked each of the ACLU's state chapters to indicate what pressing situations the committee might investigate. From North Dakota came reports that the American Legion had attempted to suppress freedom of speech. From South Carolina came an account of arbitrary arrests of labor organizers. Oregon sent stories of suppression of left-wing literature. Washington reported the use of the National Guard to quash strikes.[37] But the La Follette Committee was reluctant to broaden the scope of its investigation. Violations of academic freedom, and terror in the Midwest, disturbed the committee much less than did interference with labor organization.

With its appropriation of $15,000 the committee could plan to do little more than scratch the surface of civil liberties violations, even in labor disputes. If limited funds curtailed the range of its investigation, most staff members were inclined toward focusing the committee's activities on labor's problems rather than attempting a general survey of civil liberties infringements. The NLRB's difficulties, and the availability of its staff, encouraged this approach. Heber Blankenhorn's studies provided the committee with dramatic material, which it would have been foolish to ignore. And the preliminary hearings, which brought the committee considerable publicity, offered a solid foundation on which to build. All factors pointed in one direction: an inquiry into overt anti-union practices. By the end of July 1936 still another force, more powerful than the others but reinforcing them all, had set the La Follette Committee's bearings; the C.I.O., through the Steel Workers' Organizing Committee, made its momentous decision to organize the industry long regarded as the bastion of the open shop.

From its inception the C.I.O. made steel its first order of business. The economic power of the steel industry made it an obvious target. Furthermore, John L. Lewis considered organization in this industry crucial for the success of his United Mine Workers; their status in the captive mines, Lewis believed, remained in jeopardy while steel resisted organization. On

---

earthed" a Black Legion officer, who was interviewed by Heber Blankenhorn and John Abt. Abt doubted if the man knew much "about activities interfering with labor's or radicals' rights," and the matter was dropped (Couzens to Marie Hempel, September 2, 1936, Avrahm Mezerik to Baldwin, November 10, 1936, Baldwin to Mezerik, November 14, 1936, ACLU, Vol. 940).

[37] Baldwin to ACLU Chapters, June 12, 1936, Herbert C. Hanson to Baldwin, June 15, 1936, Charlotte Stevenson to Baldwin, June 19, 1936, R. Waldron Anderson to Baldwin, June 22, 1936, Irving M. Clark to Lucille B. Milner, June 24, 1936, ACLU, Vol. 940.

June 4 the Amalgamated Association of Iron, Steel and Tin Workers accepted C.I.O. terms for an organizing drive in the steel industry; two weeks later the Steel Workers' Organizing Committee held its first meeting. These developments profoundly affected the course of the La Follette Committee. "The force of logic of events . . . shaped the Committee," Robert Wohlforth recalled. "It was obvious from the stories in the press where we would go." [38] The C.I.O.'s decision to engage in battle with steel management thrust the La Follette Committee into the field of labor-management militancy and strengthened its commitment to securing the civil liberties of industrial workers who wished to become union members. Its initial objective, to call attention to the impotence of the National Labor Relations Board, broadened immeasurably. No longer would the committee speak solely as advocate for the NLRB. Its mandate from Congress invited it to become the cutting edge of the C.I.O.'s effort to muster public support for its campaigns and tactics. The committee did not plan an alliance with the C.I.O.; it erupted, and steel was the catalyst.

When the Steel Workers' Organizing Committee launched its organizing campaign in June, it encountered unmitigated hostility from steel companies in Pennsylvania and Ohio. The Bethlehem Steel Company hired two hundred special policemen who patrolled the streets of Johnstown armed with revolvers and blackjacks, and shouldered their way into every gathering of workers. In Aliquippa the SWOC could neither rent a hall for meetings nor secure office space. In Youngstown and Canton armed thugs in automobiles followed organizers bumper to bumper. Only after five months of effort could Philip Murray, SWOC chairman, report that "in most cases we . . . have overcome, in one way or another, most of the obstacles to exercising our constitutional rights." [39]

During the summer Clinton S. Golden, director of the SWOC's crucial northeastern region, conferred with La Follette Committee staff members in Washington. Golden had already furnished the committee with evidence of intimidation of steel workers; as former NLRB regional director of the Pittsburgh area, he enjoyed a unique opportunity to sharpen both the NLRB and the C.I.O. prongs of the La Follette investigation. [40] Golden and the committee reached specific agreement on two points: A "contact

[38] Walter Galenson, *The CIO Challenge to the AFL*, pp. 77, 79, 87; Wohlforth, COHC, pp. 6, 8.

[39] "The Problem Before the SWOC on June 17, 1936," statement by Philip Murray, November 8, 1936, C.I.O. Papers, Box 33.

[40] Cf. Golden testimony, *Hearings on S. Res. 266*, pp. 9-11; Wohlforth to Golden, July 30, 1936, LFC, Box 4.

man" would act as liaison between the two committees; and the SWOC would assist the La Follette Committee staff with secretarial help ("all we need," Wohlforth noted) and financial aid. Philip Murray instructed steel workers and SWOC members that any information "which is based on definite and accurate facts, pointing to the steel companies' tactics to deprive the workers of their civil liberties and right to organize, should be forwarded to the General Counsel at the Pittsburgh office. Such information will be made available to the La Follette Committee. . . ." [41]

The committee sent an investigator to Pittsburgh with instructions to "pick up any additional stuff that [Golden has], and be put in touch with some of the leads that are developing." Wohlforth advised him, "If you will put yourself entirely in [Golden's] hands I am sure you will get that which you are looking for." The understanding between Golden and the La Follette Committee would "go right down the line." The situation in steel, Wohlforth explained, "is such that the organizing committee has many friends, has the confidence of large numbers of people, and has the means to secure a great deal of valuable information for us. . . . In a sense the CIO is at this moment pretty much on top of the heap and they can extend to us a measure of cooperation we had not formerly anticipated. Furthermore, they want to help us and they mean business." [42]

The C.I.O. was the committee's most powerful ally, but it remained only one of several. The NLRB, its investigators dispersed throughout the country, continually alerted the committee to civil liberties infractions in labor disputes. The board, Heber Blankenhorn had suggested in the spring of 1936, "sits on its triple throne a bit like the church shorn of its right to prosecute and hang. Despite the loss of temporal power, NLRB can still thunder from the pulpit and excommunicate from the congregation of the righteous. That comforts the flock, disconcerts the heathen—and marks down the latter against the day of wrath to come." [43]

[41] Memo of conference with Clinton S. Golden, July 31, 1936, Wohlforth Papers; Philip Murray announcement, n.d., C.I.O. Papers, Box 33.

[42] Wohlforth to Golden, July 30, 1936, and Wohlforth to Allen Saylor, August 3, 1936, LFC, Box 4. Later in the year Wohlforth asked whether the committee could secure copies of affidavits collected by the C.I.O. from workers whom the steel companies discharged for their union activities during the SWOC drive (Wohlforth to Lee Pressman, December 8, 1936, LFC, Box 93).

For general comments about the committee and the SWOC organizing campaign, see New York *Post*, September 26, 1936; New York *Journal of Commerce*, October 26, 1936; Frederick H. Harbison, "Labor Relations in the Iron and Steel Industry, 1936 to 1939" (unpublished doctoral dissertation), pp. 29–30; Robert R. R. Brooks, *When Labor Organizes*, pp. 170, 174.

[43] Blankenhorn to J. Warren Madden, John M. Carmody, and Edwin S. Smith, June 16, 1936, NLRB *Hearings*, XX, 4317.

The board followed Blankenhorn's advice, and the La Follette Committee remained attentive to its sermons. When, for example, NLRB investigators returned from the West Coast with evidence that employers in Los Angeles and San Francisco had cavalierly disregarded labor's rights, the committee arranged with the NLRB for a joint investigation. The board made three of its regional attorneys available to the committee; labor relations on the West Coast subsequently comprised a major aspect of the committee's inquiry.[44]

Blankenhorn also engaged in skillful maneuvering to secure an endorsement of the La Follette investigation from the American Federation of Labor. At the federation's 1936 convention in Tampa, Blankenhorn encountered an undercurrent of hostility to the committee manifested by unwillingness to pass a resolution in support of its activities. One federation member asked Blankenhorn if he had "talked this over with Lewis before [he] came down here." Another inquired, "This La Follette thing is a C.I.O. business, started by them, [isn't] it?" Struggling against A.F. of L. coolness, Blankenhorn circumspectly delivered copies of a "model" resolution to J. J. Handley, president of the Wisconsin State Federation and a known peacemaker, and to other moderates. He wangled assurances of support from John P. Frey, president of the Metal Trades Department, and from Matthew Woll, of the federation's executive council. Finally, the Committee on Legislation decided that "there is no more important subject before this convention" than the La Follette investigation. Labor, it declared, "needs the Committee, which has full power but no funds, to continue as an aggressive weapon ready for use when labor calls upon it, and as a continuous curb on the indefensible, but so far unregulated, practices of industrial corporations." The convention adopted this report, urged that the committee receive an appropriation of $200,000, and heard President William Green announce that the federation had "played a very large part in bringing about the creation" of the committee. "These comparatively simple results," Heber Blankenhorn advised the NLRB, "were not speedily attained."[45]

Although pledges of co-operation from both major labor organizations undoubtedly pleased the committee, it did not hold its investigation in abeyance waiting for concrete help. At the end of June, Robert Wohl-

---

[44] Wohlforth to La Follette, November 5, 1936, Wohlforth memo, November 7, 1936, LFC, Box 4.

[45] Blankenhorn to NLRB, November 30, 1936, NLRB *Hearings*, XX, 4277; *New York Times*, November 22, 1936, April 30, 1940; American Federation of Labor, *Report of Proceedings of the 56th Annual Convention* (Washington, D.C., 1936), pp. 457–459.

forth drafted an outline for the first set of hearings, planned for the final week in August and the first week in September. Wohlforth listed four topics for exploration. Of paramount importance was investigation of the services offered by labor detective agencies. Using data from the preliminary hearings and from NLRB cases, the committee planned, first, to examine representative agencies in order to expose their structure, finances, clients, and activities. This phase of the investigation, Wohlforth indicated, would be "definitely related to *current* instances of interferences with the rights of labor." Second, the committee would study the anti-union behavior of manufacturers' associations and vigilante groups, for the purpose of determining what ties, if any, they maintained with detective agencies, company unions, and the labor espionage departments of large corporations. Third, the committee would investigate the anti-union activities of corporations, particularly steel, automobile, textile, and mining companies. Wohlforth hoped to learn whether high corporate officials bore responsibility for their companies' anti-union practices. Finally, the committee would probe the services offered by munitions companies as means of "resolving" labor disputes. The Nye Committee had examined the records of two firms known to be engaged in the manufacture of munitions for use in industrial controversies; Wohlforth, who was familiar with this evidence, planned to incorporate it into the La Follette investigation.[46]

In pursuing these points the committee was guided by several questions: How extensive was the use of spies, strikebreakers, *agents provocateurs*, and industrial munitions? If widely used, did they impinge upon the civil liberties of workers? Must employers utilize such techniques, or were they "the unwilling victims of a system of their own creation?" Was federal regulation necessary? The committee considered three possible approaches: labor as victim; management as customer; or detective and strikebreaking companies as agents. Limited funds and the nature of Heber Blankenhorn's data dictated the choice of the last alternative.[47]

[46] "Proposed Order of Work," memo of June 29, 1936, Wohlforth Papers; "Munitions File," *ibid.*; Wohlforth, COHC, p. 4. At La Follette's request Nye made certain of his committee records available (Nye to La Follette, January 7, 1937, LFC, Box 5). Wohlforth also looked to the experiences of the Black Committee, but for a different reason; he asked staff member David D. Lloyd to check with the Black Committee about the procedure for subpoenaing telegrams. "Watch out that we do it right," Wohlforth cautioned. "We don't want to make any mistakes." The Black Committee had made several (Wohlforth to Lloyd, August 13, 1936, LFC, Box 4). On the Black Committee, see Wolfskill, *The Revolt of the Conservatives*, pp. 236-238.

[47] U.S. Senate, Committee on Education and Labor, *Preliminary Report Pursuant to S. Res. 266*, 75th Cong., 1st Sess., 1937, p. 2.

Before the committee was swept along as a partisan in the confrontation between labor and management in the mass-production industries, it engaged in two preliminary skirmishes.[48] The first presented a serious challenge to its investigative authority. In mid-August the committee served subpoenas on five labor detective agencies, requiring them to submit all records and office documents within five days. La Follette, however, had already received the unwelcome news that one of these agencies, the Railway Audit and Inspection Company, would contest the committee's authority by refusing to produce documents or to testify.[49] At this juncture Robert Watts, associate general counsel of the NLRB, surmised that the subpoenas might frighten the detective agencies into destroying their records. In order to recapture the initiative for the committee, he devised a scheme whereby NLRB field agents would approach janitors in buildings where the recalcitrant companies maintained offices and get permission to obtain the contents of their wastebaskets. Once this maneuver was accomplished, a team of twelve girls, working in three shifts around the clock in a "secret, draftless office," pieced together the rescued fragments.[50]

Watts's stratagem served its purpose during the committee's first day of public hearings. As La Follette had suspected, counsel for the Railway Audit and Inspection Company challenged the constitutionality of Senate Resolution 266. He informed La Follette that a company stockholder had filed suit that morning to restrain its officers from appearing before the committee, and a federal judge had directed the committee to show cause why a preliminary injunction should not be issued. La Follette angrily accused the company of "the grossest kind of contumacy." The committee did not hesitate to place in evidence the mutilated records salvaged from company wastebaskets. Relying upon a law enacted in the previous session of Congress, it moved quickly for an indictment of company officials on the charge of failure to comply with a subpoena. By meeting

[48] Hearings during 1936 were held on August 21 and September 22–25, when the committee examined the activities of three labor detective agencies and two munitions companies. During nine days of hearings in January 1937, the committee focused on the labor policies of the Tennessee Coal, Iron and Railroad Company, the National Metal Trades Association, and the Chrysler Corporation. Analysis of this phase of its investigation is reserved for Chapter Five.

[49] *New York Times*, August 13, 1936; La Follette to Elbert Thomas, August 7, 1936, Thomas Papers, Box 19.

[50] Thomas I. Emerson, COHC, pp. 459–460; Emerson, in retrospect, expressed concern over the legality and ethics of this maneuver. *New York Times*, September 17, 1936.

its first challenge swiftly and efficiently, if underhandedly, the committee forestalled further attempts to stymie the investigation.[51]

In January 1937 the committee, in a preview of the evidence to follow, placed on record an account of the extent to which civil liberties had been damaged by anti-union companies. Jack Barton, a resident of Bessemer, Alabama, had been for twenty years a member of the International Union of Mine, Mill and Smelter Workers. For the last three of these years he was also a member of the Communist Party, at that time a legal party in Alabama. Bessemer, the site of a large rolling-mill operated by the Tennessee Coal, Iron and Railroad Company, a subsidiary of United States Steel, did not welcome either Communists or labor organizers, and police authorities rarely distinguished between the two. In a period of a year and a half, during which Barton encouraged workers to join the A.F. of L., he was arrested four times: as a suspected Communist, for possessing more than one item of literature advocating overthrow of the government, for vagrancy (he had thirty-five dollars in his pocket and a steady, if small, weekly income), and again for possessing seditious literature—discovered by police who entered his home with a search warrant for liquor.

After the last arrest, Barton testified, the employment manager of the Tennessee Coal, Iron and Railroad Company questioned him in the police station about "Communist" activities, both local and national. The first persons about whom he allegedly inquired were Heywood Broun and Eleanor Roosevelt. At Barton's trial on the day after his arrest, the court refused to favor him with a lawyer or a jury. It sentenced him to 180 days at hard labor and imposed a fine of one hundred dollars. When the International Labor Defense provided bail, local authorities refused to accept the bond. A writ of habeas corpus was filed and denied. Barton, who had an arrested case of tuberculosis, suffered terribly in prison; as an added indignity, the warden shackled his legs for road-gang work. (Barton told the La Follette Committee, "That had never been done before to a white prisoner.") Before long his legs became infected; after he lost fifteen pounds and could no longer work, he was transferred to a sanatorium.[52]

While Barton languished in prison, Joseph Gelders, southern representative of the National Committee for the Defense of Political Prisoners, came to Bessemer to launch a campaign for his release. There, Gelders

---

[51] *Hearings*, Pt. 1, pp. 5–6, 24; *New York Times*, August 22, 25, September 1, 22, 1936. Railway Audit and Inspection Company officials were indicted on September 21, but they were not convicted.

[52] *Hearings*, Pt. 3, pp. 758–768.

conferred with Arthur Green, an old friend, and a solicitor of the Bessemer County Court. According to Gelders' testimony, Green told him that Barton had been kept under surveillance since his arrival in Bessemer and that "the industrialists" had prevented bond from being raised on his behalf. According to Gelders, Green admitted that this procedure would not meet constitutional standards but said, "that's the way we do [it] in Bessemer. The T.C.I. controls Bessemer, and you won't get very far with your teachings here. . . ." [53]

Gelders told the committee that one evening, after I.L.D. members had met to discuss the Barton case, two men attacked him on the outskirts of town. One clubbed him with a baseball bat, another broke his nose, and together they beat him unconscious before dumping him into their automobile. After a two-hour drive they dragged him from the car, ordered him to strip, and flogged him with a leather strap three feet long and two inches wide. Whipped, beaten, and kicked mercilessly until he again lost consciousness, Gelders spent the night attempting to summon strength to seek help; he finally made his way to a hospital. He was able to make positive identification of his assailants. Moreover, both men were seen disposing of their weapons and Gelders' confiscated literature, and their car was identified. At least one of the men was understood to work as a secret investigator for the Tennessee Coal, Iron and Railroad Company; he had an unlisted telephone in company offices. Notwithstanding this evidence, a grand jury twice failed to indict. An Alabama state police officer, assigned to the case by the governor, explained this failure to the La Follette Committee: "The T.C.I. owns or controls about fifteen-sixteenths of that country around there. . . ." [54]

In their treatment of Barton and Gelders Alabamans had disregarded at least seven guarantees of the federal Bill of Rights. Either one or the other had been denied the right to speak, the right of peaceable assembly, the right to be secure against unreasonable searches and seizures, the right to counsel and to an impartial jury, and the right not to have excessive bail required nor an excessive fine imposed. Both men were denied their liberty, and very nearly their lives, without due process of law.

But the furor in some segments of the Southern press which accompanied the Barton-Gelders hearing caused the La Follette Committee some

[53] *Ibid.*, pp. 772–779.
[54] *Ibid.*, pp. 779–788, 792; Calkins, *Spy Overhead*, pp. 278–301; *New York Times*, January 15, 1937.

concern.[55] The *New Leader* reported a "very definite movement" in
Washington to stifle the investigation by blocking further appropriations.[56] Consequently the committee never again ventured south in its
probe of civil liberties infractions. Certain of its authority and cognizant
of the practical limits of its inquiry, the committee concentrated on those
anti-union practices which for decades had undermined the civil liberties
of industrial workers. The approaching confrontation between labor and
management in the mass-production industries prompted Senator Thomas
to tell Robert Wohlforth, "I think the pressure to go on will be greater
than the pressure to stop." [57] Thomas' prophecy was accurate. The committee turned from the civil liberties of two Alabama radicals to the civil
liberties of thousands of industrial laborers.

[55] E.g., Birmingham (Ala.) *News*, January 16, 1937; Greensboro (N.C.) *News*,
January 16, 1937; Decatur (Ala.) *Daily*, January 18, 1937, clippings in ACLU, Vol.
994. The Greensboro *News* wondered if the Gelders investigation portended an
inquiry into lynching. If so, it predicted "a crescendo of oratory, of constitutional
protest and of technical differentiations from southern statesmen."

[56] *New Leader*, January 16, 1937, clipping in ACLU, Vol. 994. On January 27
Senator Thomas introduced S. 70, authorizing a further appropriation of $50,000,
Three weeks later the Senate approved the resolution after a cut of $10,000 by the
Audit and Control Committee.

[57] Thomas to Wohlforth, January 11, 1937, LFC, Box 5.

V

The Instruments of Industrial Warfare

"MAY I humbly warn the Senate," John L. Lewis thundered, with few audible signs of humility, in a New Year's Eve radio address on December 31, 1936, "that labor wants [the La Follette] investigation pressed home and wants industry disarmed lest labor men on their march to industrial democracy should have to take by storm the barbed-wire barricades and machine-gun emplacements maintained by the rapacious moguls of corporate industry."[1]

To chroniclers of labor relations in the New Deal, military metaphors have seemed particularly appropriate. If labor was, as Lewis suggested, marching toward industrial democracy, then he was its general and the La Follette Committee its aide-de-camp. By collecting information about the enemy's tactics, it sustained morale at the front and helped labor to win its battle for public opinion. While the antagonists maneuvered for position during the winter of 1936–1937, the La Follette Committee began its examination of four anti-union practices that had frustrated labor organization for decades: espionage, stockpiling of munitions, strikebreaking, and intimidation by armed private police. These accoutrements of industrial strife represented the underside of American industrial relations. Their frequent use convinced the La Follette Committee that management was conducting "a colossal, daily drive in every part of the country to frustrate enunciated labor policy. . . ."[2]

Espionage is indispensable in every war; since the 1870's spies had sapped the strength of American unions by covertly observing and reporting attempts to organize. In 1937 the La Follette Committee discovered espionage "to be a common, almost universal, practice in American industry." Management knew of no more efficient method to prevent the formation of a union, to weaken a newly organized union, or to wreck a

[1] *New York Times*, January 1, 1937.
[2] U.S. Senate, Subcommittee of the Committee on Education and Labor, *Preliminary Report Pursuant to S. Res. 266*, 75th Cong., 1st Sess., 1937, p. 15.

union when it tested its strength. The list of companies resorting to espionage read "like a blue book of American industry. . . . From motion-
picture producers to steel makers, from hookless fasteners to automobiles,
from small units to giant enterprises—scarcely an industry . . . is not fully
represented in the . . . list of clients of the detective agencies." The
committee found a correlation between the decline of labor unions and
company expenditures for espionage, and it concluded that collective
bargaining could not succeed while the industrial spy plied his trade.[3]

Labor spies had developed efficient techniques for destroying unions.
Frequently the representative of a detective agency came to an industrial
community and gained the confidence of local labor leaders or union
members. By transmitting useful information to the employer, he was able
to secure a contract for his company's services; then another agent—the
spy—would be assigned to infiltrate the union and disrupt its efforts to
organize. The latter was achieved by a process known as "hooking," a
term coined by a labor spy who perceived the similarity between his
technique of baiting the hook and the less pernicious practice of fishing
for catfish in the Mississippi River. As one former spy, adept at hooking,
explained, "Well, first you look your prospect over, and if he is married
that is preferable. If he is financially hard up, that is number two. If his
wife wants more money or he hasn't got a car, that all counts."[4]

The hooked man was led to believe that co-operating with the "hooker"
would further the interests of his fellow workers. Hookers persuaded
victims that their reports were desired by minority stockholders, insurance
adjusters, or federal agencies bent on ending company mismanagement.
The spy transmitted his estimate of union strength and his lists of active
union members to the detective agency, which edited them and forwarded
them to its client, who was thus forewarned of strikes and apprised of
strike plans and union weaknesses. Spies wreaked havoc on union locals;
generating mistrust, the spy, according to the La Follette Committee, "in-
cites to violence, preaches strikes, inflames the hot-headed and leads the
union to disaster."[5]

[3] U.S. Senate, Committee on Education and Labor, *Industrial Espionage*, Report
No. 46, Pt. 3, 75th Cong., 2d Sess., 1937, pp. 2, 22, 23, 74. The committee examined
five labor detective agencies: Pinkerton's, Railway Audit and Inspection Company,
Corporations Auxiliary Company, William J. Burns International Detective Agency,
and National Corporation Service, Inc.

[4] *Ibid.*, p. 33; *Hearings*, Pt. 1, pp. 135, 201.

[5] *Industrial Espionage*, pp. 28, 37–38, 63.

Employers and detective agency officials advanced several justifications for espionage: protection against radicalism, prevention of sabotage, detection of theft, and improvement of labor-management relations (euphemistically called "human engineering"). Those who admitted using espionage rarely pondered its ethical implications. La Follette pressed the vice-president of De Soto to distinguish between espionage used to secure another company's industrial secrets—a practice which the officer deplored—and espionage to obtain information about unions. The senator was told: "I think the difference is in the use that is made of the information." The general manager of the Associated Industries of Cleveland insisted: "Spying always will be an essential part of warfare. . . . When a man has reason to fear that the work of a lifetime is going to be struck at by some attack . . . he is going to forewarn himself in order to forearm himself if he can." [6]

The history of organization efforts by automobile workers in Flint, Michigan, presented a paradigm of the destructiveness of industrial espionage. In 1934 the Federal Union of Automobile Workers boasted 26,000 members in General Motors plants in that city. But of thirteen members of the union's executive board at least three were spies; one served as chairman of the organizing committee, and another represented the local at a convention where plans for new organizing drives were formulated. Within two years membership in the Flint local fell to 120. When UAW organizers came to Flint they found workers who were afraid to participate in overt union activities. Clandestine meetings were held at night with the lights out, for the frightened men were unwilling to risk being identified. The La Follette Committee concluded that through espionage "private corporations dominate their employees, deny them their constitutional rights, promote disorder and disharmony, and even set at naught the powers of the Government itself." [7]

[6] *Ibid.*, p. 9; *Hearings*, Pt. 4, pp. 1220–21, Pt. 22, p. 9457.

[7] *Industrial Espionage*, pp. 70–71, 73. The publicity given to labor espionage by the La Follette Committee produced salutary results. In April 1937 Pinkerton directors resolved to discontinue industrial espionage. In May the National Metal Trades Association discontinued its espionage services. The Corporations Auxiliary Company liquidated its entire business (*ibid.*, pp. 73–74; Baltimore *Sun*, March 17, 1937; Robert Wohlforth to Roger Rutchick, September 8, 1937, LFC, Box 87). A prospective spy was told by the manager of a detective agency, "You, of course, realize with the La Follette investigating committee functioning, that we are not putting any men to work on investigations that would have anything to do with labor difficulties or labor unions" (*Hearings*, Pt. 57, p. 20875). Governors Lehman of New York and Benson of Minnesota demanded strict regulation of detective agencies on the basis of La

When espionage failed to deter organization, management invested in tear and nauseating gas, machine guns, gas bombs, and billy clubs, in anticipation of labor trouble.[8] Capitalizing on the fear of communism to sell their wares, munitions companies transformed every impending labor crisis into a harbinger of revolution. One company purchased and distributed to prospective clients 1,500 copies of Elizabeth Dilling's *The Red Network*, an anti-New Deal diatribe. Stirred by apprehension, employers responded militantly to union demands for recognition; but by stockpiling munitions they frequently prompted workers to strike, thereby bringing about the very result they had hoped to forestall. During strikes company police and hired strike-guards constantly usurped the public police power by venturing away from company property, weapons in hand, to maintain "law and order." They scattered picket lines and disrupted union meetings. "The possession and use of industrial munitions by employers," declared the La Follette Committee, "is the logical end of a labor-relations policy based on nonrecognition of unions. . . ."[9]

Munitions salesmen appreciated that labor unrest was necessary to their business. In 1935 one of them told his sales manager: "Wish a hell of a strike would get under way." When strike prospects improved, he wrote, "I hope that this strike develops and matures and that it will be a damn bad one, we need the money." Another agent facetiously wondered about the propriety of "a restraining order on the President of the United States to prevent him from stopping all these strikes. It seems to me that his actions are absolutely in restraint of trade—that is as far as we are concerned." In anticipation of a Communist-led hunger march a salesman hoped for "an opportunity to demonstrate the use of our clubs and baby

Follette Committee findings (Lehman message to N.Y. Legislature, January 6, 1937, copy in LFC, Box 85; American Federation of Labor *Weekly News Service*, November 17, 1937). For an exchange between Senators La Follette and Thomas and the *New York Times* over the veracity of the committee's espionage report, see *New York Times*, December 24, 1937, January 2, 1938.

[8] Evidence presented before the Nye Committee revealed that corporations had stockpiled munitions for use in industrial disputes. Robert Wohlforth's knowledge of this practice led to this phase of the La Follette investigation (Wohlforth, COHC, p. 4; *Progressive*, February 29, 1936). Since a House committee had investigated Pinkerton's in 1892, at least four congressional committees had revealed the existence of private industrial arsenals (U.S. Senate, Committee on Education and Labor, *Industrial Munitions*, Report No. 6, Pt. 3, 76th Cong., 1st Sess., 1939, pp. 5–13). The three munitions companies examined by the La Follette Committee were Federal Laboratories, Inc., the Lake Erie Chemical Co., and the Manville Mfg. Corp.

[9] *Industrial Munitions*, pp. 61, 108, 157, 189.

giants." During the 1934 strike of longshoremen in San Francisco, a representative of the Federal Laboratories Company related how he "shot a long-range projectile into a group, a shell hitting one man and causing a fracture of the skull, from which he has since died. As he was a communist, I have no feeling in the matter and I am sorry that I did not get more." His superior commended him for a "splendid" report.[10]

The diligence of munitions salesmen was amply rewarded. Between 1933 and 1937 Republic Steel, United States Steel, Bethlehem Steel, and Youngstown Sheet and Tube each purchased more gas equipment than did any law enforcement agency in the country. Republic, with 52,000 employees, purchased more than ten times as many gas guns and more than twenty-six times as many gas shells and projectiles as did the Chicago police department, which was responsible for the safety of 3,300,000 persons. Republic's arsenal included 552 revolvers, 64 rifles, 245 shotguns, 143 gas guns, 4,033 gas projectiles, 2,707 gas grenades, and an undetermined number of night sticks and gas revolvers. "Our general experience," explained a Republic vice-president, "has been that during these strikes it is well to have your plants sufficiently armed and in proper shape to repel an invasion." Scanning the hearing room, he commented on the presence of armed policemen, as in Republic plants. La Follette dryly assured him, "We want you to feel that you are in a homelike atmosphere." [11]

Representatives of munitions companies and corporation officials agreed that gas provided "the most humane way" of handling labor disputes. "We are out to sell gas," declared the president of Federal Laboratories, "as a humane means of protecting property from destruction or protecting life from injury. . . ." The sales manager of another munitions company believed that through the sale of gas, "I am not only improving industry but improving society." Walter Gordon Merritt, counsel for the Anthracite Institute, explained: "The whole theory of the use of gas is that it makes it unnecessary to use bullets. I am sorry we have to have strikes. I am sorry we have Communists in the country." [12]

The La Follette Committee could not begin to estimate the number of persons whose civil liberties were abridged by armed agents of corpora-

[10] *Hearings*, Pt. 2, pp. 399–400, Pt. 7, p. 2439, Pt. 15-D, p. 7219, Pt. 7, p. 2726. In 1933 Federal Laboratories sold tear gas and gas equipment to the Amtorg Trading Co., the Soviet Union's American purchasing agent. A company official explained that the company had no controversy with communism in Russia (*ibid.*, p. 2503).

[11] *Industrial Munitions*, pp. 41, 46, 57; *Hearings*, Pt. 23, p. 9760.

[12] *Hearings*, Pt. 7, p. 2437, Pt. 2, pp. 420–421; *New York Times*, September 25, 1936. See also *Hearings*, Pt. 2, p. 413, Pt. 23, p. 9787.

tions. It noted, however, that "the exercise of constitutionally guaranteed rights of freedom of speech and of assembly necessarily involves freedom to conduct uninterrupted meetings and gatherings in public and private places." The practice of dispersing strikers and union sympathizers with gas weapons obviously mocked these rights. The committee did not condemn the possession of pistols and rifles for necessary policing purposes. It did urge, however, that corporations not be permitted to acquire machine guns and offensive gas weapons of such potency that only responsible public authorities should be entrusted with their use. The committee concluded that "munitions, and especially gas, are usually purchased by employers for the purpose of intervening in the policing of picket lines and the conduct of strikes. Through them the employer . . . exercises physical coercion upon his own employees in his economic struggle with them." [13]

When use of spies and munitions failed to quash labor militancy, anti-union employers again turned to detective agencies for a supply of strike-breakers—hired men who temporarily replaced striking workers to hasten the end of a strike. The strikebreaker, once glorified as an "American hero" by Harvard president Charles W. Eliot, had an obvious interest in intensifying the strike that he was hired to break; his wages depended upon his doing so. Since the time of Jack Whitehead's "Forty Thieves" in the Gilded Age, workers had confronted professional strikebreakers in countless labor controversies. During the great railroad strikes of 1877, and in Homestead fifteen years later, Pinkerton strikebreakers contributed to union defeats. By the turn of the century, nearly every large city had strikebreaking agencies, ready to respond to, and exacerbate, labor unrest.[14]

Federal commissions periodically condemned professional strikebreakers, but Congress remained immune to their requests for federal legislation against strikebreaking. Fourteen states required full disclosure of strikebreaking activities, but this legislation had little effect. Only Wisconsin required detective agencies engaged in espionage or strikebreaking to obtain licenses. In 1936 the federal government finally responded; the Byrnes Act made it a felony to transport any person in interstate commerce with intent to employ him to interfere with peaceful picketing or organization for collective bargaining. But the act, badly drafted, contained many loopholes; it did not, for example, define "intent" or apply sanctions to

13 *Industrial Munitions*, pp. 36, 73, 190.
14 Daniel Bell, "Industrial Conflict and Public Opinion," *Industrial Conflict*, ed. Arthur Kornhauser, *et al.*, p. 244; Levinson, *I Break Strikes*, pp. 15–33.

strikebreakers themselves. Only one prosecution was brought under it: Pearl Bergoff, who applauded Section 7(a) because "I can see so much strife ahead I don't know which way to turn," was acquitted of violating the act, although he operated one of the largest strikebreaking agencies in the country.[15]

The La Follette Committee's hearings on strikebreaking reminded one newspaper editor of "Dante's vision of the Inferno." [16] A vast underworld of strikebreakers thrust unsavory mercenaries into industrial controversies. At Ninth and Euclid in Cleveland, at Broadway and 42nd Street in Manhattan, in the Loop at Randolph Street in Chicago, detective agencies, employers' associations, and individual entrepreneurs recruited men to serve as strikebreakers and strike-guards. Many were convicted criminals. "Chowderhead" Cohen, for example, was wanted in Baltimore for grand larceny, for which he had already been arrested five times in New York. Chowderhead, a surly, corpulent veteran of industrial warfare, had also served time in Sing Sing for burglary and in a federal penitentiary for conspiracy. Other strikebreakers presented similar credentials; their self-chosen sobriquets underscored their outstanding character traits: "Snake-Eyes Kid Steinie," "Stinkfoot" McVey," Eat-em Up" Jack Fisher, "Bennie the Fink" Gross, and "The Brass Monkey." [17]

Strikebreakers and strike-guards evolved into distinct occupational types: "finks," "nobles," and "missionaries." "Finks," or strikebreakers, served as industrial shock troops to encourage strikers to return to work; they distinguished carefully between their activities and the work of "scabs," who permanently replaced strikers. The strike-guard, or "noble," protected the strikebreakers, the loyal workers, and plant property. Strike "missionaries" mingled with strikers to provoke violence and circulated among noncombatants to propagandize against the strike. For most of its practitioners, strikebreaking was a career; men rose from the ranks to

[15] Homer Cummings to FDR, December 22, 1936, FDRL, OF 407; "Industrial Strikebreaking—The Byrnes Act," *University of Chicago Law Review*, IV (June 1937), 657–666; "Employer Interference with Lawful Union Activity," *Columbia Law Review*, XXXVII (May 1937), 831–837; Harry A. Millis and Royal E. Montgomery, *Organized Labor*, pp. 610–611; Edward Levinson, "Strikebreaking Incorporated," *Harper's Magazine*, CLXXI (November 1935), 719–730; "Strikebreaking," *Fortune*, XI (January 1935), 92. In 1938 Congress amended the Byrnes Act to make strikebreakers liable for their own activities.

[16] Washington *Post*, September 25, 1936.

[17] U.S. Senate, Committee on Education and Labor, *Strikebreaking Services*, Report No. 6, Pt. 1, 76th Cong., 1st Sess., 1939, pp. 73–74, 78, 83.

become strike "lieutenants" who recruited strikebreakers and commanded them on the job. Some strikebreakers, apparently, hoped eventually to establish their own agencies and become successful entrepreneurs.[18]

"The almost inevitable effect of employing [strikebreakers]," the La Follette Committee reported, "is to produce resentment, bitterness, violence, and bloodshed." The character of the men and the intensity of the strikers' animosity toward them ensured this result, for strikebreakers understood that when a strike lagged or appeared likely to end they must "heat up the job." A former strikebreaker told the La Follette Committee: "[The] best thing [to] do is slug a picket or two . . . or go in and throw a rock through a business representative's window, or something like that." Detective agencies naturally were eager that a labor dispute provide employment for as many of their men as possible. Fierce interagency competition prevailed when a strike was imminent, and occasionally an agency used reports of its spies to justify its strikebreaking services.[19]

Perhaps inevitably, when a company retained the services of strikebreakers it ceased to control the struggle, as the experience of the RCA Manufacturing Company of Camden, New Jersey, indicates. After a strike call had been issued, seventeen detective agencies offered their services. An officer of the Sherwood Agency presented a letter of introduction from the governor of New Jersey; impressed, the company hired twenty-five men for "missionary" work and two hundred strike-guards. Violence broke out almost immediately; in a series of riots several employees were seriously injured. The company reconsidered its decision and terminated its contract with the agency.[20]

Although employers lost control of strikebreakers' tactics, they could not evade responsibility for them. Few employers were unaware of the caliber of men whom they hired as strikebreakers. Some recognized the probability of violence; those contracting with the Burns Detective Agency insisted on signing an agreement exempting themselves from liability for their hirelings' conduct. Frequently employers insisted that their strike-guards present themselves armed; in other instances employers purchased weapons for them. (One company official explained that an unarmed strike-guard is "just a chunk of meat. . . .") The employer, declared the La Follette Committee, "is the key to the strikebreaking problem. . . ." He should be held responsible "for the tactics of aggression, intimidation,

18 *Ibid.*, pp. 2, 65, 74.
19 *Ibid.*, pp. 94–95, 97; *Hearings*, Pt. 22, p. 9383.
20 *Ibid.*, Pt. 8, pp. 2881–2908.

provocation, deception, and brutality, carried out by irresponsible mercenaries which have cost the Nation so much in human life, suffering, bitterness, and misery. . . ." [21]

The final weapon available to the anti-union employer was a private police force. With geographical expansion and industrial development, private policing had become fashionable, for local police departments simply could not meet the special needs of railroads, mines, or lumbering districts. Private police forces functioned so efficiently that they became instruments of private economic policy, invariably with an anti-union animus. Unlike public police, responsible to elected officials and restricted by constitutional safeguards, private police were rarely accountable to anyone but their employers. Private police power reached its apogee in company towns, where conditions approximated industrial peonage. A company town, declared the La Follette Committee, "is an autocracy within a democracy. . . . It is an offense against duly constituted authority." The committee examined private police systems in company towns and factories; it warned that "when the armed forces of the employer are injected into the delicate relations of labor and management, the consequences seriously threaten the civil rights of citizens and the peace and safety of whole communities." [22]

The Republic Steel Corporation provided a dismal example of the perversion of police power in private hands. Republic police were the chief

[21] *Ibid.*, Pt. 7, p. 2380; *Strikebreaking Services*, pp. 105–106, 138. Cf. Edward Levinson, "The Right to Break Strikes," *Current History*, XLV (February 1937), 77–82; "The 'Fink' Racket," *Nation*, CXLVIII (February 11, 1939), 165–166; Hamilton Basso, "Strike-Buster: Man Among Men," *New Republic*, LXXXI (December 12, 1934), 124–126.

[22] U.S. Senate, Committee on Education and Labor, *Private Police Systems*, Report No. 6, Pt. 2, 76th Cong., 1st Sess., 1939, pp. 2–7. The committee confined its investigation of private police systems almost entirely to Harlan County and to the Republic Steel Corporation. The Harlan findings will be discussed more extensively below, in an analysis of the committee's services to the C.I.O.

For a survey of private police practices in one state see "Report of the Commission on Special Policing in Industry to Governor Gifford Pinchot of Pennsylvania" (1934). In the Foreword Pinchot declared that private police "ought to rest with the dinosaur and the great auk . . ." (copy in ACLU, Vol. 754). Pennsylvania (in 1937) and Kentucky (in 1938) prohibited the appointment of any person as a special police officer who had been convicted of, or indicted for, a crime involving moral turpitude. The Pennsylvania law also required a sheriff to select his deputies from a list of qualified individuals. West Virginia prohibited private compensation to deputies for the performance of their official duties. But, the La Follette Committee noted, "State regulation . . . is totally inadequate throughout most of the Nation" (*Private Police Systems*, pp. 215–216).

instruments of company labor policy. The police superintendent instructed new recruits that union activity was detrimental to company interests; consequently, company police tapped telephone wires, read personal mail, confiscated union literature, and intimidated and attacked organizers. Committee hearings indicated that during a 1935 strike in Canton, Ohio, Republic police left plant property and "sallied forth into the city of Canton attacking with ferocity employees, nonemployees, strikers, pickets, bystanders, women, and children, with the same impartiality and lack of discrimination as the attacks on defenseless civilians in contemporary warfare." These guards, a witness told the committee, "were rushing around the people, and beating the people to the brick pavement, and then beating them after they were down. . . . It did not occur to me that in a community that was supposed to be civilized such things could occur." [23]

When the Steel Workers' Organizing Committee launched its campaign, Republic responded by enlarging its police force. It increased from 270 men in the spring of 1936 to 348 by January of the following year.[24] Organizers were kept under constant surveillance; two of them gave these accounts to the La Follette Committee:

". . . I was followed constantly. They would follow me when I would leave the hotel, go out to breakfast or lunch or dinner. If I went out and got my car they would follow me there. . . . It got so that I couldn't stop and talk to anybody without they was right behind me."

"[A guard] came up to me and circled around me several times, continually looking at my shoe. . . . When this happened about three or four times Mr. Wimmer, my buddy, started circling around him. After five or six revolutions around me, he started after Mr. Wimmer, and circled around him. . . . When he started going around him I started going around Sergeant Riggins, and after several more attempts he stepped back and laughed at us and walked into the plant." [25]

Such harassment frightened away prospective union members, made organizers wary of approaching new recruits, prevented the distribution of union literature, and crippled the SWOC organizing drive.

Testimony concerning the company towns of eastern Kentucky con-

[23] *Private Police Systems*, pp. 125, 178, 187–188; *Hearings*, Pt. 24, p. 9993, Pt. 34, pp. 13828–31.
[24] *Ibid.*, Pt. 26, p. 11007.
[25] *Ibid.*, pp. 11009–10, 11042.

vinced the La Follette Committee "that violations of civil liberties ensue whenever private police systems are used as instruments of labor policy to thwart self-organization of workers." In Lynch, the United States Coal and Coke Company, a subsidiary of U.S. Steel, owned everything but the schools and churches. Company police, the only law enforcement officers in town, refused to permit organizers to enter Lynch, interfered with their attempts to address miners on the public highways, destroyed their literature, and openly threatened union sympathizers. A UMW organizer told the committee how deputy sheriffs followed him to the front door of miners' homes and snatched his handbills from them. The miner-organizer of a Lynch local testified that a policeman met him daily at the mouth of the mine, followed him wherever he went, and "would not allow me to speak to anybody. . . ." Twenty-four-hour-a-day surveillance was maintained at his home; deputy sheriffs ordered his sister-in-law, visiting from Berea College, to leave town the morning after her arrival. In High Splint, under the pretext of possessing a search warrant for 1,100 pounds of stolen meat, Harlan County deputies ransacked the house of a resident, looking for the "meat" in his dresser drawers. They did not find it—nor did they find the real object of their search, UMW literature.[26]

The La Follette Committee issued a vigorous indictment of private police systems as instruments of anti-union policy, charging that they abridged civil liberties; violated the statutory rights of workers; spawned violence and bloodshed; endangered public safety; fostered labor-management bitterness; encouraged private usurpation of public authority; and perverted representative government.[27] Like espionage, munitions stockpiling, and strikebreaking, private police systems testified that industrial autocracy was incompatible with civil liberty.

At the hearings, the sheer weight of the testimony concerning oppressive labor practices encouraged an obsessive fascination with the flotsam of American industry: hooked workers, miscreant strikebreakers, tyrannical deputy sheriffs, and callous merchants of labor discord. "Always tinged with a hint of melodrama," observed the *Christian Science Monitor*, the hearings "sounded at times like a dime store novel. . . ."[28]

But the hearings transcended melodrama by means of the backdrop

26 *Private Police Systems*, pp. 15, 48–54, 208; *Hearings*, Pt. 11, pp. 3907, 3915, 4247.
27 *Private Police Systems*, p. 214. Cf. "Industrial Policing and Espionage," *Harvard Law Review*, LII (March 1939), 793–804.
28 *Christian Century*, February 24, 1937, clipping in ACLU, Vol. 994; *Christian Science Monitor*, February 8, 1937.

against which they were set. Although the La Follette Committee's exposure of antilabor activities revealed little that had escaped the attention of the Industrial Relations Commission or the Interchurch inquiry, the committee exerted influence far beyond that of its predecessors, for its investigation coincided with, and derived its vitality from, the C.I.O.'s efforts to organize America's mass-production industries.

During the first six months of 1937 the wave of industrial unionism reached its crest. Months of careful preparation and diligent effort brought the Steel Workers' Organizing Committee, the United Automobile Workers, and the United Mine Workers within sight of their goal. While John L. Lewis negotiated secretly with Myron Taylor of United States Steel, and automobile workers in Flint engaged in a sit-down strike, and UMW organizers resumed their perennially hazardous mission to Harlan County, the La Follette Committee called corporate officials to account for their anti-union practices.

The committee hardly attempted to construct a rounded account of labor-management relations. The predilections of its staff disposed it toward selection of those incidents lending maximum support to the contention that antilabor employers were engaging in relentless class warfare against exploited workers. Committee hearings and reports tended to exaggerate the percentage of workers eager for industrial unionization and involved in union organizing efforts. Similarly, the communities selected by the committee for investigation seemed to present, too neatly perhaps, precisely the stark alignment of forces that the Left would expect to find: a besieged minority of pro-union workers overwhelmed by predatory employers and hired mercenaries. The La Follette Committee certainly did not fabricate its findings; through its choice of incidents and witnesses, however, it painted a picture that indicated occasional blindness to shadings of gray. Nuances and complexities were obscured by the committee's zeal to accelerate and justify C.I.O. organizing drives.

The committee warmed to its task as the confrontation between U.S. Steel and the SWOC approached a showdown. Its hearings in January on the Barton-Gelders debacle in Bessemer exposed the practices of a subsidiary of U.S. Steel. Few informed observers doubted the committee's intention to lock horns with U.S. Steel itself. When Myron Taylor made his dramatic announcement that U.S. Steel would sign a contract with the C.I.O., the committee's presence in the wings was amply credited for Taylor's decision. Its revelations, declared the *Amalgamated Journal*, "were unquestionably a large factor" in the unionization of Big Steel. The

C.I.O.'s counterespionage system, reported *Fortune*, fed the La Follette Committee with information "just as distasteful to the gentlemen on the Board of U.S. Steel as it was to their Chairman." [29]

In Little Steel, however, and in automobiles and mining, the C.I.O. encountered much stiffer opposition. These temporary stalemates gave the La Follette Committee an opportunity to utilize its varied resources. It cautioned, cajoled, and censured in a versatile display of investigatory expertise. The committee's treatment of General Motors is particularly illuminating. Throughout 1936, automobile workers risked their jobs, their constitutional rights, and occasionally their lives to organize. They were "under a constant fear of being watched," reported a UAW official, "and [did] not dare to speak to one another in the plant concerning unions." [30] The members of one local expressed their feelings in doggerel:

> But there's no beast in swamp or lair
> That can in loathsomeness compare
> With men who belly-crawl to do
> The dirty-work that all despise.
>
> Who sell their birthrights and their souls
> To operate as labor spies!

An anonymous GM worker at the Saginaw Malleable Iron Corporation could not treat the situation so lightly. He told Senator La Follette: "[General Motors] so completely run this town and have it so well propagandized to their own good that one don't even dare talk here. You have no liberties at all. You couldn't belong to a union and breathe it to a soul. That soul would probably be a spy." [31]

Even before the Senate approved Resolution 266, La Follette and Heber Blankenhorn had learned of General Motors' exorbitant expenditures for espionage. Delmond Garst, UAW secretary in St. Louis, sent La Follette a clipping from the Chicago *Tribune* that cited General Motors' report

[29] *Amalgamated Journal*, September 2, 1937; "It Happened in Steel," *Fortune*, XV (May 1937), 179; Walter Galenson, "The Unionization of the American Steel Industry," *Unions and Union Leadership*, ed. Jack Barbash, p. 127; Edward Levinson, *Labor on the March*, pp. 199–200. The other factors generally cited as contributing to Taylor's decision include Roosevelt's 1936 victory, pending NLRB hearings, and the potential cost of a strike when U.S. Steel had begun to earn substantial profits for the first time since 1930.

[30] William L. Munger to John Brophy, October 20, 1936, C.I.O. Papers, Box 23.

[31] N.A.F.I. *Workers News*, January 15, 1937, copy in LFC, Box 121; "Employee" to La Follette, July 15, 1937.

to the Securities and Exchange Commission of $167,586 paid to Pinkerton's for plant protection. "As soon as the subcommittee lays out a definite plan of action," La Follette promised, "our investigators will go to work." Blankenhorn received two copies of the same clipping; one was from an NLRB attorney in St. Louis who said "Let me know of any action by the Senate on the investigation. I am wild to have a hand in busting up the racket"; the second was accompanied by a prediction from another NLRB attorney: "I bet you can pull some fine rabbits out of that SEC hat." [32]

During the late summer and early fall, committee investigators interviewed UAW officials, who offered evidence of GM blacklists and espionage.[33] In September the committee served a subpoena on the company. Gradually the shape of a hearing on General Motors emerged; it promised to be brief and undramatic. But on December 18, in the wake of a sitdown strike at the Fisher Body plant in Kansas City to protest the discharge of an employee for union activity, John L. Lewis announced that the United Automobile Workers would demand a collective bargaining agreement with General Motors. Lewis' statement, committee counsel Abt realized, "lends added significance to our G.M. hearing." He advised Charles Kramer in Detroit to "line up one of the union boys to appear in Washington and testify as to the tactics of the corporation in fighting the union." [34] On December 19 the committee announced that it would inquire into labor conditions in General Motors plants; Abt denied any connection between Lewis' and the committee's announcements, but the disclaimer fooled no one. Ten days later, when the sit-down strike spread to the Fisher Body and Chevrolet plants in Flint, the committee discovered that it had a mission.[35]

[32] Delmond Garst to La Follette, June 5, 1936, La Follette to Garst, June 24, 1936, David Shaw to Blankenhorn, June 5, 1936, John D. Moore to Blankenhorn, June 3, 1936, LFC, Box 124.

[33] Unsigned memo, September 10, 1936, LFC, Box 121. Charles Kramer reported to Wohlforth that Homer Martin's group "has not been terribly helpful. . . . [Martin is] so rushed with his own work that he is unable to pitch in and help us any. We get farther dealing with his locals directly" (September 14, 1936, LFC, Box 125); "General Motors—Pontiac Motors Division—Conference, 10/29/36," LFC, Box 124.

[34] *New York Times*, December 19, 1936; Abt to Kramer, December 19, 1936, LFC, Box 102; Abt to Kramer, Boland, Frazer, *et al.*, December 19, 1936, LFC, Box 121.

[35] *New York Times*, December 20, 1936; Laird Bell, "Probes," *Atlantic Monthly*, CLX (July 1937), 23; Saul Alinsky, *John L. Lewis*. Alinsky writes: "Throughout the course of events that followed, the Senate Civil Liberties Committee constantly pursued General Motors and repeatedly uncovered information damaging and acutely embarrassing to the corporation, actually performing yeoman service for the CIO

In response to Judge Edward Black's injunction restraining the Flint sit-down strikers, UAW president Homer Martin urged the La Follette Committee to dispatch observers to Flint immediately. But the committee had anticipated this request, and investigators, who had been in Flint since the outbreak of the strike, not only kept the Washington staff fully informed of developments but also became participants in the struggle. Committee representatives instructed union rank and file in "methods of procedure" for reporting alleged stool pigeons. Following "The Battle of the Running Bulls" on January 11, when strikers in Fisher Body Plant No. 2 repulsed Flint police, a committee staff member entered the plant and assembled fifty strikers to tell their story. In his reports to Washington H. D. Cullen, the committee investigator assigned to Flint, shamelessly favored the sit-down strikers; "The explosion is coming, sure as God made little green apples," he predicted on January 21, "unless those damn fools of GM get busy and give up!!!!" "The biggest thing this Committee can do this year," Cullen continued, "would be to drive this GM thing out into the open and thus create a public sentiment that would FORCE the right action. A complete back-down by GM would not only be best, from our standpoint, but for the whole damn country as well. . . ." [36]

Cullen became ubiquitous in Flint. He obtained progress reports on the activities of the Flint Alliance, an anti-UAW organization, from observers at its meetings. He learned that the lieutenant of detectives of the Flint police department maintained his own espionage system and infiltrated spies into the ranks of sit-down strikers. He sat in as an observer at a meeting called by the prosecuting attorney of Genessee County to discuss peaceful measures for reopening GM plants. He followed closely the advice of Charles Kramer: "I believe that if it becomes known that you are in town watching [anti-union] activities, they will tend to decrease." [37] Cullen's final chore was to find promising witnesses for the hearings. Under instructions from Robert Wohlforth, he briefed UAW organizer Robert Travis on the points the committee wished to develop ("discrimi-

---

offensive against GM" (p. 109). On the sit-down strike, see Sidney Fine, "The General Motors Sit-Down Strike: A Re-examination," *American Historical Review,* LXX (April 1965), 691–713.

[36] *New York Times,* January 3, 1937; Minutes, 1/3/37, Local #7, UAW-CIO, Nick Di Gaetano Collection, Box 3; Harold Cranefield to Wohlforth, February 10, 1937, H. D. Cullen to Wohlforth, January 21, 1937, LFC, Box 124.

[37] Cullen to Wohlforth, January 26, 1937, LFC, Box 124; Cullen to Wohlforth January 31, 1937, LFC, Box 122; Cullen to Wohlforth, January 31, 1937, LFC, Box 124; Kramer to Cullen, January 27, 1937, LFC, Box 125.

nation cases, union discharges, the Flint welfare and relief outfit, the bands tightening in on the union, relations with factory managers, etc.") and made certain that union witnesses would arrive in Washington in time for the committee to review their testimony.[38]

The General Motors hearings began on February 15, four days after the strike's dramatic end. Their timing did not escape notice. Considering the bad feeling created by union tactics in Flint, observed the Washington Post, the hearings afforded an opportunity "to preserve a due sense of proportion at a moment when balance in judging the labor problem is everywhere needed." Other editors viewed the hearings less kindly. The Portland (Me.) Press-Herald, for example, declared them to be "nothing that most people will get excited about." After all, just as department stores employed plainclothesmen, and congressional committees used investigators, so business spied on labor.[39]

Clearly, the committee intended the hearings to counter unfavorable public reaction to the sit-down strike and to influence pending negotiations between GM and the automobile workers. For seven days it dissected General Motors' labor policy, jousted with company officials, and provided the UAW with a national forum. The committee found itself, La Follette said, "in a sort of mystic mist . . . about who actually does determine labor policy" at GM.[40] But it entertained no doubts about the operation or results of that policy. From 1934 until mid-1937 fifty-two members of the UAW were Pinkerton spies, reporting on unionization

[38] Wohlforth to Cullen, January 26, 1937, LFC, Box 124. News from Flint, Charles Kramer told Travis when union victory seemed imminent, "sounds perfectly swell. . . . You guys seem to be about the only ones who are really doing a job." Kramer might well have been referring to Cullen and to the La Follette Committee (Kramer to Travis, February 1, 1937, LFC, Box 124). UAW attorney Maurice Sugar was worried lest the La Follette investigation prove too successful; he was afraid that union members would lose their self-reliance and look only to Washington for assistance (Sugar to Victor Reuther, February 10, 1937, Victor Reuther Papers).

[39] Washington Post, January 25, 1937; Portland (Me.) Press-Herald, February 16, 1937. See also Richmond (Va.) News Leader, February 20, 1937; Washington News, February 12, 1937; Baltimore Sun, February 13, 1937. A rider attached to the Relief Deficiency bill, inserted on the eve of the La Follette Committee's GM hearings, and providing that no funds could be used to pay the salaries of WPA employees who were loaned to congressional committees, was seen as a direct slap at the committee. In response to administration pressure the Senate altered the bill to permit committees to hire anyone, provided their names were reported to Congress (Madison [Wis.] Capital Times, February 3, 1937; Marissa [Ill.] Progressive Miner, February 12, 1937, clippings in ACLU, Vol. 994; Rose Schneiderman to FDR, February 2, 1937, FDRL, OF 1581).

[40] Hearings, Pt. 7, p. 2317.

efforts in General Motors plants. One became president of a Chevrolet local in Flint; another was vice-president of a Fisher Body local in Lansing. GM's fear of collective bargaining, the committee concluded, caused it "to surrender to a group of unknown adventurers an increasing responsibility in [its] relations with [its] employees." The company even hired Pinkerton agents to spy on its Corporations Auxiliary Company spies, in the belief that the latter had passed trade secrets to one of GM's competitors. At various times General Motors kept under surveillance labor leaders William Green, John P. Frey, Homer Martin, and Walter Reuther, sociologist Edward A. Ross, and Assistant Secretary of Labor Edward McGrady. Between January 1934 and July 1936 the company paid $839,764.41 to labor detective agencies.[41]

Harry W. Anderson, GM labor relations director, explained why his company invested in espionage: "We were interested to know if there was any particular labor organization going on in town, and if so, why? The thing I was interested in was what was there about the plant operation that would give any need for an outside organization." Senate authorization of the La Follette investigation had prompted Anderson to eradicate all traces of the company's interest in union activities. He examined the files of William Knudsen and Charles E. Wilson and eliminated every scrap of evidence likely to come under a Senate subpoena. He told the committee that GM had discontinued all Pinkerton services; the La Follette hearings, he explained (with questionable logic), "gave us an opportunity to wipe it out." Alfred Marshall, director of personnel relations at Chevrolet, contended that GM's expenses for espionage were "thrust on the corporation . . . by outside organizations." Marshall told the committee, "We are not all bad. We are not vicious. We are not vicious toward the unions. . . . [But the Chevrolet union] was based upon a great deal of radicalism. . . ." General Motors was not afraid of organized labor, Marshall insisted, quickly adding the qualification, "properly organized." [42]

The La Follette Committee invited renegade Pinkerton spies and UAW organizers to tell their side of the GM labor story. (In fact, portions of the committee's report on industrial espionage read like a UAW brief against General Motors.) Arthur J. Dubuc, self-styled "Fighting Frenchman from the Wolverine" and a former spy in Flint, regaled the senators and spectators with stories of espionage. Dubuc, a garrulous, colorful character, prefaced his sentences with "By golly" or "Wottahell," and

---

[41] *Industrial Espionage*, pp. 26, 44, 47; *Hearings*, Pt. 6, pp. 1879, 1992.
[42] *Hearings*, Pt. 6, pp. 1878, 1894–97, 1922–25, 2049, 2050, 2082.

relished the opportunity for vengeance on his former employers.[43] Another Pinkerton spy recounted his experiences in a Lansing local that disintegrated to the point where it had five officers—all of them Pinkerton spies—and no members. Joseph B. Ditzel, UAW organizer in Flint and Saginaw, itemized abridgments of his civil liberties: He could not rent a hall in Saginaw to address the automobile workers; in Bay City a gang of toughs forcibly detained him in his hotel room; he was trailed constantly in Flint where his car was sideswiped and three organizers were sent to the hospital with serious injuries.[44] Robert Travis gave circumstantial evidence pointing to the presence of spies among the sit-down strikers. He told how, during the strike, company *agents provocateurs* created disturbances intended to damage the union's reputation. Even GM's settlement with the UAW had not ended the harassment of union members; on the contrary, Travis insisted, "it has been more vicious. . . . Men are being framed" and reported to company superintendents for union sympathies.[45]

Exposure of GM's espionage expenses, of its surveillance of labor and government officials, and of the harsh treatment it meted out to union organizers did not increase toleration for the sit-down strike but did help to demonstrate the legitimacy of union grievances. Sit-down strikers menaced law and order, commented one newspaper, and espionage "smacks of the methods of Fascists and Communists and is hostile to the principles of democracy." Another editorial severely condemned both practices as "devious devices." [46]

Congressional debate in April 1937 indicated how the La Follette Committee hearings restored balance after the sit-down strike. Dispute erupted over Senator Byrnes's amendment to the Guffey-Vinson bill; the amendment read: "That it is the sense of the Congress that the so-called sit-down strike is illegal and contrary to sound public policy." Robert F. Wagner immediately suggested the inclusion of a statement demanding that employers recognize the jurisdiction of the NLRB and other government agencies in the peaceful settlement of labor disputes. "I heard no great indignation," Wagner admonished the Senate, "when the La Follette committee brought out the manner in which workers were exploited by means of the spy system, the machine guns, and all the other methods used

[43] See Washington *News*, February 19, 1937; Baltimore *Sun*, February 20, 1937.
[44] *Hearings*, Pt. 6, p. 2104, Pt. 7, pp. 2308–12.
[45] *Ibid.*, pp. 2327–29.
[46] Trenton (N.J.) *Gazette*, February 23, 1937; Galveston (Tex.) *News*, February 15, 1937.

to oppress them while collective bargaining was completely denied them. ... We ought to look at the whole picture." Senator Joseph Robinson of Arkansas led administration forces in opposition to the Byrnes amendment, which failed to pass by twelve votes.

After its defeat Key Pittman of Nevada introduced a new resolution condemning both the sit-down strikes and industrial espionage as "contrary to sound public policy." Robinson, pointing to the La Follette hearings, strengthened the Pittman resolution by inserting a paragraph denouncing the refusal of employers to bargain collectively and condemning their use of any unfair labor practice, as defined in the Wagner Act. After some quibbling the Senate approved the Pittman resolution with the Robinson amendment; the vote was 75–3. Three days later the House of Representatives concurred.[47] The La Follette Committee, in effect, was vindicated.

The committee's second major thrust in 1937 was on behalf of the United Mine Workers. In two weeks of hearings on anti-unionism in Harlan County, Kentucky, it performed yeoman service for John L. Lewis' miners. The Harlan bituminous coal fields, the sole mining area of importance still unorganized in 1937, were crucial to the United Mine Workers; unless the union organized the Harlan miners and secured a contract with the coal operators, union officials believed, neighboring fields would find it impossible to maintain union standards and the unionization drive in coal would collapse.[48] But Harlan, known as "that little ugly running sore," resisted unionization with a vengeance. Its residents lived in company houses within company towns; they were obliged to purchase at company stores; they received their wages in scrip; and they entertained guests, traversed public highways, and used the federal mails at the whim of management. Their dingy and decrepit villages, commented one shocked observer, needed "only castles, draw-bridges, and donjon-keeps to reproduce to the physical eye a view of feudal days." [49]

Harlan County first gained national notoriety in 1931 when deputy sheriffs and picketing miners clashed in a bloody battle near Evarts. The

[47] *Congressional Record,* 75th Cong., 1st Sess., 1937, Vol. 81, pp. 3131, 3135–36, 3233, 3236, 3248; "Congress and the Sit-Down Strikes," *Congressional Digest,* XVI (May 1937), 133.

[48] Galenson, *CIO Challenge,* pp. 194–204; F. Raymond Daniell, "Behind the Conflict in 'Bloody Harlan,'" *New York Times Magazine,* June 26, 1938, pp. 1–2, 11.

[49] Lawrence Grauman, Jr., "That Little Ugly Running Sore," *Filson Club Historical Quarterly,* XXXVI (October 1962), 340–354; *Private Police Systems,* pp. 17–26; Bernstein, *Lean Years,* pp. 362–366.

Kafka-esque trial of the miners prompted an invasion of Harlan County by writers, communists, theologians, and students. The Kentucky miners, they observed, "have become the rebellious protestants of His Majesty, King Coal." [50] But in 1932 not a single miner belonged to the UMW, and the coal operators, proud of their record, were determined to maintain it. A horde of deputies eagerly implemented the sheriff's declaration of "open season on organizers." For attempting to assist miners in exercising their constitutional rights, organizers were forced to skulk around the public highways like hunted animals.

Encouraged by NRA and by the Wagner Act, the union poured men and money into Harlan, only to be routed by the coal operators. Churches were dynamited, organizers were kidnaped, sympathetic law-enforcement officers were assassinated, the National Guard was shuttled in and out— and the UMW drive collapsed completely. The series of unsolved murders prompted the sardonic quip that in Harlan County death from shooting had long been regarded as "death from natural causes." A special commission, appointed by the governor in 1935, reported: "It is almost unbeliev-able that anywhere in a free and democratic Nation . . . conditions can be found as bad as they are in Harlan County. There exists a virtual reign of terror. . . ." [51]

The La Follette Committee hearings on Harlan County opened two days after the Supreme Court upheld the Wagner Act and just as the United Mine Workers, responding to that decision, dispatched a new wave of organizers to Harlan. The hearings presented quite a spectacle. Deputy sheriffs, wearing broadbrimmed black hats and "uncomfortable store clothes," entered the hearing room with pistol holsters under their jackets. Two Kentuckians, on their first visit to a city, spent most of their time riding the Senate elevators. John L. Lewis glowered from the audi-ence. "Watch closely," a reporter suggested, "when the photographers flash . . . their bulbs. All over the room there will be men who automati-cally clutch swiftly at their hips, in the manner of men reaching for their

[50] The National Committee for the Defense of Political Prisoners sponsored a group led by Theodore Dreiser; Waldo Frank led a delegation of writers; Reinhold Niebuhr brought a group of clergymen; Columbia economist Donald Henderson re-cruited students from New York colleges ("All Around the Liberty Pole," *Survey Graphic*, XXV [July 1936], 426; Grauman, "That Little Ugly Running Sore," pp. 348–349; Murray Kempton, *Part of Our Time*, p. 304; Theodore Dreiser, ed., *Harlan Miners Speak*, p. 19 and *passim*).

[51] *Private Police Systems*, pp. 13, 57–77; *Hearings*, Pts. 10–12; *Progressive*, July 30, 1938.

guns. Then they look around slowly to see if they've been noticed."
Everyone knew, observed *Newsweek*, that La Follette's primary intentions
"were to arouse public anger and to help his friend John L. Lewis organize the miners." Yet this knowledge hardly mitigated the spectators' in-
credulity at Harlan conditions, for the hearings depicted anti-unionism
"at its exceptional worst." [52]

Philip Murray, vice-president of the United Mine Workers, presented
the union's major grievance: "The refusal of the authorities, the duly
constituted and accredited authorities, to recognize the Mine Workers'
civil liberties. . . ." [53] He recounted the most recent effort, in January, to
unionize Harlan; the coal operators had resisted with every weapon at
their command. "They have discharged [miners], they have discriminated
against them, they have coerced them, they have intimidated them, they
have beaten them up, they have thrown them in jail, and they have shot
them. . . ." Encouraged by the *Jones & Laughlin* decision, the union once
again had sent field organizers into Harlan. "We are going to expect and
demand," Murray told the committee, "that the Government of the United
States of America protect the lives and limbs of our people. . . . We are
here demanding that the Government see to it that these acts of brutality,
these killings, these kidnapings, and this letting of blood in Harlan County
be stopped." [54]

Deputy sheriffs, Harlan residents, and union officials depicted the chaotic terror of life in Harlan County. The key to the situation was the
deputy sheriff system. Theodore Middleton, sheriff of Harlan County,
apparently selected his deputies for their criminal record. His brother, a
deputy in 1934 and 1936, had been indicted seven times in two years on
a variety of charges, including carrying concealed weapons and stealing a
ballot box. Eight deputies, who still held office when Middleton testified
before the La Follette Committee, had served prison terms for man-
slaughter, and three had done so for murder. Since 1934, thirty-seven of

[52] *New York Times*, April 16, 1937; Washington *Star*, April 27, 1937; Washington
Post, April 25, 1937; *Progressive*, April 24, 1937; *Newsweek*, May 15, 1937, p. 15;
Time, May 3, 1937, p. 13.

[53] *Hearings*, Pt. 10, p. 3447. Ben Allen, a committee staff member, had briefed
Murray thoroughly the day before: It was "essential" that Murray recount the history of the UMW, the benefits to its members, the control exercised over Harlan
captive mines by "foreign" corporations (e.g., U.S. Steel and Ford), the menace of
deputy sheriffs to civil liberties, and the danger of one unorganized county to
national wage scales (Allen to Murray, April 13, 1937, LFC, Box 89).

[54] *Hearings*, Pt. 10, pp. 3448, 3450; Washington *Star*, April 14, 1937.

his deputies had been convicted of felonies and sixty-four had been in-dicted at least once.

Middleton entertained curious notions of law and order; declaring he would "put up with no labor disturbances here," he once filed suit to enjoin the National Guard from preserving the peace in Harlan on the ground that it was his function to do so. To Middleton's dismay, the Supreme Court of Kentucky ruled that the sheriff did not possess a prop-erty right in preserving law and order.[55]

The coal companies of Harlan County acted as ruthlessly as the deputy sheriffs, with whom they frequently conspired to deprive miners of their rights. On one occasion, under instructions from the vice-president of the Harlan-Wallins Coal Corporation, a foreman fired all union men. He ad-mitted to belonging to a "thugging" gang, which went "out hunting for union men, organizers, and so forth. . . ." When asked to explain why virtually no UMW local ever succeeded in organizing one of the com-pany's mines, vice-president Pearl Bassham replied, "Our people have never seemed to want the union." Bassham required his workers to sign yellow-dog contracts. Independent merchants could not open stores in Harlan town; the company store returned 170 per cent profit on the investment of its owners during its first year of operation. Bassham's most diabolical device to mulct his employees was a semimonthly second-hand car lottery; Bassham forced miners to buy chances by checking off their wages. He disposed of eight of his own used cars in this manner, at a profit of nearly two thousand dollars annually. When Senator Thomas asked Bassham why he did not enter the raffle business, Bassham replied candidly, "I would not be able to sell the chances, sir, if I did not have the mine." [56]

With coal operators and deputy sheriffs acting in concert against them, union organizers were frustrated. Marshall Musick, UMW field represen-tative in Harlan, traveled throughout the county under continual surveil-lance by deputy sheriffs; occasionally they refused to permit him to return home at night, and he would remain with the miners until day-break. Within three days after he had managed to organize a local in Pearl Bassham's Harlan-Wallins mine, company spies had relayed membership lists to the coal operators, who discharged every union leader. In May

[55] *Hearings*, Pt. 10, pp. 3561–69, Pt. 11, p. 3830; *Private Police Systems*, pp. 29–35, 75.

[56] *Hearings*, Pt. 12, pp. 4355–57, Pt. 10, p. 3597, Pt. 13, p. 4499; *Private Police Sys-tems*, pp. 20–24.

1934 Musick was arrested for violating Kentucky's criminal syndicalism statute; that fall Sheriff Middleton told him that as long as he "had anything to do with the racketeering labor organization," he would receive no protection from law enforcement officers.

One Sunday evening during the UMW organizing drive in January 1937, Musick and his wife were returning home from a visit with friends when they were caught in an enfilade of bullets, but they miraculously escaped injury. The police judge of Evarts warned Musick to leave Harlan County if he wished to remain alive. Musick followed his advice: "I left on the train and when I got off that train at Pineville there was a message in the hotel that my boy was killed. . . ." Armed gunmen had murdered Musick's nineteen-year-old son, and wounded his wife and another son, in their own house. Musick appealed for a police escort into Harlan, but the sheriff of Bell County told him, "Possibly you and me both would be killed. . . ." The following day the surviving members of the Musick family left Harlan County.[57]

When the Harlan hearings ended early in May, the La Follette Committee looked to the governor and "the public conscience of Kentucky" to halt the terror in the Harlan coal fields; the national government, the committee observed, could do little "to restore the elementary rights of Americans" to its citizens.[58] But the committee underestimated its own achievements and the potential power of an aroused federal government; even before the hearings ended, counsel for the Pioneer Coal Company in Pineville, Kentucky, admitted to a committee investigator that "the presence of you fellows in Pineville is very largely responsible" for the company's decision to sign a contract with the United Mine Workers. Conditions in Harlan County improved noticeably; a week after the hearings ended, two mass meetings were held without incident.[59]

[57] *Hearings*, Pt. 11, pp. 3812–18, Pt. 12, pp. 4230–38; *Private Police Systems*, pp. 79–105.

[58] *New York Times*, May 7, 1937.

[59] Jack B. Burke to Wohlforth, March 30, 1937, LFC, Box 89; William Turnblazer to James F. Byrnes, July 6, 1937, LFC, Box 87; Galenson, *CIO Challenge*, p. 204. The Harlan hearings, in general, sacrificed depth for spectacle. For the most part, the committee did not explore the nature of the captive mine situation, in which labor policies were set hundreds of miles away by controlling corporations. "Middleton and his crew," reads a memo in the committee papers, "are merely the hired thugs of the big bandits that sit behind the great companies that own the mines of Harlan, and deliberately finance and promote the conditions . . . in which Middleton and his crowd are rather puny figures" (unsigned memo, n.d., LFC, Box 89). La Follette was accused of using the Harlan hearings as the foundation for a third party, to be active

When signs of deterioration set in, another branch of the federal government decided to step into the breach. On May 19 the Department of Justice ordered agents of the Federal Bureau of Investigation into Harlan County to investigate charges that the coal operators had violated the Wagner Act by conspiring to thwart union organization. Attorney General Homer Cummings linked this investigation to the La Follette Committee disclosures and to complaints made by John L. Lewis.[60] In September a federal grand jury indicted twenty-four coal mining officials, twenty-three law enforcement officers, and twenty-two coal mining corporations for conspiring to deprive American citizens of rights guaranteed them by the Constitution and federal statutes. The Justice Department, relying on the Wagner Act and on Section 51, Title 18, of the United States Code (the restatement of a provision of a Reconstruction statute of 1870 making it a crime to deprive a citizen of any right or privilege secured by the Constitution or by federal law), acknowledged for the first time that the statutory right of workers to organize was also a civil liberty that the government would sue to protect. Although the trial of the Harlan defendants ended with a hung jury and the declaration of a mistrial, the Harlan County Coal Operators' Association signed a contract with the United Mine Workers to become effective on September 1, 1938. In response to this action the government dropped its prosecution. Four months later the UMW secretary-treasurer in Harlan thanked Senator La Follette and his committee "for bringing peace to Harlan County. . . ."[61]

By the middle of May 1937 the La Follette Committee could take considerable pride in its record. In mining, as in steel and autos, it had demonstrated its ability to function simultaneously as protector of the Bill of Rights, instrument of government labor policy, and adjunct to the C.I.O. organizing drive. The National Labor Relations Board, having survived

in the elections of 1940, which he and John L. Lewis would presumably have led (Oshkosh *Northwestern*, June 22, 1937, clipping in Legislative Reference Library, Madison).

[60] *New York Times*, May 20, 1937.

[61] *New York Times*, April 17, 1938; *Newsweek*, May 30, 1938; *C.I.O. News*, September 3, 1938, October 9, 1939; M. Nelson McGeary, *The Developments of Congressional Investigative Power*, pp. 90–91; *Private Police Systems*, pp. 112–114. The NLRB also joined in the attack on the Harlan coal operators; in November 1937 it ordered the Clover Fork Coal Company to cease co-operating with the Harlan County Coal Operators' Association and to reinstate sixty men discharged for union activities (*ibid.*, pp. 111–112).

the challenge to its constitutionality, no longer needed the La Follette Committee as a prop. The C.I.O. had reached the zenith of its strength and power and John L. Lewis repeatedly said that the committee's investigations materially aided the C.I.O.'s development.[62]

La Follette seriously considered terminating his investigation. The senator, Gardner Jackson told Roger Baldwin, "is fed up with his investigation and wants to taper it off to a close quite soon. . . ." This prospect dismayed Jackson, who noted, "He has not ventured into the rural areas and has failed to do any investigation into the general Civil Liberties situation involved in the patrioteering and red-baiting organizations." Jackson urged Baldwin to muster ACLU support for further investigations. Baldwin, who knew of La Follette's "disinclination to carry on the Committee work," promised to do what he could "to get pressure brought tactfully." The ACLU circulated the committee's preliminary report, and its board of directors commended La Follette and requested "continuance of the committee's work with a view to creating a permanent investigating body." In a personal appeal Baldwin told La Follette, "Historically [your investigation] is the best piece of work that has ever been undertaken on behalf of minority rights." [63]

La Follette finally yielded, but not to ACLU entreaties. At the end of March the Steel Workers' Organizing Committee had requested signed contracts with Bethlehem Steel, Republic Steel, Inland Steel, and the Youngstown Sheet and Tube Company—but these giants of Little Steel refused. On May 26 the SWOC struck Republic, Inland, and Youngstown. Four days later, on Memorial Day, occurred one of the most brutal and senseless clashes in American labor history. In the course of the "Memorial Day Incident" (known to labor as the "Memorial Day Massacre")

[62] Gardner Jackson, COHC, p. 669.

[63] Jackson to Baldwin, May 13, 1937, Baldwin to Jackson, May 14, 1937, ACLU Board of Directors, Minutes, May 17, 1937, Baldwin to La Follette, May 24, 1937, ACLU, Vol. 981. There is evidence that the ACLU was not completely satisfied with the committee's scope. In March its board of directors urged the committee to investigate Ku Klux Klan terrorism in Florida; in June it grew restive over La Follette's failure to investigate the Arkansas sharecropper situation; in October it urged an investigation of the Shoemaker beating in Tampa (ACLU Board of Directors, Minutes, March 8, 1937, ACLU, Vol. 1035; Mary Fox to ACLU Executive Board, June 7, 1937, ACLU, Vol. 981; ACLU News Release, October 21, 1937, ACLU, Vol. 1035). La Follette, Robert Wohlforth recalled, "was ready to quit every time we ran out of money, and it was Blankenhorn who did all the legwork and all the politicking in order to get us additional funds" (Wohlforth, COHC, p. 16).

outside the gates of Republic's South Chicago factory, ten people were killed and one hundred injured when Chicago police, fearing an assault on the plant, dispersed a large group of marching strikers with gas and bullets. La Follette, according to Robert Wohlforth, "didn't want to touch" the Memorial Day incident. But the hue and cry against the strikers, despite their disproportionate suffering, and the sharp conflict over responsibility for the disaster galvanized the committee staff. Its zeal overcame La Follette's reluctance.[64]

Initially the Memorial Day incident may have seemed hardly worth investigating. The New York Times carried an unequivocal three word headline: "STEEL MOB HALTED." Its story told of union demonstrators, "armed with clubs, slingshots, cranks and gear shift levers from cars, bricks, steel bolts and other missiles," who attacked the police and, after being repulsed, "tried to reassemble for another attack on the plant. . . ." The Chicago Tribune described the "attack" as an invasion by "a trained military unit of a revolutionary body." In fact, most newspapers and weeklies sharply censured the strikers, displaying hostility toward the victims rather than toward their assailants. Furthermore, President Roosevelt seemed indifferent to the strikers' suffering, and few congressmen defended C.I.O. tactics. Labor militancy was equated with labor irresponsibility.[65]

Initially there were few dissenters. Paul Y. Anderson, a correspondent for the St. Louis Post-Dispatch, went to Chicago after the holiday weekend and spent a week piecing together a story entirely different from the prevailing account. While Anderson gathered material in Chicago, committee secretary Wohlforth learned that a Paramount News photographer had filmed the incident. Wohlforth hurried to New York, applied pressure on a friend at Paramount, secured a print of the film, and held a private screening for La Follette, Thomas, and the committee staff. (Paramount News refused to release the film, claiming that its showing "might very well incite local riots. . . .") In exchange for the name and story of a prize witness, ferreted out by Anderson, the committee permitted Anderson to see the film; he was the only reporter present. In an anonymous scoop for the Post-Dispatch Anderson wrote that spectators at the secret première "were shocked and amazed by scenes showing scores of uniformed

[64] Wohlforth, COHC, p. 53.

[65] New York Times, May 31, 1937; Chicago Tribune, June 6, 1937; Donald G. Sofchalk, "The Chicago Memorial Day Incident: An Episode of Mass Action," Labor History, VI (Winter 1965), 26–32.

policemen firing their revolvers pointblank into a dense crowd of men, women and children, and then pursuing and clubbing the survivors unmercifully as they made frantic efforts to escape." [66]

In mid-June Wohlforth and John Abt, accompanied by several committee agents, arrived in Chicago to direct a ten-day investigation of the Memorial Day incident. Many of the facts were relatively undisputed. On May 26, the first day of the strike, police had dispersed a group of strikers and sympathizers for hollering at nonstriking workers and calling policemen "scabs" and "finks." Twenty-three people were arrested and charged with unlawful assembly and disorderly conduct. But during the next forty-eight hours Mayor Kelly issued a public statement assuring the strikers that peaceful picketing would be permitted, and the police commissioner told union attorneys that the strikers could maintain as many peaceful pickets as they wished. Despite these assurances the police shunted pickets two blocks from the plant entrance and limited their number to six. On May 28, when the strikers attempted to picket en masse, a brief scuffle resulted in injuries to six policemen and the arrest of an equivalent number of strikers. The SWOC called a meeting for the afternoon of Memorial Day to protest police treatment.[67]

At 3 P.M. on a warm, sunny Sunday afternoon two thousand strikers, their families, and sympathizers assembled outside union headquarters at Sam's Place, a former tavern located one block east and five blocks north of the Republic factory gate. From a speakers' truck SWOC organizers addressed the gathering, which included divinity students, writers, and ministers who had come as observers. Speakers condemned police restrictions on their right to picket and whipped up support for the C.I.O. organizing drive in steel. At the conclusion of their remarks a motion was made and carried to establish a picket line in front of the plant. Two men raised American flags flanking the truck and led the marchers down Green Bay Avenue to 114th Street, then onto a dirt road that led to the factory entrance.[68]

[66] C.B.S. National Headliners Club Broadcast, July 10, 1937, script in LFC, Box 87; Wohlforth, COHC, p. 54; St. Louis *Post-Dispatch*, June 17, 1937; *Progressive*, June 26, 1937; W. Carrol Munro, "Cameras Don't Lie," *Current History*, XLVI (August 1937), 37–40. Of Paramount's refusal to show the film, Munro wrote: "In this instance the goddess of truth was not raped, she was strangled" (p. 40).

[67] U.S. Senate, Committee on Education and Labor, *The Chicago Memorial Day Incident*, Report No. 46, Pt. 2, 75th Cong., 1st Sess., 1937, pp. 4–6.

[68] *Memorial Day Incident*, pp. 4, 8, 10–13; *Hearings*, Pt. 14, pp. 4920–21; Mary Heaton Vorse, *Labor's New Millions*, p. 121. See also Meyer Levin, *Citizens*, pp. 11,

Interpretation of the march and the ensuing incidents formed the crux of the La Follette Committee's task. Did the marchers launch an attack on the police, who responded with such force as was reasonably necessary to defend themselves and disperse the crowd? Or did the police, without justification, attack citizens who were peaceably asserting their constitutional rights? The committee could choose from a range of interpretations. For Tom Girdler, president of Republic Steel, "This crowd was being organized to force its way into our steel plant to drive the men out." The marchers, he said, were "playing parts in a drama written, directed, and produced by revolutionists." Joseph P. Kamp, author of *Join the C.I.O. and Help Build a Soviet America*, depicted an "agitated and inflamed" mob, composed of "blind followers of [John L.] Lewis bent on supplanting government by mob rule and anarchy"; in the Chicago police, the mob had encountered the "good, old-fashioned type of American government established by our forefathers. . . ." [69]

At the other extreme, an editorial in *Worker's Age* accused the Chicago police of acting "with true clerico-fascist 'Social Justice.' . . ." Howard Fast described the violence as "a focal point for the theory and the technique of reactionary capitalism. . . ." Mary Heaton Vorse interpreted police tactics as "part of a country-wide plan . . . to take from labor its recent gains. . . ." For their own reasons all these chroniclers probably would have concurred in *Fortune*'s description of the Memorial Day incident as "a story as savage as any in the dark annals of American labor struggles." [70]

The La Follette Committee concluded "that the sole objective of the meeting and the parade was to march past the plant gate or establish a mass picket line in front of it. . . ." It rejected the police contention that the marchers sought to storm the plant; the presence of women and children in their ranks, and the strikers' knowledge that 1,300 nonstrikers and armed guards were inside the factory gates, convinced the committee that such a venture was never seriously entertained. Nor did the committee accept the police argument that SWOC speakers had incited the marchers

51; Howard Fast, "An Occurrence at Republic Steel," *The Aspirin Age*, ed. Isabel Leighton, pp. 384, 386.

[69] Tom M. Girdler, in collaboration with Boyden Sparkes, *Boot Straps*, pp. 251, 263; Joseph P. Kamp, *The Hell of Herrin Rages Again*, pp. 25, 26, 30.

[70] *Worker's Age*, June 12, 1937; Fast, "An Occurrence at Republic Steel," p. 399; *Progressive*, July 17, 1937; "The Industrial War," *Fortune*, XVI (November 1937), 172.

to violence or that the marchers were so generally armed as to indicate their intention to attack the police. It also rejected the union claim that its march was spontaneous, for a number of SWOC placards and several Red Cross signs clearly indicated premeditation.[71] The events preceding the confrontation between marchers and police convinced the committee that the marchers had acted within their rights. But it heard diametrically opposed versions of the action that followed.

As the marchers approached the police line, Sergeant Lyons observed them moving "as if under commands." La Follette pointed to a picture showing the advancing group in a somewhat random column, with scores of stragglers, and asked if it resembled any military formation that Lyons had ever seen. Indeed it did; it resembled, Lyons said, "the army of the 'Reds,'" or perhaps "the Mexican Army." Patrolman Igoe labeled the marchers "typical agitators." Many of them, he thought, "were under the influence of marihuana cigarettes." His evidence was their "monotonous chant 'C.I.O., C.I.O.'"[72]

After several moments of heated discussion between police officers and the marchers, Captain Kilroy heard a shot fired from the rear of the marchers. "Suddenly," he reported, "from the crowd a shower of bricks and revolver shots were hurled at the police. The front rank of the mob surged forward, policemen were struck with clubs, short pieces of pipe, and two by four boards." The police returned fire, shooting only in self-defense. According to Captain Mooney the strikers let loose "a barrage of bricks, all kinds of missiles," and the police retaliated with tear gas. The demonstrators "acted like wild people. . . . They acted out of their heads, completely wild." Mooney observed his officers shooting into the air; several of the policemen, forced to the ground, shot to protect themselves until the mob retreated. The battle, Mooney suggested, was "between us and the Communists." But of the strikers' fatal wounds not one was frontal, and La Follette wondered about Mooney's embattled officers shooting in self-defense; he thought it "improbable that [marchers] who were surrounding a [police]man, beating him and attacking him would be doing it with their backs turned toward him."[73]

Marchers and observers completely contradicted the police story. Ralph Beck, a reporter for the Chicago *Daily News*, heard the marchers ask

[71] *Memorial Day Incident*, pp. 9, 13, 18; *Hearings*, Pt. 14, pp. 4852–55, 4893.
[72] *Ibid.*, pp. 4761, 4768, 4821.
[73] *Ibid.*, pp. 4648, 4692–94, 4707–20, 4734–39.

Captain Mooney for permission to establish a picket line. Then he saw a tree branch hurled from behind the line of marchers toward the police. After a warning cry, "the next thing I heard was a shot from the rear of me, . . . and I turned around and saw a policeman's revolver pointing in the air over the heads of the other officers." Following the first shot came a "rain of rocks and clubs" from the strikers and a volley of several hundred shots from the police. Beck saw policemen at the front of the line "fire point-blank into the crowd." Then, as the marchers broke and fled, the police "started to work with their clubs." [74]

John Lotito, a flag-bearer, was talking to a policeman when "I got clubbed . . . and I went down, and my flag fell down, and I went to pick up the flag again, to get up, and I got clubbed the second time. . . . I started to crawl away, . . . half running and half crawling. . . ." Approximately thirty-five yards from the police line Lotito was shot in the calf. Harry Harper, in the front row of marchers, saw men fall "as though being mowed down with a scythe." Dr. Lawrence Jacques, observing from Sam's Place, saw the crowd "reverse itself almost like slats of a venetian blind" in its haste to escape. None of the ten dead marchers was shot in the front of his body; seven were shot in the back. Of forty gunshot wounds, four were frontal and twenty-seven were from behind. [75]

Mrs. Lupe Marshall, the witness discovered by Paul Y. Anderson, was a social worker who marched with the strikers. She heard "a dull thud toward the back of . . . my group, and as I turned around there was screaming . . . and simultaneously a volley of shots. . . . I turned around to see what was happening, and the people that were standing in back of me were all lying on the ground face down. I saw some splotches of blood on some of the fellows' shirts." Mrs. Marshall tried frantically to escape but "somebody struck me down from the back again and knocked me down. As I went down . . . a policeman kicked me on the side. . . . After he kicked me I tried to get up, and they hit me three times across the back, and then somebody picked me up and took me to the patrol wagon." Police piled the wounded on top of each other, "half dragging them and half picking them up. . . . Some had their arms all twisted up, and their legs twisted up, until they filled the wagon up, and one man said, 'Well, I guess that's all.' . . ." [76]

[74] *Ibid.*, pp. 4855–58.
[75] *Ibid.*, pp. 4939–40, 4961, 4986–97.
[76] *Ibid.*, pp. 4950–55; *Memorial Day Incident*, pp. 29–30.

On the morning of the third and final day of hearings the La Follette Committee showed the suppressed Paramount News film. It climaxed the hearings and demolished virtually every claim made by the police. Except for two brief intervals during which lenses were changed, the film captured the entire incident. It revealed that after the initial volley of shots the police had charged the marchers, swinging their riot sticks and throwing tear-gas grenades. Only one marcher could be seen to resist the police onslaught. Policemen surrounded isolated marchers and beat them insensible. One man tried to run the gantlet of officers; he was clubbed until he fell unconscious. Another, shot in the back and paralyzed below the waist, was forced to climb into a patrol wagon, until he collapsed from the effort. Only two words from the sound track were clearly audible: "God Almighty!" [77]

The film ended, Paul Anderson wrote, as a disheveled policeman, "his coat open, a scowl on his face, approaches another who is standing in front of the camera. He is sweaty and tired. He says something undistinguishable. Then his face breaks into a sudden grin, he makes a motion of dusting off his hands, and strides away." Congressman Maury Maverick hurried from the Senate hearing room to the House of Representatives, where he interrupted debate to declare, "This was one of the most uncommonly brutal things I have ever seen in my life. . . . [It is] one of the most shameful occurrences in the history of any civilized country." [78]

The La Follette Committee's report on the Memorial Day incident declared it "clearly avoidable," and placed responsibility for the disaster on the Chicago police. "The nature of the police injuries," said the committee, "does not argue that the marchers put up marked resistance to the police; the medical testimony of the nature of the marchers' wounds indicates that they were shot in flight." Although the police claimed to have shot into the air, "shooting in the air cannot explain 40 gunshot wounds, the majority in the back," nor could back wounds be reconciled with a claim of self-defense. The police treated the wounded with "the most callous indifference to human life and suffering. Wounded prisoners of war might have expected and received greater solicitude." The police, the committee charged, had directed their energies not toward an impartial investigation, but toward building a case against the marchers on the basis of their alleged Communist affiliations. Had the police permitted the parade to proceed to the plant gate, "the day would have passed without

[77] St. Louis *Post-Dispatch*, June 17, 1937.
[78] *Ibid.; Congressional Record*, 75th Cong., 1st Sess., 1937, Vol. 81, pp. 6766–67.

violence or disorder. . . ." The committee believed that "it might have been possible to disperse the crowd without the use of weapons"; in any case, gas would have sufficed. "From all the evidence" concluded the committee, "we think it plain that the force employed by the police was far in excess of that which the occasion required. Its use must be ascribed either to gross inefficiency in the performance of police duty or a deliberate effort to intimidate the strikers." [79]

The close of hearings on the Memorial Day incident on July 2, 1937, marked the end of the La Follette Committee's first and most active phase. In the judgment of the American Civil Liberties Union, "no more signal service to civil liberties has been rendered in years than the searching inquiries of the Committee. . . ." [80] Indeed, the committee had enjoyed a remarkably successful year. It had based its hearings on reliable data gathered over a period of time that began before World War I. It drew sustenance from labor and civil libertarian supporters in order to surmount the hurdle of skimpy appropriations. It capitalized upon the great upheaval within the labor movement and wisely wagered its future on the success of the C.I.O.

Yet the committee, during its first year, never ceased to function as a partisan instrument.[81] The reason is obvious. Just as the Wagner Act was one-sided because the source of the difficulty that it attacked was unilateral, so the La Follette Committee's bias was a reaction against management's response to industrial unionization.[82] The sorry state of labor-management relations before 1937 made the Wagner Act necessary, shaped the

[79] *Memorial Day Incident*, pp. 33, 35, 36, 37, 39. In a supplementary statement Senator Thomas wrote: "The encounter of May 30 should never have occurred. . . . Police and marchers defended their actions on the basis of right, but those who died were not martyrs to a cause. They were victims of circumstances, lack of sound judgment and inexpedient actions. . . . The use of police officers in such a way that they seem to be allied with either side of a labor dispute destroys their effectiveness as peace officers representing the public" (*ibid.*, p. 41). A coroner's jury in Chicago returned a verdict against the police of "justifiable homicide."

[80] American Civil Liberties Union, *Let Freedom Ring! The Story of Civil Liberty, 1936–1937*, p. 3.

[81] The committee's friends appreciated this from the beginning. In the spring of 1937, for example, Kenneth Haycroft, Farmer-Labor candidate for mayor of Minneapolis, was informed: "[Representative] Henry [Teigan] has tried to get the La Follette Committee to break the Citizens Alliance inquiry before the June election. There is a possibility this might be done" (Teigan's secretary to Haycroft, May 18, 1937, Henry G. Teigan Papers, Box 16). Professor William E. Leuchtenburg kindly called this item to my attention.

[82] Bernstein, *New Deal Collective Bargaining Policy*, p. 146.

resolution authorizing the La Follette investigation, and determined the La Follette Committee's course.

Like the Industrial Relations Commission a generation earlier, the La Follette investigation underscored the persistence of violence in American labor disputes. The committee, however, exposed only one side of this violence; it never considered the intimidation of nonunion employees by union members, strikers, and organizers. The committee's interpretation of its mandate, and the pattern of labor developments during 1937, consigned civil liberties infractions by organized labor to the background. For this omission employers and their spokesmen, understandably, judged the committee harshly.

Yet violence perpetrated by union members must be seen in the context of labor's position. Organized labor was a minority faction, and would remain so until employers ceased to treat unions as a curse to be exorcised. Government told workers that they had a right to organize, but anti-union employers prevented their doing so. Completely frustrated, denied the opportunity to express their grievances legitimately, workers occasionally borrowed the violent tactics of their employers. But when confronted by Pinkertons, armed guards, arsenals, and strikebreakers, workers suffered disproportionately.

To be sure, union witnesses did not appear before the La Follette Committee with clean hands, and the committee did not attempt to tell both sides of an often sordid story. Its sole concern was investigation of the violence generated by hostility to unionization; this side the committee told comprehensively. But the conditions responsible for the La Follette investigation, and the commitment of committee personnel to industrial unionism, prevented impartiality.

Committee hearings did indicate, however, that when labor's only effective representative—the union—was presumed to be illegitimate, violence became the sole alternative to submission. Strikes were called by minority factions because employers' opposition to unionization made a pro-union majority inconceivable in many factories. Before the sit-down strike in Flint, for example, the United Automobile Workers "was a small, struggling organization, with great ambitions but few members." [83] The sit-down strike, like more conventional strikes elsewhere, enabled a pro-union minority to wield power disproportionate to its numbers and thereby to pave the way for mass unionization. Workers did not strike *after* obtain-

[83] Galenson, *CIO Challenge*, p. 134. Six months after the strike, Galenson notes (p. 148), the UAW claimed more than half a million dues-paying members.

ing majority support; they used strikes as weapons to forge majorities. Employers, of course, had their weapons too; local police, the state militia, and the National Guard seemed interested solely in protecting property, at the expense of workers' rights. Infiltration of union meetings, assaults on union headquarters, suppression of union literature, and intimidation of union members goaded workers beyond endurance. Workers felt, quite rightly, that their civil liberties were entitled to defense. When they realized that no institution existed to protect their rights they chose to fight rather than surrender. The hostile power of employers and the sullen anger of workers generated frequent explosions. The first phase of the La Follette investigation constituted an implicit warning that the consequences of opposition to organization and collective bargaining could no longer be tolerated.

VI

The Ideology of Industrial Warfare

THE La Follette Committee concluded the first phase of its investigation on a note of triumph, but after the hearings on the Memorial Day incident the committee entered a period of transition. It had virtually exhausted Heber Blankenhorn's material on overt anti-union practices. Several staff members, loaned by other government agencies, returned to their original posts; with the Wagner Act and the National Labor Relations Board constitutionally secure, NLRB personnel no longer regarded the committee's success as their primary responsibility. Even more significantly, while the committee was plotting its future course, forces beyond its control deprived it of the most conspicuous advantage of its 1937 hearings—immediacy.

The strike in Little Steel, a catastrophic experience for the Steel Workers' Organizing Committee, stalled the C.I.O. organizing drive. On the heels of this setback came a sharp recession, the most severe decline in American history; the recession, according to William E. Leuchtenburg, "halted the momentum of industrial unionism and dissipated its quasi-revolutionary potential." [1] The C.I.O., which had seemed invincible a few months earlier, saw its fortunes ebb. Consequently, the La Follette Committee, which did not reinterpret its role as labor's ally, suffered a parallel decline. It could no longer blaze a trail for the C.I.O.; at best, it could attempt to redress the balance that swung so sharply against the C.I.O. during the summer of 1937.

The committee tried to use the Little Steel strike to restore the C.I.O.'s lost stature. Hearings on the strike, held nearly a year after its termination, represented a belated but determined effort to condemn the victors in a struggle that the union had lost, apparently irretrievably.[2] The strike

[1] Leuchtenburg, *Franklin D. Roosevelt and the New Deal*, p. 254. Cf. Kenneth D. Roose, "The Recession of 1937–38," *Journal of Political Economy*, LVI (June 1948), 241.

[2] For accounts of the Little Steel strike see Donald G. Sofchalk, "The Little Steel Strike of 1937" (unpublished doctoral dissertation), pp. 55ff.; Galenson, *CIO Challenge*, pp. 96–109; Louis Leotta, Jr., "Republic Steel Corporation in the Steel Strike of 1937" (unpublished master's thesis).

had pitted the aggressive SWOC against the uncompromising steel companies—especially Bethlehem, Republic, and Youngstown Sheet and Tube—which refused to recognize the union as bargaining agent in their plants. It involved nearly two hundred thousand workers, paralyzed a dozen industrial communities, and earned a well-deserved reputation as one of the bloodiest and costliest conflicts in American labor annals. Republic's Tom Girdler had declared his willingness to "raise apples and potatoes" before dealing with John L. Lewis. For the union Philip Murray insisted, "Labor is entitled to recognition and labor is going to get its full measure of recognition." [3] In 1937 Girdler's intransigence proved more enduring.

"With magnificent thoroughness," wrote columnist Kenneth G. Crawford, the La Follette Committee "stripped away the curtain of pretense and told the real story" of the Little Steel strike. The committee's thoroughness still had strongly partisan overtones, however; at times it seemed to be conducting a vendetta against Girdler and Republic Steel. But committee hearings on the role of citizens' committees and employers' associations during the strike constituted more than a union apologia; they exposed, starkly and effectively, the rationalizations of industrial leaders for their anti-union policies. Some businessmen tried to mold their anti-unionism into an ideology; more often than not, their explanations seemed to be a conditioned reflex to legitimate labor aspirations. The La Follette Committee's Little Steel hearings left a voluminous record to document the paucity of business thought during a period in which the actions of business leaders most desperately needed a reasoned defense.[4]

The committee selected six communities for detailed analysis: Monroe, Michigan; Johnstown, Pennsylvania; and Youngstown, Warren, Canton, and Massillon, Ohio. A common pattern characterized them all. At the outset of negotiations the companies had refused to sign any written agreement with the SWOC, an action that was tantamount to a refusal to bargain at all. "The strike arose," declared the La Follette Committee, "out of this one issue." Charles White, vice-president of Republic Steel, explained the policies of his company, policies which the other Little Steel

---

[3] *Hearings*, Pt. 23, p. 9738; quoted in Sofchalk, "The Little Steel Strike of 1937," pp. 55, 74.

[4] Kenneth G. Crawford, *The Pressure Boys*, p. 131. U.S. Senate, Committee on Education and Labor, *The "Little Steel" Strike and Citizens' Committees*, Report No. 151, 77th Cong., 1st Sess., 1941. In March, April, July, and August 1938, the committee held hearings on the Little Steel strike, employers' associations, and citizens' committees. Of 37 days of hearings nearly 19 were devoted to testimony regarding the policies and activities of Republic Steel.

companies had adopted: "We had a very fine relation with our men, so we thought. Later events, I think, proved that. And we could not understand this situation. . . . We were unable to see, Senator, why it was necessary to have a contract to carry out a publicly announced policy of our corporation. We just couldn't understand that. . . . [Our employees believed] that if we signed the contract that it was going to divest them of their natural rights. . . ."[5]

While none of the steel companies eschewed traditional anti-union practices, they all added a modern refinement, the organization and manipulation of public opinion. As one executive explained to the La Follette Committee, "strikebreakers and violence and things of that kind [are] things of the past. . . . The way to win or combat a strike was to organize community sentiment."[6] Organization of community sentiment invariably meant the formation of a citizens' committee, ostensibly neutral but in fact the mouthpiece for corporate policy. What companies would not risk doing openly they accomplish through these committees, which acted under the guise of preserving law and order.

Citizens' committees were particularly effective in the cities affected by the Little Steel strike, where a single industry dominated the economic life of the community. They appealed to public opinion, but they made certain that public opinion could exercise only one choice. An NLRB official declared: "Seeking peace, [the citizens' committee] creates violence; in protecting law and order, it resorts to disorder; in preserving democracy, it denies its every corollary." Citizens' committees generally advocated law and order, constitutional liberty, and conciliation and mediation between parties to the dispute. But a disillusioned rabbi, who had joined the Johnstown committee, testified: "The actual objectives . . . were, first, to get as many men back to work as possible, and to get them back as soon as possible. Second, to break the strike. Third, to break the union."[7]

In Canton, where Republic Steel operated the major manufacturing plants, a Law and Order League was organized at a mass meeting held two weeks after the strike began. "That which confronts us tonight," warned a local minister, "is but the advance guard of Communism. . . ." "You do not need to be a student of history," declared a local attorney,

---

[5] *"Little Steel" Strike*, p. 321; *Hearings*, Pt. 27, pp. 11272, 11275.

[6] Quoted in Louis G. Silverberg, "Citizens' Committees: Their Role in Industrial Conflict," *Public Opinion Quarterly*, V (March 1941), 27.

[7] *Ibid.*, pp. 18, 22, 23.

"to recognize that the situation exists in this country today which parallels that of the French Revolution." The league professed to subscribe to the fondness of President McKinley, Canton's most honored resident, for "concord, not conflict." But its animus was apparent; "It is our intention," wrote the league's chairman, "to educate the public to disapprove of the organization methods used by the C.I.O. . . ." The Law and Order League promoted a back-to-work movement and conducted a back-to-work vote through the mail, in order to embarrass the union; it secured a temporary injunction, subsequently made permanent, against picketing.[8]

The John Q. Public League of Warren, and the Mahoning Valley Citizens' Committee in Youngstown, pursued similar objectives. Pledged to "the American way of living," they urged that "outside agitators" (union organizers) be run out of town. The director of the John Q. Public League invited Silver Shirt leader Spencer J. Warwick to one of its meetings; the Youngstown committee was organized by the president of the bank that carried the payroll account of the Youngstown Sheet and Tube Company. After the Little Steel strike ended, the treasurer of Republic Steel stated: "The very earnest work done by the real citizens of Warren and Youngstown has been very effective in bringing about what now appears to be a quite satisfactory outcome." [9]

Once citizens' committees made their presence felt through overt resistance to unionization, strikers confronted the hostile power of the entire community. In Canton, Republic police and nonstriking employees provoked and assaulted pickets. The National Guard chased pickets from the streets, arrested union leaders, and prevented reporters from gathering news within the strike area. In Massillon, Republic secured the assistance of the city police department to break the strike. In the chief's absence, a retired army major and a Republic police officer led special deputies and city police "in an unprovoked and murderous attack" on C.I.O. headquarters. This raid resulted in the death of three strikers, the arrest, without warrants, of 165 people, and the demolition of union headquarters. It also demoralized the union and broke the strike.[10]

In Youngstown, an SWOC organizer tried to secure radio time, and the station representative refused, claiming, according to one witness, "that he would only get in wrong with the corporations . . . as well as the business-

8 *Hearings*, Pt. 25, p. 10589, Pt. 32, p. 13077, Pt. 39, p. 15430, Pt. 25, p. 10596; "*Little Steel*" *Strike*, pp. 221–222, 224, 226.
9 *Ibid.*, pp. 183, 209, 212; *Hearings*, Pt. 29, p. 12156, Pt. 31, p. 12777.
10 "*Little Steel*" *Strike*, pp. 218, 228, 252; *Hearings*, Pt. 33, pp. 13428–515.

men . . . if he permitted any such speeches going out over the radio which . . . [were] 'communistic,' trying to organize the employees." A Youngstown pastor told the La Follette Committee that one of his parishioners, an employee of the Youngstown Sheet and Tube Company, left the church after a series of sermons on religion and labor because his employer told him "that it would be inadvisable if he wished to continue his job, to continue attending my church." The pastor testified to the financial dependence of churches in industrial areas upon corporate officials, who withheld support "from anyone whose views they disagree with. . . ."[11]

A series of events in Monroe demonstrated to the committee's satisfaction "the impotence of a minority group in the face of the extension of employer influence and domination throughout the community. . . ." The SWOC had secured a tenuous foothold in Monroe when a few workers made furtive contacts with Detroit organizers and met with them on roads outside of the city to form a local. After the Little Steel strike began in the other Republic plants, 125 SWOC members in Monroe voted unanimously to leave their factory. They picketed several hundred feet from plant property and made no attempt to interfere with the movements of other workers. After Memorial Day, however, an independent union generated pressure for a back-to-work movement. The mayor recruited his own army, armed and financed by Republic Steel. An angry mob assaulted C.I.O. organizer Leonidas McDonald in broad daylight; he raced them to the city limits, where union members, afraid to enter Monroe, met him and rushed him to a hospital. The beating of McDonald galvanized the pickets, who armed themselves with rocks, steel bars, and tree branches. While American Legionnaires patrolled the business district, the picketing strikers were dispersed by tear gas and pursued and beaten with clubs and baseball bats by the mayor's special police. The Republic plant reopened with the strike irrevocably broken.[12]

In Johnstown, Pennsylvania, Bethlehem Steel subsidized the local citizens' committee, which became the nucleus of a national citizens' organization. On June 11 two-thirds of Bethlehem workers went out on strike. Sporadic outbursts of violence during the next two days prompted the mayor to threaten to "bring out unlimited numbers of legionnaires to protect our city against invaders." City officials and prominent Johnstown businessmen joined forces to promote "law and order." Mayor Shields deputized five hundred vigilantes, armed them with night sticks, and in-

11 *Ibid.*, Pt. 26, p. 11030, Pt. 27, pp. 11216–17.
12 *"Little Steel" Strike*, pp. 132–161.

structed them to patrol residential areas in taxicabs and private automobiles. In a radio address he told his constituents that "Communism and
anarchy are in evidence in our city today." According to the La Follette
Committee, "The rights of workers to strike and to picket were at no
time the concern of the mayor. He and the citizens' committee were more
conscious of the economic loss resulting from the strike than of the exercise of rights of free speech and assembly." [13]

When the governor of Pennsylvania invoked martial law in Johnstown,
thereby discontinuing picketing and closing the plant, Mayor Shields and
the citizens' committee suddenly discovered that no emergency existed
and that law and order had never been in jeopardy. They demanded the
immediate reopening of the plant. The citizens' committee retained Thorn-
ley and Jones, an advertising agency, to generate support for an end to
martial law. Forty thousand people on the agency's mailing list received
a "Fellow American" letter, warning that "unless public opinion is aroused,
our elected representatives will continue to give in weakly to the threats
of noisy minorities." The agency called for the organization of a Citizens'
National Committee "to defend the right of local self-government and the
right of every worker to pursue his occupation peaceably and within the
law." On July 15, two hundred people from seventy-three cities gathered
in Johnstown and pledged themselves to preserve the "inalienable constitutional right to work." One delegate, chairman of the Massillon Citizens'
Committee, brought down the house by shouting, "Thank God for Tom
Girdler. . . . I think we ought to send him a telegram congratulating him
for smoking out those Communists—John L. Lewis, Madame Perkins and
President Roosevelt." [14] If ever a strike "was broken by public opinion,"
announced the *Labor Relations Bulletin* of the National Association of
Manufacturers, it was the Little Steel strike in Johnstown. When the governor lifted martial law, a vigorous back-to-work movement commenced
and within ten days the SWOC conceded defeat. [15]

The La Follette Committee issued a penetrating analysis of the role of
citizens' committees in circumscribing civil liberties during the Little Steel
strike. The committee discovered "a new alinement of forces in the field
of civil liberties." The Wagner Act "started a great hunt by the first
party, the industrialist, for a third party to do to labor on industry's

13 *Ibid.*, pp. 255, 256, 263, 268, 269; *Hearings*, Pt. 19, pp. 8394, 8639.
14 "*Little Steel*" *Strike*, pp. 275–277, 285–287; *Hearings*, Pt. 19, pp. 8484–85, 8498;
New York Times, July 16, 1937.
15 N.A.M. *Labor Relations Bulletin*, July 15, 1937; *Hearings*, Pt. 19, p. 8261.

behalf what the individual employer himself could no longer do legally." Citizens' committees, potentially the most dangerous "third party," had become "an invisible super-government" in many communities. Under the cloak of maintaining law and order they aroused, or co-operated with, a spirit of vigilantism that stifled the legitimate efforts of workers to exercise their constitutional and statutory rights. "In a country whose history provides evidence of vigilantism," cautioned the committee, "it is a matter of no little public concern when business organizations, influential and moneyed, seize on and foster such movements to the attainment of their own ends." [16]

The La Follette Committee warned of the tendency of majority opinion to ride roughshod over individual rights. Its findings might well have convinced civil libertarians that they had slain the ogre of federal coercion only to discover even more ominous local tyranny. The history of citizens' committees, wrote an NLRB official in 1941, indicated "that a vast portion of our people are so unconcerned with the preservation of civil liberties that they can be easily induced to withdraw them from what, at the moment, 'public' sentiment stamps as an objectional group in the community." [17]

Citizens' committees, law and order leagues, vigilante groups, and private police forces bypassed responsible law-enforcement agencies and implemented their own concepts of liberty. Vigilantism was, in fact, vigorously defended by those who practiced it. William Frew Long, of the Associated Industries of Cleveland, told the La Follette Committee: "There are things happening today that if they had happened 50 years ago you and I and everyone else would have grabbed a shotgun and gone out and done something. But we are getting apathetic and soft. . . . Where the people of a city or town rise in righteous indignation about a situation they don't like, it is a very healthy sign." [18]

"In the ill-defined, loosely articulated structure of American life," Daniel Bell has written, "public opinion rather than law has been the more operative sanction against nonconformists and dissenters. . . . During periods of extreme excitement . . . the punitive sanctions of opinion quickly supercede law." Labor relations during the New Deal presented one such period of extreme excitement, and the result confirms Bell's thesis. The

[16] *"Little Steel" Strike*, p. 293; U.S. Senate, Committee on Education and Labor, *Interim Report*, Report No. 46, Pt. 4, 75th Cong., 3d Sess., 1938, pp. 2, 3.
[17] Silverberg, "Citizens' Committees," p. 37.
[18] *Hearings*, Pt. 20, p. 8879.

constitutional, or judicial, definitions of specific civil liberties yielded to the restrictions imposed by local majorities. The La Follette Committee's findings foreshadowed a new civil libertarian formula: Federal power, so long the source of libertarian fears, might be needed to counteract local, and private, power, which in fact, if not yet in libertarian theory, often acted as the final arbiter of the Bill of Rights.[19]

The expected climax to the hearings on the Little Steel strike was the confrontation between the committee and Tom Girdler, whom *Fortune* labeled "the avatar of the old-style, unsocialized competitive order. . . ."[20] This acknowledged leader of Little Steel employers was a veteran of thirty-five years in the industry. He had made his reputation at Jones and Laughlin's Aliquippa plant, called by workers "the Siberia of America." (Aliquippa, Girdler admitted in his autobiography, resembled a "benevolent dictatorship.") Girdler had become chairman of the board of Republic Steel the day before the stock market crashed in 1929, and for the next eight years he had struggled to save his company from financial disaster, from unions, and from "the great force that seemed bent on our destruction," the United States government. Girdler reminded one historian of "a character from Dickens or even one from melodrama." In perhaps his most characteristic statement he once asked, rhetorically, "With free water and cheap soap who, other than poorly trained children, really is obliged to live in filth?"[21]

Philip Murray set the stage for Girdler's appearance when he told the La Follette Committee that Republic Steel, "so far as its labor policies are concerned constitutes the filthiest industrial cesspools of labor relations in America." On August 11, 1938, the final day of hearings on Little Steel, Girdler testified before an overflow crowd in the Senate Office Building. But the Girdler–La Follette confrontation, Paul Y. Anderson wrote, "turned out to be pretty much of a flop." Girdler admitted to many mistakes but insisted that he knew nothing of Republic's more reprehensible antilabor practices. La Follette, Anderson charged, failed to present many facts that would have embarrassed Girdler. "Bob has got into the habit,"

[19] Daniel Bell, "The Dispossessed—1962," *The Radical Right*, ed. Daniel Bell, p. 31. Andrew Hacker suggests that in the struggle for individual and minority rights "the proponents of democracy had best not rely on the principle of majority-rule. For that battle cry is on the other side" ("The Indifferent Majority," *New Leader*, XLVI [March 18, 1963], 21).

[20] "Fifteen Businessmen," *Fortune*, XVII (March 1938), 73.

[21] Girdler, *Boot Straps*, pp. 5, 177, 195, 214, 224–226; Broadus Mitchell, *Depression Decade*, p. 295.

he wrote, "of leaning over backward so far that he is constantly losing his balance." [22]

La Follette did question Girdler closely about an article, published in the St. Louis *Post-Dispatch*, describing labor conditions in Aliquippa during Girdler's tenure there. Girdler apparently had complimented the author for "a God-damned-near-perfect picture." The picture included espionage extending into schools, churches, and homes, use of company police, "escorts" for union organizers, and distribution by foremen of marked sample ballots. As one worker explained, "We were treated like pig iron. We were just a commodity." Girdler admitted that Aliquippa "was not a popular place for professional union men, and that was because of the men themselves, who did not want professional union men there." [23]

At Republic, as in Aliquippa, Girdler testified, employees opposed outside unions. Girdler did not believe that there existed "a happier, better satisfied set of steel employees in the United States than the Republic employees working under the employee-representation plan" (that is, under a company union). Girdler conceded that times had changed. "You were commended [in 1919] if you had close relations with your men . . . and you told them what you thought. Today, if you tell them anything, it is an unfair labor practice." Girdler grasped the essence of this change, but he did not respond to it; "A terribly *disorganizing* influence is at work at the base of all industry in America," he later wrote. "The boss is no longer the boss. . . ." [24]

In a prepared statement Girdler accused the La Follette Committee of raking over "the dead ashes of past disputes, in search of the minutest mistakes made by industry." [25] Girdler's charge was not entirely groundless, but the committee's Little Steel hearings, in conjunction with its earlier investigations, did more than expose industry's "minutest mistakes." They also offered insight into the American capitalist mentality during a period of pervasive unrest. Industrial magnates had enjoyed decades of virtually unchallenged hegemony in labor relations, but within a few years a surging labor movement had established a beachhead and become

[22] *Hearings*, Pt. 25, p. 10423; Paul Y. Anderson, "La Follette Pulls His Punches," *Nation*, CXLVII (August 20, 1938), 170. "For some strange reason," Anderson wrote, La Follette "has become imbued with the notion that the most important purpose of his investigation is to 'make a record.'" Anderson was not the only "liberal" to criticize La Follette for being too fair.

[23] St. Louis *Post-Dispatch*, June 29, 1937; *Hearings*, Pt. 34, pp. 13789–90, 13903–6.

[24] *Ibid.*, pp. 13792–93, 13842–43, 13786; *Boot Straps*, pp. 449–450.

[25] *Hearings*, Pt. 34, pp. 13972–73.

a serious competitor for traditional managerial prerogatives. The La Follette Committee hearings revealed the ideological as well as the physical defenses erected by management as means of maintaining the *status quo ante.*

The most common explanation for resistance to unionization, advanced by management and detective agencies alike, linked labor organization by "outside" unions to communism. The specter of communism was used to justify everything from the confiscation of union literature to the killing of Memorial Day marchers. As the most active "outside" union, the C.I.O. suffered most from the Red scare. Asher Rossetter, Pinkerton vice-president, neatly defined communism for the La Follette Committee as "absolute control by committees of organized workers in all matters pertaining to labor, social relationship, religion, and so forth." The supervisor of Pinkerton's Atlanta office insisted that his industrial investigations focused on "radical agitation" and "communistic activity"; when pressed by La Follette, he conceded that he had yet to uncover his first Communist. Dan G. Ross, general manager of the Corporations Auxiliary Company, believed that a "spurt in Communism" resulted from passage of the Wagner Act. Raymond J. Burns, president of the Burns Detective Agency, acknowledged that "when a community is infested with . . . Communists . . . the client is more susceptible to service at that time." In a letter filled with portents of doom, Corporations Auxiliary warned Republic Steel: "Ominous as the vibrant throb of jungle drums are the disquieting notes coming from the various gatherings of labor organizations. . . ." It told of Communists in the A.F. of L., in the C.I.O., and even in company unions, and urged every industrialist to pay "profound attention if he is not to be caught napping while the other fellow is keenly wide awake." [26]

What originated as sales propaganda for detective agencies was quickly absorbed by management and just as quickly filtered down to company underlings. During the Little Steel strike Tom Girdler advised his employees that the sole issue was: "Must Republic and its men submit to the communistic dictates and terrorism of the C.I.O.?" Republic vice-president Charles White excused the actions of company police "because of the organizing campaign which carried with it a very large number of known law violators and Communists. . . ." Not surprisingly, a Republic

[26] *Ibid.,* Pt. 2, pp. 536, 540–541, Pt. 4, p. 1134, Pt. 8, p. 2738, Pt. 25, pp. 10824, 10827.

police sergeant justified his surveillance of union organizers with the statement, "Well I, being a family man, with nine children—I didn't want to see anything turn communistic in Youngstown." Another Republic police officer shadowed an SWOC organizer and confiscated his literature because "he is known commonly and professionally as a Communist and an atheist." The secretary of the Citizens' National Committee, who referred to the C.I.O. as the "C(ommunist) I(nternational) O(rder)," described union activities in Johnstown as "a scheme of communistic dictatorship, the most revolting and oppressive with which this Nation has ever been threatened, or man debased." [27]

Apart from their alleged function as advance agents of communism, unions threatened one of the shibboleths of management dogma, "industrial harmony." For years business leaders had proclaimed, "The interests of labor and capital also of management and public are inseparable and practically indistinguishable." [28] The Depression, and labor militancy during the New Deal, did nothing to shake this belief. In fact, they reinforced it, at the very moment when management's own behavior evinced the widest possible gap between assertion and action. Businessmen, suggests one student of their New Era ideology, carried with them into the thirties "an acute distrust of any power with a popular base." [29] Their program to promote harmony was a socially acceptable expression of this distrust. Erected on a tottering framework of managerial authority, its object was to perpetuate the image of the businessman as instructor and leader of his workers, who would patiently look to him for guidance. [30] Businessmen may have preached harmony and law and order, but their often unlawful acts created constant disharmony and disorder.

The general manager of Chrysler's De Soto branch told the La Follette Committee that as a result of Chrysler's expenditures on espionage

[27] *Ibid.*, Pt. 29, p. 12144, Pt. 26, pp. 11093, 11024, 11063, Pt. 31, pp. 12948–49. For a discussion of more recent corporate obsessions with Communist infiltration, see Alan F. Westin, "Anti-Communism and the Corporations," *Commentary*, XXXVI (December 1963), 479–487.

[28] Address of John E. Edgerton, president of the National Association of Manufacturers (1929), quoted in James W. Prothro, *Dollar Decade: Business Ideas in the 1920's*, p. 97.

[29] *Ibid.*, p. 175.

[30] Robert A. Brady, *Business As a System of Power*, p. 287. Brady compares harmony programs in the United States, Germany, Japan, France, and Italy and argues: "The accepted large-scale employer version of 'harmony' in labor relations, . . . could lead only to 'the servile state.' "

($275,000 between 1933 and 1936), "our labor relations with our employees are in very good shape." Espionage could be justified "from the fact that we do have and have had proper employee relations." Lewis G. Seaton, a General Motors labor relations expert, insisted that "the interest of the employer and the employee are the same in the end." But his company's expenditures for espionage prompted La Follette to make a sardonic promise: "If we discover that spying . . . is a helpful principle, that it makes for better manhood, that it builds up a better citizenry, that it makes for more efficient shops, and that it actually saves industrialists money, you may rest assured that our report . . . [will commend] the great work that is being done by spying organizations. . . ."[31]

Detective agencies insisted that they did their part to promote harmonious conditions in industry. "Our service," wrote the representative of one agency, "is a curative and preventive measure, and constructive in every respect!" The president of the Corporations Auxiliary Company told the committee that "we assist in harmonizing conditions in a plant." How was this accomplished? "Well, we would place one of our people in the plant and ask him to get all the information he possibly can concerning all dissatisfaction, discord, nepotism, . . . and we [would give] that information to our clients. . . ." Another representative of that agency could not see "where our men are really doing anything that is detrimental to a union. We do not put men in the unions for the purpose of disrupting them and tearing them down and putting class up against class. . . . Our work is strike prevention." In fact, said this representative, Corporations Auxiliary spies functioned as "a human suggestion box."[32]

In order to secure "peace in industry," the National Metal Trades Association established a defense fund upon which it drew to pay strikebreakers, proselytize against the Wagner Act, furnish munitions, and circulate blacklists. Its commissioner, Homer D. Sayre, claimed that "our primary interest . . . is to try and get the employer and employee to believe that their interests are mutual." Labor difficulties presented "the worst thing that can possibly happen"; workers must realize "that the best interests of both management and employees lies in the control of management over the fundamental policies of management. . . ."[33]

---

[31] *Hearings*, Pt. 4, p. 1219, Pt. 6, pp. 1893–94.

[32] *Ibid.*, Pt. 25, p. 10806, Pt. 4, pp. 1105, 1165, 1168.

[33] *Ibid.*, Pt. 3, pp. 820, 830–831, 836; U.S. Senate, Committee on Education and Labor, *Labor Policies of Employers Associations*, Report No. 6, Pt. 4, 76th Cong., 1st Sess., 1939, pp. 44–101.

Management preached harmony, but the La Follette Committee, Heber Blankenhorn wrote, "found war." [34] Businessmen perceived that unions and the government threatened their principles as well as their profits. Arguing that economic freedom was a natural right, they refused to grant legitimacy to labor unions as social institutions because unions challenged their traditional prerogatives. Whether or not unionism did in fact aim to overthrow managerial authority, businessmen believed that it did. Their belief helps to explain, if not to excuse, their conduct.[35] Similarly, management realized that government regulation threatened its hegemony. The "psychic cost" of regulation may have troubled businessmen even more than the economic cost. New Deal regulatory measures, particularly the Wagner Act, challenged the image of the businessman as leader and, one study suggests, "deprived businessmen of psychologically important increments of deference and self-respect." [36] With their authority undermined, many businessmen developed patterns of behavior that indicated slight concern for the personal rights of others.[37]

The La Follette Committee hearings revealed characteristic business responses to threats from the "outside." Even in its heyday American business had resorted to extreme measures to squelch incipient unionism. During the thirties, while unions themselves grew stronger, business increased its activities and developed new techniques, such as the citizens' committee, to shore up its crumbling defenses. The apparent hostility of government intensified these efforts. But all the while businessmen, and those who served them, preached harmony. They insisted upon their right to maintain the power that made "harmony" acceptable to them, and they called "communistic" any group seeking to share that power. The committee's record exposed management's frantic search for stability during a period in which continual change destroyed old certitudes.

[34] "The Struggle of Labor," *Religion and Public Affairs*, ed. Harris F. Rall, p. 47. Cf. "Labor Should Have Civil Rights," *American Federationist*, XLVI (July 1939), 691–692, in which it is argued that some American employers "have done more than Karl Marx could accomplish in creating the impression that an irreconcilable conflict exists between Capital and Labor."

[35] Daniel Bell, "Industrial Conflict and Public Opinion," *Industrial Conflict*, ed. Arthur Kornhauser, *et al.*, pp. 240–256; Lois Macdonald, *Labor Problems and the American Scene*, p. 602; Prothro, *Dollar Decade*, p. 139; Richard C. Wilcock, "Industrial Management's Policies Toward Unionism," *Labor and the New Deal*, ed. Milton Derber and Edwin Young, p. 280.

[36] Robert E. Lane, *The Regulation of Businessmen*, pp. 19–38.

[37] Alfred Winslow Jones, *Life, Liberty, and Property*, p. 180. See also Thomas Paul Jenkin, *Reactions of Major Groups to Positive Government in the United States, 1930–1940*; Francis X. Sutton, *et al.*, *The American Business Creed*.

The committee's examination of the labor policies of employers' associations complemented the exposure of business ideology. Sixteen years earlier Clarence Bonnett had called these associations "the most powerful organizations in the business and industrial world." Their primary function was to promote employers' interests in labor-management relations; they assisted employers to negotiate with, or to fight, a union. In 1922, in the classic study of employers' associations, Bonnett had predicted "that the conflict [between associations and unions] will be conducted on a continually enlarging scale, . . . and probably with increasing intensity." [38] For its investigation, which was to update Bonnett's study and confirm his prophecy, the La Follette Committee selected three associations whose activities had hampered New Deal labor policy: Associated Industries of Cleveland, a locally organized group of employers in various industries; the National Metal Trades Association, which comprised employers in a particular industry; and the National Association of Manufacturers, with members in diverse manufacturing industries.

Employers' associations, declared William Frew Long of Associated Industries of Cleveland, "are the best friends the unions ever had. . . ." Members of Associated Industries employed one-third of all workers engaged in manufacturing in the Cleveland area. Their role of "best friends" included refusal to bargain collectively with unions, purchase of the services of spies and strikebreakers, and evasion of Section 7(a) of the NIRA, and the Wagner Act, whenever possible. Two years after passage of the Wagner Act, and after the sit-down strikes, the capitulation of United States Steel, and the outbreak of the Little Steel strike, Associated Industries of Cleveland told its members that "there is every evidence that the American workman is not inclined to unionize." [39]

Associated Industries tolerated only the company union. Association members, William Frew Long insisted, had "the right to know and in some cases must ask, if employees belong to a union." In conjunction with the National Association of Manufacturers, Associated Industries devised an individual employment contract which all employees were obligated to sign. The contract required them to indicate whether they wished to bargain with their employer "directly," or collectively through a union, or collectively through representatives chosen by them. If an employee

[38] *Employers' Associations in the United States: A Study of Typical Associations*, pp. vi, 13, 558.

[39] *Hearings*, Pt. 20, p. 8843, Pt. 38, p. 15262; *Labor Policies*, Pt. 5, pp. 2, 34–35, 182–185.

chose the second alternative, he identified himself as a union sympathizer and invited discharge. If he selected either of the other alternatives, his employer could use his contract to resist the claim of a union to speak for plant employees.[40]

Employers' associations did not confine their activities to members' factories. When the board of directors of Associated Industries learned that Socialists had been holding meetings in the Cleveland YMCA, one of the directors contacted YMCA officials and reported back that the YMCA would reconsider permitting radical groups to use its facilities. Associated Industries exerted similar pressure on local churches.[41]

The language of the association's information bulletins contrasted sharply with its declared purpose, "the improvement of employment relations and the betterment of industrial conditions." One bulletin preached, "Preparedness is always a deterrent." Another suggested, "Through years of experience in facing one particular type of foe—enemies of American conditions of employment—[Associated Industries] is best equipped to shield your business from closed shop domination." Senator La Follette commented on the juxtaposition of "harmony" rhetoric and military metaphors: "First you refer to [the association] as a 'defense' and then you refer to it as a 'shield' . . . and it rather seemed to me that you were psychologically in the frame of mind of a staff officer in a war." [42]

The National Metal Trades Association counted among its members General Motors, Chrysler, and Republic Steel. It was, according to one of its pamphlets, a voluntary association of metal manufacturers who believed that "the Open Shop is beneficial to both employers and employees . . . and should be maintained and extended." But a preliminary analysis by the La Follette Committee indicated that the association "has devised a philosophy and method which are the most invulnerable and ominous toward organized labor in the country today." The association stated unequivocally in its Declaration of Principles: "We will not admit of any interference with the management of our business." [43] In fact, the only right retained by employees was the right to quit. Association members would not tolerate strikes, nor would they discuss wages, hours, or working conditions. No strike could be settled without the consent of the association's administrative council; a member pursuing an independ-

[40] *Ibid.*, pp. 107, 112.

[41] *Ibid.*, p. 135.

[42] *Hearings*, Pt. 20, pp. 8772, 8776.

[43] *Labor Policies*, Pt. 4, p. 6; "Preliminary Analysis of National Metal Trades Association," LFC, Box 106; *Labor Policies*, Pt. 4, p. 17.

ent course was subject to suspension or expulsion. The association insisted upon absolute power to determine the methods for preventing or ending a strike. Collective bargaining never became one of them.[44]

The National Metal Trades Association denounced the Wagner Act as "revolutionary" and urged members to oppose it on grounds of "patriotism." Members who did not comply were threatened with immediate expulsion. Thirty per cent of the membership dues went into a defense fund which the association administered. It furnished strikebreakers, and guards to protect them, and procured labor spies when asked to do so. Commenting on the activities of the association, the La Follette Committee concluded, "When the interest of society in freedom of association for workingmen has found statutory embodiment, the persistence of the National Metal Trades Association in its avowed program presents a challenge to government itself." [45]

For the La Follette Committee, the National Association of Manufacturers, combining characteristics of Associated Industries and the NMTA, epitomized organized employer attitudes toward New Deal labor policy. The majority of American businessmen, the committee conjectured, acquiesced in the policy enunciated in Section 7(a) and in the Wagner Act. But "an intransigent minority of powerful corporations" still opposed organization and collective bargaining, and these corporations occupied dominant positions in the NAM. Guided by "this small but powerful minority of corporations," the NAM persisted in its traditional policies of opposition to unions and to government action intended to improve working conditions. The committee condemned the NAM's "deliberate action . . . to promote organized disregard" for the Wagner Act, and deplored its failure to adapt to changing times and new laws.[46]

In 1911 the association's president had charged that the American Federation of Labor "is engaged in an open warfare against Jesus Christ and His Cause"; for the next twenty-five years the ideal union, for the NAM, was that between employer and employee. Executive vice-president Walter B. Weisenburger insisted, "Much of the effort of this association is directed toward producing industrial peace . . . . I do not want the impression to go out here that this association is simply an antilabor organization." [47]

[44] *Ibid.*, pp. 17–19, 39–44.
[45] *Ibid.*, pp. 44–46, 69, 117.
[46] *Ibid.*, Pt. 6, pp. 221–222.
[47] *Ibid.*, pp. 19, 28; *Hearings*, Pt. 17, p. 7418, Pt. 18, pp. 7824–25.

The NAM's efforts to produce industrial peace interested the committee and comprised the most revealing facet of its investigation of the association. After 1934 the NAM conducted a program of education, "to cope with the issue of unscrupulous unionism and radicalism. . . ." Unlike the NMTA and Associated Industries, the NAM confined itself to lobbying, distributing propaganda, and providing legal advice. It relied upon press releases, cartoons, editorials, films, and radio broadcasts to defend unregulated private enterprise. It blamed changed patterns of industrial relations on "Communists," "impatient reformers," "disturbers," and "teacher propagandists." It appealed to "public understanding" to resist incursions on managerial prerogatives. What the NAM really wanted, declared the La Follette Committee, was to retard unionization and "to render public opinion intolerant of the aims of social progress through legislative effort." [48]

In 1936 the NAM initiated one of its most ambitious projects. It sponsored a series of thirteen advertisements, entitled "Prosperity Dwells Where Harmony Reigns," which received nationwide circulation. The advertisements featured pithy statements reminiscent of the Horatio Alger success myth. "From the ranks of today's workers," suggested one, "will come thousands of the *leaders* of the future. . . ." The NAM attributed this phenomenon to "the spirit of good will among all classes," and warned against the danger of "destructive influences—often guided by hands across the sea. . . ." Another advertisement requested workers to "put *yourself* in his place!" Most corporation leaders, the NAM maintained, began their careers in the factory; therefore, "they can't help but understand [workers'] responsibilities and have a desire to relieve them as much as competition will allow." Teachers, preachers, editors, and business and professional men were advised to "guard carefully each act and each utterance to see that it cannot be misconstrued to give aid or comfort to enemies of the public welfare. If evidence of false or harmful propaganda comes to their attention they should aid quickly in its wise suppression." The NAM advised all citizens that "with so many destructive 'isms' and creeds being printed and preached—youth will welcome your help in pointing out the pitfalls of false and un-American doctrines." [49]

Clarence Bonnett had indicated that belligerent associations could combat unions by furnishing munitions to member organizations, engaging in lobbying, breaking strikes, accumulating blacklists, encouraging corporate welfare work, or conducting propaganda campaigns. The La Follette

[48] *Labor Policies*, Pt. 6, pp. 154–175.
[49] *Hearings*, Pt. 18, pp. 7896–908.

Committee hearings confirmed that these practices persisted, despite the passage of legislation making labor organization and collective bargaining the cornerstone of national labor policy. In their campaign against the Wagner Act, Associated Industries of Cleveland, the National Metal Trades Association, and the National Association of Manufacturers bore responsibility, charged the committee, "for one of the greatest campaigns of nullification ever waged against any Federal statute." [50] Although the Wagner Act presumably blanketed American workers with First Amendment guarantees of free speech and assembly, many employers refused to accept the new congressional definition of civil liberty. The La Follette Committee hearings offered an excellent vantage point for observing the struggle between labor and management to interpret the meaning of the First Amendment in industrial relations.

As the hearings on employers' associations and the Little Steel strike neared an end, La Follette submitted another resolution to augment the committee's appropriation and to extend its life.[51] Once again the request for appropriations invited friends and foes of the committee to wrangle over its achievements and shortcomings. And once again Senator James F. Byrnes, presiding over the Committee to Audit and Control the Contingent Expenses of the Senate, stood athwart the La Follette Committee's progress. Byrnes accused committee staff members of lobbying on behalf of the new resolution; he was, Gardner Jackson told Roger Baldwin, "reported to be sore as Hell." But Byrnes's anger, Jackson believed, was "merely an excuse . . . for him to try to stymie the appropriation." Baldwin fired letters off to James M. Landis, Dean of the Harvard Law School, and to Samuel I. Rosenman, Roosevelt's adviser, requesting them to ask the President to use his influence with Byrnes to ensure favorable action on the resolution.[52]

The committee faced an uphill struggle. According to the St. Louis *Post-Dispatch*, its investigations "have been striking some tender and sensitive spots, so the lobbyists are busying themselves in an effort to block continuance of [its] work. . . ." During late April and early May the

[50] Bonnett, *Employers' Associations*, p. 550; *Labor Policies*, Pt. 5, p. 185.

[51] *Congressional Record*, 75th Cong., 3d Sess., 1938, Vol. 83, p. 5468. The resolution authorized an additional appropriation of $60,000. The committee had already received $105,000.

[52] Jackson to Baldwin, April 28, 1938, Baldwin to Landis, May 9, 1938, Baldwin to Rosenman, May 9, 1938, ACLU, Vol. 1091.

press came to the committee's defense. "It is impossible," declared the Birmingham (Ala.) *Post*, "to put a cash value on what the civil liberties committee of the U.S. Senate has done in the last two years . . . this has been one of the wisest, most profitable investments of public money." The Madison (Wis.) *Capital Times* commended the committee for doing "more to bring back freedom of speech to oppressed groups in this country than any other governmental agency." And the *New Republic*, one of the committee's stanchest supporters, asked, "Who interferes with liberty in this country and how? The greatest single contribution ever made toward an answer to this question has come from the Civil Liberties Committee. . . ." [53]

On May 10 Senator Byrnes reported the La Follette resolution without recommendation; the appropriation would therefore appear on the Senate calendar as unfinished business, requiring administration pressure for its consideration. On May 13 Roger Baldwin asked Morris Ernst to speak to President Roosevelt about the resolution. Four days later Baldwin reported happily to Gardner Jackson that La Follette had spent the weekend with Roosevelt. On May 18, when the Senate considered the resolution, La Follette promised that the $60,000 appropriation would suffice to complete the committee's investigation. La Follette assured the Senate that his committee would issue its final report and legislative recommendations on or before January 15, 1939. His pledge evidently disarmed the opposition, for the Senate quickly approved the measure.[54]

With its new appropriation, predicted the *Progressive*, the committee would investigate infringements of civil liberties in Jersey City, Mayor Frank Hague's bailiwick. In January Lee Pressman, C.I.O. general counsel, had filed forty affidavits with the committee accusing Hague of repressing every trace of unionism in Jersey City. The *Progressive* anticipated another "team play" between the committee and the Justice Department, as had occurred in Harlan County. When hearings on the Little Steel strike ended, said "a source close to the committee," the Jersey City investigation would begin. But La Follette, who conducted the hearings

[53] St. Louis *Post-Dispatch*, May 4, 1938; Birmingham (Ala.) *Post*, May 6, 1938, clipping in ACLU, Vol. 2001; Madison (Wis.) *Capital Times*, April 26, 1938, clipping in ACLU, Vol. 1091; "The Committee Should Go On," *New Republic*, XCIV (April 27, 1938), 344.

[54] *Congressional Record*, 75th Cong., 3d Sess., 1938, Vol. 83, pp. 5468, 6522, 7050; Baldwin to Morris Ernst, May 13, 1938, Baldwin to Jackson, May 17, 1938, ACLU, Vol. 1091; letters urging support for the appropriation in FDRL, OF 1581; *New York Times*, May 19, 1938.

alone during August while Elbert Thomas was engaged in a primary campaign, never displayed much enthusiasm for the project. Although La Follette, according to one newspaperman, provided "Washington's best show of the summer," he took his pledge to the Senate seriously; his evident weariness of the investigation, now entering its third year, undoubtedly contributed to his unwillingness to undertake a new venture. In mid-September he announced that the committee would leave Jersey City to the Justice Department because an investigation would add little to the information already available.[55]

The second phase of the La Follette Committee investigation, which ended so anticlimactically with Tom Girdler's testimony on August 11, 1938, lacked the excitement of the 1937 hearings. By 1938 the committee had achieved most of the labor objectives set for it two years previously. Furthermore, the committee's conception of its task remained static. The decision to confine its investigations to labor disputes, which had once opened up so many possibilities, now made the committee seem a victim of inertia. As Robert Wohlforth admitted, "We should have closed . . . up [the investigations] on the Memorial Day massacre. . . . We just lived too long." [56] Perhaps his judgment was too harsh, for the committee's later findings, though less dramatic, were no less significant. In fact, one of the committee's vital contributions was its exposure of the power of private individuals, acting in concert, to determine the meaning of specific provisions of the Bill of Rights within a particular community. Whether or not the La Follette Committee, or any agency of the federal government, would act to correct this situation remained to be seen.

[55] *Progressive*, January 22, May 28, July 9, August 27, September 17, 1938; *C.I.O. News*, January 14, 1938. Robert Wohlforth denied that La Follette's reluctance to investigate Jersey City had any political overtones (Wohlforth, COHC, pp. 12–13).
[56] Wohlforth, COHC, p. 51.

VII

The Committee and Class Struggle

FRANKLIN D. ROOSEVELT has been depicted as the skillful captain who steered the New Deal along a middle course, guiding it safely past the Scylla of irresponsible individualism and the Charybdis of totalitarianism.[1] But New Deal rhetoric often outran New Deal action, particularly in moments of economic stress. At such times the Roosevelt administration seemed to tack decisively to port. The recession of 1937–1938, for example, rekindled the antipathy of Roosevelt and the New Dealers for the "money-changers" and the "economic royalists." Old slogans were refurbished and new alarums were sounded over the ominous concentration of economic power in the hands of a few antisocial industrialists.

In December 1937 Secretary of the Interior Harold L. Ickes warned members of the American Civil Liberties Union of the "corporate overlords" who had interposed themselves between the citizen and his state. Economic power, Ickes insisted, was vested in "an irresponsible and self-constituted corporate oligarchy, benevolent and paternalistic at its best, despotic and predatory at its worst." Americans must beware of those who, "pretending that they would save us from dreadful communism, would superimpose upon America an equally dreadful fascism."[2] Three weeks later, Assistant Attorney General Robert H. Jackson told the American Political Science Association that an autocratic "economic oligarchy" was menacing political and economic freedom. The New Deal, Jackson said, had saved business from ruin but had restored it to arrogance. "Today," he observed, "we have in command of big business . . . the same Bourbons who were in command of the defeat of 1929 and who since then have learned nothing and forgotten nothing."[3] In his message to Congress of April 29, 1938, President Roosevelt announced, "Among

---

[1] Arthur M. Schlesinger, Jr., *The Politics of Upheaval*, pp. 647–657.

[2] Harold L. Ickes, "Nations in Nightshirts," *Vital Speeches*, IV (January 1, 1938), 180–181.

[3] Robert H. Jackson, "The Philosophy of Big Business," *Vital Speeches*, IV (January 15, 1938), 209–210.

us today a concentration of private power without equal in history is growing." Liberty was threatened, the President declared, because "concentrated private economic power . . . is struggling so hard to master our democratic government."[4]

These administration jeremiads revealed the occasional fondness of New Dealers for the rhetoric of the Left. In a decade when Americans tended to exaggerate the menace of domestic fascism, the antilabor activities of businessmen frequently seemed the harbinger of totalitarianism.[5] New Deal rhetoric was not without purpose, however; whether rooted in conviction or in convenience, it made enactment of moderate reforms less difficult. But in order to succeed, it had to contain at least a measure of truth. During Roosevelt's first two terms, no New Deal agency contributed as much grist to the antibusiness mill as did the La Follette Civil Liberties Committee.

By 1938 the committee had amassed a body of testimony that constituted a damning indictment of American industrialists. Labor relations, its findings suggested, had been poisoned by the cruel acts of predatory employers. Oppressive labor practices, and an ideology of callous indifference to labor's legitimate demands, seemed to confirm the most pessimistic Marxist forebodings about the nature of capitalistic society. The La Follette Committee did not warn of the imminence of class warfare; it documented its existence. The committee had originated, to be sure, as the instrument of a nonideological liberal administration; its supporters in Congress and in administrative agencies had hoped primarily to implement the mandate of the Wagner Act. But the committee's personnel and the "objective situation" in which it found itself pushed it increasingly to the left. Its hearings and reports were variations on one theme: class warfare. In this struggle employers were armed with the deadliest weapons. Committee disclosures pointed to class war as the dominant fact of American life.

The commitment of the committee to this motif shaped reactions to its work; neutrality in regard to its investigations was virtually impossible. Responses to the committee polarized along a Left-Right axis, with representatives of both extremes extracting precious nuggets of evidence to support their preconceived notions. Committee hearings reinforced the belief of American Marxists that liberal democracy could not resolve its

[4] *The Public Papers and Addresses of Franklin D. Roosevelt*, ed. Samuel I. Rosenman, VII, 306, 308.

[5] Cf. Leuchtenburg, *Franklin D. Roosevelt and the New Deal*, pp. 275–276.

internal problems. The hearings also convinced spokesmen for industry that the New Deal, and particularly the labor movement, had infected the country with the germ of communism. The La Follette Committee, aided immeasurably by its allies and adversaries, emerged as a representative New Deal symbol of the struggle between exploiters and the exploited.

For obvious reasons the C.I.O. sang paeans to the La Follette Committee. General counsel Lee Pressman, in a letter sent to every senator, commended the committee for uncovering "a vast conspiracy against the civil rights of workers throughout broad sections of American industry. The exposure of this conspiracy has been of great assistance not only to organized labor, but to all democratic and progressive forces in the United States." At the C.I.O. convention in 1938, the Committee on Legislation, comprising Pressman, Sidney Hillman, Philip Murray, and Homer Martin, offered its "grateful acknowledgment" to the committee for its "tireless probing into the organized suppression of the rights of workers." The entire convention approved a resolution stating that the La Follette Committee, more than any committee in Senate history, deserved the appreciation of American workers.[6]

Editorials in the *C.I.O. News*, probably written by Len De Caux, painted a glowing picture. The committee had proved itself "a vigilant defender of American liberties. . . . Without fear or favor, it has held up to public scrutiny all who participate in the sordid business of terrorizing and preying upon the poor." In August 1938 De Caux, whose columns consistently reflected Communist Party policy, wrote that the committee "has put the puppets on the stand one after another and . . . revealed the mechanics of the money-strings that make them jump." The committee, he declared, served as a model of "even-handed justice and democratic procedure"; its reports "are as fair and accurate as is humanly possible."[7]

The American Civil Liberties Union, while occasionally critical of the committee's restricted focus, zealously supported its investigations. In its

[6] Pressman to Elbert D. Thomas, March 24, 1939, LFC, Box 3; Congress of Industrial Organizations, *Proceedings of the First Constitutional Convention*, pp. 72, 186.

[7] *C.I.O. News*, April 23, 1938, August 6, 1938, February 6, 1939. By contrast, the American Federation of Labor, following its declaration of support in 1936, remained extremely cool to the committee; not until 1939 did an A. F. of L. convention again take substantial note of it. The federation was the only organization which the author found to support both the Dies and the La Follette investigations (American Federation of Labor, *Report of Proceedings of the Fifty-Ninth Annual Convention*, pp. 132, 410).

review of civil liberties developments during 1936 the ACLU singled out
Senate Resolution 266 as "the most significant of all measures affecting
civil liberties." A year later it hailed the committee's investigation as "the
most striking single development in civil liberties during the year." Committee exposures, the ACLU noted, had contributed to a sharp reduction
in anti-union violence; conditions in communities investigated by the
committee "have materially improved," it concluded. Roger Baldwin, in
retrospect, praised the La Follette Committee for "a job magnificently
done. . . ." [8]

The liberal and labor press continually bestowed encomiums upon the
committee. At the very least it won plaudits for its procedural fairness.
The committee, declared the *New Republic*, "has been a model of what
a Congressional investigation should be." The San Francisco *Chronicle*
praised it for providing "an exemplary illustration of what a congressional
investigating body can be when it tries." The New York *Post* commended
the committee for its "painstaking and brilliant probe." And the Philadelphia *Record* hailed its historic work and suggested that it be made into
a standing committee, "ready to jump into any situation where constitutional guarantees are denied and fight the situation with the great
weapon of publicity." [9]

The substance of the committee's findings earned equal praise. Because
of committee investigations, declared Benjamin Marsh's People's Lobby
Bulletin, "spokesmen for the oppressed and disinherited can be assured a
nationwide sounding board." The Minnesota *Leader*, lauding the committee as "A Defender of Democracy," declared that next to the National
Labor Relations Board no other New Deal agency had made such a vital
contribution to the cause of social justice. Henry Zon thought that the
committee "has done as valuable a piece of work as any committee in the
history of the Senate." A correspondent for the *Christian Century* doubted
"whether any other chapter in the history of the American labor struggle
can match the cool, calculating treachery, the callous brutality and the

[8] American Civil Liberties Union, *How Goes the Bill of Rights? The Story of
the Fight for Civil Liberty, 1935–1936*, p. 15; American Civil Liberties Union, *Let
Freedom Ring! The Story of Civil Liberty, 1936–1937*, pp. 3, 19; American Civil
Liberties Union, *Eternal Vigilance! The Story of Civil Liberty, 1937–1938*, p. 25;
Roger Baldwin, COHC, p. 202.

[9] "Shape of Government," *New Republic*, CII (May 20, 1940), 702; San Francisco
Chronicle, February 3, 1940; New York *Post*, July 7, 1937; Philadelphia *Record*,
August 4, 1937, clipping in Elbert Thomas Papers, Scrapbooks, "1937–8 Labor,"
Vol. 6.

deliberate sabotage of the democratic process which the La Follette investigating committee has exposed. . . ." Further to the left, one writer praised the committee for demonstrating the attempts of "Fascist-minded industrialists" to destroy unionism. According to Duane Wilson, the committee "has etched in acid lines the inhuman philosophy as well as the methods employed by this cancerous growth [labor espionage] which has fattened on the wealth of industry and thrived on the blood of workers." [10]

The La Follette Committee hearings and reports elicited a torrent of congratulatory messages from leftist individuals and organizations, whose worst forebodings the committee had confirmed. A "simple citizen" praised Senator La Follette for his efforts and commented, "Finally the liberty that the gentlemen of the Liberty League espouse is being held up for public gaze." A history professor told La Follette, "You have done a work of transcendent value to the cause of social justice. . . ." Joseph P. Lash, executive secretary of the American Student Union, wrote to Senator Wagner, "We believe that the central task of our generation is extending the frontiers of democracy in the economic realm. The La Follette Committee has been invaluable. . . ." Paul Kellogg, editor of *Survey Graphic*, regarded the committee's work "as a salty, significant and tremendously useful shaft of light thrown into deep-seated industrial abuses out of joint with American life." "Many of us," declared Mary Hillyer of the League for Industrial Democracy, "feel that this is the most important investigation that has been made in Washington." [11]

Very early in its life the committee became a source of inspiration to proletarian novelists, writers of nonfiction, film producers, and playwrights. Even before its most dramatic hearings, its preliminary findings provided raw material for left-wing artists. In October 1936 the executive secretary of the Chicago Repertory Group informed La Follette of the production of Albert Maltz's *Black Pit*, a play depicting coal miners' efforts to unionize in the face of espionage, company unions, and terror-

[10] People's Lobby *Bulletin*, VII (September 1937), 4, in Benjamin C. Marsh Papers; *Progressive*, December 17, 1938; Henry Zon, "La Follette's Work Should Continue," *Brewery Worker*, LIV (January 7, 1939), 6; *Christian Century*, March 16, 1938, p. 330; Ruben Levin, "Big Business Finances War on Labor," *Railroad Telegrapher*, LVII (January 1940), 3; *Labor*, October 6, 1936.

[11] Isadore Rader to La Follette [September 1936], LFC, Box 130; Wood Gray to La Follette, February 27, 1937, LFC, Box 131; Lash to Wagner, January 12, 1939, LFC, Box 3; Kellogg to Elbert Thomas, January 12, 1939, LFC, Box 3; Hillyer to La Follette, March 4, 1937, LFC, Box 131. See also National Council for Civil Liberty to Roger Baldwin, February 6, 1939, ACLU, Vol. 2081; Arthur C. Eyre to La Follette, December 6, 1940, LFC, Box 3.

ism. "We feel that a theatre like ours . . . can really help in publicizing and dramatizing the work that you are doing," the secretary wrote.[12] In 1938 Frontier Films, an organization dedicated to making "progressive films for America," prepared a feature film dramatizing "the American heritage of freedom" and based largely on committee findings. According to its synopsis, the film "indicates how the anger and resentment of American opinion created the . . . Committee, how the agencies of espionage and civil violence lied and destroyed evidence. . . ." First shown at the Third American Writers' Congress in 1939, the film "exposed dramatically" the antilabor network of espionage, strikebreaking, munitions, and vigilantism.[13]

The first phase of the committee's investigation inspired two works of nonfiction. In 1937 Clinch Calkins' *Spy Overhead* and Leo Huberman's *The Labor Spy Racket* popularized the committee's espionage findings. For Calkins, the industrial worker had played "a tragic and curious part" in American history; once "a lone figure having some strength to strike a bargain with men who needed and respected him," he had been "boiled down . . . to his fullest economic helplessness." Committee hearings convinced Calkins that class war existed in the United States. "Like actors the witnesses come, speak their pieces, and go," she wrote. "For the moment of his appearance each witness becomes the apotheosis of his part, the embodied antagonist in a war of impersonal forces." [14]

Leo Huberman used the committee's espionage hearings to register a vigorous plea for labor organization. He, too, perceived one theme in the La Follette investigation: class war. "The line-up in this war," he wrote, "is employers vs. workers, Capital vs. Labor." The committee, Huberman declared, had presented a shocking story which should "shame" American industrialists and "arouse our workers." All fair-minded citizens must "rise up in their wrath and demand that immediate steps be taken to prevent what has happened here from ever happening again." Labor's voice, Huberman insisted, "must be a collective voice." In the United States, he concluded, "there is no room for tyrants. To get rid of the tyranny in

---

[12] Alice Evans to La Follette, October 1, 1936, LFC, Box 85.

[13] Paul Strand to Elbert Thomas, April 4, 1938, Thomas Papers, Box 19; Paul Strand to Dr. Clarence A. Dykstra, January 10, 1939, Presidents' File, Box 396, University of Wisconsin; *New York Times*, June 4, 1939. According to the *Progressive* (September 3, 1938), Pare Lorentz was also preparing a film from committee material.

[14] *Spy Overhead*, pp. 4, 5, 9, 19.

American industry is the job of the workers of America. There is only one way to do it—ORGANIZE." [15]

The first of two novels based in part upon the work of the La Follette Committee was published in 1939. Benjamin Appel's *The Power-House*, wrote one reviewer, could have been, and probably was, written directly from the transcript of the committee hearings.[16] *The Power-House* chronicled the activities of Bill Trent, an enterprising young racketeer who discovered lucrative opportunities in industrial espionage and strikebreaking. Appel depicted virtually every anti-union tactic exposed by the La Follette Committee. A "hooked" worker needed money to pay his wife's hospital bills; his company hired strikebreakers; the local judge issued an injunction to halt mass picketing; the Red scare was used to justify the formation of a citizens' committee. "That was the formula," Appel wrote: "To handle men as things." He indicted the giant industrial magnates who, collectively, comprised the "Power-House," controlling corporation executives, judges, mayors, and police. "Only the damn workers," Appel lamented, "had the gall to put up a fight," but they rarely possessed the strength to win.[17]

Meyer Levin's *Citizens*, perhaps the most successful literary representation of the La Follette Committee's activities, appeared in 1940. Levin, a spectator at the Memorial Day clash between Republic strikers and Chicago police, wrote his novel, he explained, not "as an exposure but as an interpretation." "The inner human truths of motive and compulsion," Levin declared, "can be found by examining experiences of reality. By using only actual, attested events as materials, the writer reduces the possibility of arriving at false conclusions." [18]

Levin sought an explanation for the events of that Memorial Day afternoon:

"The picture stood again in his mind; two lines like two rows of . . . toy soldiers; move one line up into position, stand the other against it, then the first line goes bang bang bang and the second line is all knocked down. . . . That was the simple picture. Out of that he had to find a meaning." [19]

At times the dialogue of Levin's characters was almost a verbatim repro-

[15] *The Labor Spy Racket*, pp. 1, 139, 160, 163.
[16] Otis Ferguson, "It Reads Like Fiction," *New Republic*, XCIX (May 24, 1939), 78.
[17] *The Power-House*, pp. 393–454.
[18] Levin, "A Note On Method," *Citizens*, pp. 649–650.
[19] *Ibid.*, p. 73.

duction of testimony taken by the La Follette Committee. "In some instances," Levin explained, "such recorded statements were so pure that
I felt the novelist's art, at least this novelist's art, could arrive at nothing
more revealing. . . ." [20] Levin perceived not class war but two governments in opposition, one represented by Tom Girdler, the other represented by the committee.[21] He failed, however, to discover the meaning
he hoped to find. Although he tried to advance beyond the committee's
literalness, his efforts, like those of Calkins, Huberman, and Appel, were
overshadowed by the committee's factual record.

The composite image of the committee molded by its friends resembled
a knight errant slaying the dragon of industrial iniquity. Roused by an
alarmed citizenry, it had ventured forth to defend liberty, succor the industrial worker, ensure social justice, and expose the fascistic conspiracies
of malevolent employers. The many critics of the La Follette Committee
believed otherwise. Instead of exposing a conspiracy, the committee was,
they thought, the agent of one. Organized clandestinely, they alleged, it
had been a nuisance in its best moments, and more often than not a vin-
dictive partisan of the C.I.O. and the Communist Party.

Two of the mildest yet most perceptive criticisms came from Southern
newspapers. The Chattanooga *News*, observing that the committee enjoyed a "field day at the expense of some of the big corporations," reminded it of the many civil liberties infringements that it had ignored,
particularly intimidation by the Ku Klux Klan and violence directed
toward tenant farmers and sharecroppers. The committee, declared the
Lynchburg (Va.) *News*, "is not seeking what it may find, but seeking
something specific." An editorial in that newspaper urged that the suppression of civil liberties, "not the suppression of civil liberties by one
class of men, or by one class of organization, should be the subject of
inquiry. When the real subject of inquiry is one group and the real purpose is to discredit that group, the suppression of civil liberties is a subject
likely to be neglected." [22]

The committee was chastised most frequently for its excessive partisan-

---

[20] *Ibid.*, p. 645.

[21] Levin, Harold Strauss wrote in the *New York Times Book Review* (March 31,
1940, p. 2), "has struck the shackles of photographic realism from the strike novel."
In retrospect, it seems that Levin was imprisoned by those very shackles.

[22] Chattanooga (Tenn.) *News*, March 3, 1937; Lynchburg (Va.), *News*, February 20, 1937. For charges that the La Follette Comittee was a nuisance to businessmen, see Macon (Ga.) *Telegraph*, April 27, 1938, clipping in ACLU, Vol. 1091;
"Business and Senate Subpoenas," *Business Week*, July 23, 1938, pp. 20–21.

ship. As early as November 1936 businessmen suggested that the La Follette investigation had served its purpose and should be terminated. Edward S. Cowdrick, secretary of the Special Conference Committee, a group comprising executives of a dozen large corporations, asked Assistant Secretary of Commerce Ernest G. Draper if the administration would initiate steps toward a rapprochement with business. Business leaders, Cowdrick wrote, "consider that they have been rebuffed and scolded every time they have tried to cooperate with the government on a self-respecting basis." President Roosevelt, Cowdrick suggested, might consider amending one or two New Deal laws in accord with business wishes. "It might be well also," Cowdrick stated, "to call off the La Follette 'labor spy' investigation. That has already achieved most of its political objectives and its continuance can have little effect except to keep up irritation and unrest."[23]

Attacks on the committee mounted once it plunged into the labor-management turmoil of 1936–1937. The committee, charged the *New York Times*, never thought to expose the tactics of labor organizers and probably would not consider "acts of tyranny and even brutality" by union officials. The committee's espionage report, the *Times* conceded, performed "an essential service." But its very sweep aroused suspicion about its accuracy. "What would be thought," the *Times* asked, "of a referee who penalized only the fouls committed by one of the contestants and deliberately shut his eyes to those committed by the other? Such umpiring is not calculated to bring industrial peace."[24]

The La Follette Committee's interest in civil liberties, warned the New York *Herald Tribune*, was merely "a cloak for a smear-employer campaign. . . ." The *Wall Street Journal* accused the committee of telling only "Half of a Drab Story." Its hearings had revealed intolerable practices, to be sure, but there was virtually no difference between the tactics of either side "in what has been in all essentials an open war." Committee reports, charged one newspaper, represented "another of those favorite

[23] Cowdrick to Draper, November 5, 1936, *Hearings*, Pt. 45, pp. 16897–98.
[24] *New York Times*, January 29, December 23, 1937. On February 4, Senator Thomas replied to the January 29 editorial. Thomas rejected the *Times*'s implication that to be on the employees' side was good politics: "In my particular case I think that politically my position on this Civil Liberties Committee is a very, very bad one for me. . . . Not a single word concerning any of our hearings has appeared in the newspapers of my home town, Salt Lake City" (Thomas to Editor, *New York Times*, February 4, 1937, Thomas Papers, "Labor," Box 19). As late as August 31, 1939, Thomas expressed gratitude to one of his constituents for discovering "that I am a member of the Committee" (Thomas to Robert G. Price, August 31, 1939, Thomas Papers, Box 17).

'leftist' attempts to assume a monopoly on virtue." The committee had restricted the meaning of liberty to "the liberty of labor unions to do as they please," declared a Wilmington (Del.) newspaper. Representative Clare Hoffman (R-Mich.) demanded that the committee cease its "witch hunting and persecution." [25]

Accusations of partiality shaded easily into imputations that the committee bowed slavishly to C.I.O. commands. The committee "was a CIO brain child," according to the New London (Conn.) *Day*. An editorial in the Chicago *Tribune*, entitled "La Follette's GPU," portrayed the committee as "an official partisan of John Lewis and the C.I.O. . . . [It] defends no constitutional rights. It subverts them." La Follette's "so-called inquiry," wrote a Tribune correspondent, "was conceived by John L. Lewis . . . and used to intimidate, harass, and smear employers opposed by the C.I.O." Joseph P. Kamp, whose Constitutional Educational League was the subject of one hearing, called the committee a "veritable adjunct" of the C.I.O. and "the culmination of a conspiracy entered into between John L. Lewis, representatives of Communist, and other red organizations, and . . . Senator La Follette." The committee and the NLRB, said Clare Hoffman, "have made a hell on earth for one industry after another. . . . [They] have been the most effective recruiting agent of the C.I.O." [26]

In the spring of 1938, when La Follette's request for additional funds was pending before the Audit and Control Committee, Congressman John C. Nichols (D-Okla.) received a three-page memorandum, presented to that committee, enumerating the La Follette Committee's shortcomings. "As far as appears to the disinterested out-sider," wrote his correspondent, "the so-called La Follette Committee has been nothing but a trouble breeding advertising plan serving as an adjunct to the CIO and the Labor Board and adding to the general chaos and demoralization." The memorandum accused the committee of having become "personalized." By "a cunning use of propaganda," it had indicted all of American industry. Its Harlan inquiry, directed by the United Mine Workers, "was a witch-

25 New York *Herald Tribune*, August 26, 1939; *Wall Street Journal*, September 25, 1936; Jersey City (N.J.) *Jersey Journal*, August 17, 1939; Wilmington (Del.) *Evening Journal* [1939], clippings in ACLU, Vol. 2092; *Congressional Record*, 76th Cong., 1st Sess., 1939, Vol. 84, p. 3867.

26 New London (Conn.) *Day*, February 11, 1937, clipping in ACLU, Vol. 994; Chicago *Tribune*, April 26, October 17, 1938; *Progressive*, October 29, 1938; Joseph P. Kamp, *The Hell of Herrin Rages Again*, p. 32; *Congressional Record*, 75th Cong., 3d Sess., 1938, Vol. 83, p. 1230; Milwaukee *Journal*, August 1, 1937, clipping in Legislative Reference Library, Madison.

hunt, not an investigation." It had suppressed controversial evidence and permitted a number of "flat untruths" to mar its record. It threatened or conducted a smear campaign "whenever the unions of John L. Lewis have been restrained or have been unsuccessful." The committee, the C.I.O., and the NLRB "have cooperated or conspired to produce the savage labor strife of the past two years. . . ." The committee "is as much an organizing weapon of the CIO as the regularly salaried field organizers." Termination of its investigations "would be taken as a hopeful sign by business and would allay much fear of the results of the alliance of government with the CIO and the radical labor element."[27]

Once the La Follette Committee and the C.I.O. were coupled, the committee inevitably faced the accusation that it, like the C.I.O., functioned as an agent of the Communist conspiracy. In January 1938 Mrs. Elizabeth Dilling, author of numerous publications branding the New Deal as communistic, published a pamphlet entitled "Dare We Oppose Red Treason?" Ostensibly quoting from Communist literature, Mrs. Dilling "proved" the La Follette Committee's Communist antecedents and motivation. Guests at the Cosmos Club dinner in 1936 were "well known radicals," Mrs. Dilling stated. She accused Dorothy Detzer of the Women's International League for Peace and Freedom and Gardner Jackson—both of whom had attended the dinner—of belonging to Communist organizations; she declared that John L. Lewis, also present, was "the hero of the Communist press." "Beware!" Mrs. Dilling warned. "The La Follette Committee may get you if you don't watch out! Is this a joke? Indeed, it is not." She demanded that no further funds be allocated for the committee's "infamous, Red-supported activities. . . ."[28]

Three months later, in April, the New York *Herald Tribune* embellished Mrs. Dilling's story. It reported that the La Follette Committee's Senate critics had received copies of an article in *Fight,* the publication of the American League Against War and Fascism, enumerating the "Communists" who had allegedly been present at the Cosmos Club dinner: John L. Lewis, Gardner Jackson, Roger Baldwin, Dorothy Detzer, Earl Browder, Max Bedacht (secretary of the International Workers Order), Clarence Hathaway (editor of the *Daily Worker*), James W. Ford (the Communist Party's vice-presidential candidate in 1936), Mother Bloor

[27] John Brookes to Nichols, May 2, 1938, Nichols Papers, Division of Manuscripts, the University of Oklahoma, Norman. Professor William E. Leuchtenburg called this item to my attention.

[28] Elizabeth Dilling, *Dare We Oppose Red Treason?* (1937), pp. 1, 13–14; Union City (N.J.) *News,* January 1938, clipping in ACLU, Vol. 2001.

(a veteran left-wing agitator), Gil Greenberg (president of the Young Communist League), and Israel Amter (New York organizer for the Communist Party).[29]

After the *Herald Tribune* published this account, the Reverend William B. Spofford, secretary of the Church League for Industrial Democracy and a bona fide guest at the dinner, checked with the editor of *Fight*, who affirmed that none of those named by the *Herald Tribune* had in fact been named in the article. Two days after its original story appeared, the *Herald Tribune* printed a retraction, stating that the erroneous list of names had apparently been circulated by the Silver Shirts, a fascistic organization opposed to the continuation of the La Follette investigation.[30]

The charge of Communist affiliation did not disappear as readily as did the *Herald Tribune*'s story. The Los Angeles *Examiner* had already compared the La Follette Committee's conception of civil liberties to "that of the HITLER GESTAPO and the STALIN OGPU." "While the Lewis communists attacked the properties," announced the Chicago *Tribune*, "the La Follette committee was to attack the property owners." The committee, the *Tribune* continued, "was to picture the revolutionaries as abused persons, to arouse class hatreds, to impose upon persons easily deceived, and to give all this disorder and lawlessness the appearance of a noble struggle for human rights, whereas it was a vicious assault upon democratic principles of law, order, justice, and equity." The Communists, the C.I.O., the La Follette Committee, the National Labor Relations Board, and the National Committee of the Democratic Party, charged Tom Girdler, had conspired to conduct a "cold-blooded plot" against business.[31]

Fringe hate groups persistently tried to exploit the La Follette Committee's alleged Communist ties. The national organizer of the National Gentile League asked La Follette whether the committee he chaired bore any relation to the Civil Liberties Committee "that is a faction of the Communist movement." The National Gentile League tried to discourage "any and all isms in this country," the national organizer explained, "excepting the one brand of Americanism." Field Marshall William Zachary of the Silver Shirts charged that the committee had attempted to subpoena

[29] New York *Herald Tribune*, April 24, 1938.

[30] William B. Spofford, "Talking It Over," *Witness*, VII (May 5, 1938), 4; New York *Herald Tribune*, April 26, 28, 1938; "Two to Make a Rumor," *New Republic*, XCIV (May 4, 1938), 380.

[31] Los Angeles *Examiner*, September 25, 1936; Chicago *Tribune*, November 28, 1938; Girdler, *Boot Straps*, p. 368.

his organization's records "simply to turn [them] over to the Jews." And the *Weekly Liberation*, the organ of the Silver Legion, told "How La Follette Has Squandered Senate Money For A Sub-Committee Wildly Approved By The Jewish Reds." The committee, it declared, represented a bloc of "Communist politicians *or* Gentile Fronts for Jews" and had assisted "the foreign Moscovite Jewish Clique to bring atheistic Communism upon this country via the route of disrupted Trade Unionism!" [32]

In the wake of the La Follette Committee's investigation of the activities of an Ohio Silver Shirt official during the Little Steel strike, the Silver Legion of Utah excoriated Senator Thomas. "Suddenly, from my own state," Thomas told a constituent, "come protests that the Committee is 'Communistic,' misled and an embarrassment to the people of Utah, and that I am unaware of the 'genesis' of the Committee, which by implication is supposed to be somehow connected with subversive organizations." [33]

One Utah woman considered Thomas' activities for the La Follette Committee "wholly un-American." Another constituent, warning of "a Secret Jewish World Government," predicted, "You'll find young La Follette is rated by those well informed to be a friend of Communists. . . ." A member of the Silver Legion, the motto of which was "For Christ and Constitution," told Thomas, "[I] find at the rate the home folks are awaking to the Jewish question and their connection to Communism that you are now being branded as a red. . . ." "Did we send Senator Thomas to Washington to be a stooge for Stalin," asked this patriot. "Of course not. I think it is time that every real red-blooded American residing in Utah write Senator Thomas and tell him we do not approve and will not tolerate his Red Activities." [34]

[32] Donald Shea to La Follette, March 19, 1937, LFC, Box 83; U.S. House of Representatives, Special Committee on Un-American Activities, *Hearings, Investigation of Un-American Propaganda Activities in the United States*, 75th Cong., 3d Sess., 1938, 1, 45; *Weekly Liberation*, III (February 7, 1938) 6, clipping in Elbert Thomas Papers, "Civil Liberties Committee."

[33] Thomas to W. R. Fairborn, February 15, 1938, Thomas Papers, Box 19.

[34] Bess Epperson to Thomas, February 4, 1938; E. Hollings to Thomas, January 20, 1938; C. F. Allen to Thomas, January 21, 1938; Deseret (Utah) *News*, n.d., Thomas Papers, "Civil Liberties Committee." In 1950 Senator-elect Wallace F. Bennett, who had just defeated Thomas' bid for a fourth term, replied to a question about the Communist issue in the campaign: "Senator Thomas's writings and his appearances on programs sponsored by Communist-front organizations, and the part of the Communists in the La Follette Committee investigations—these were all thoroughly discussed. . . . I think it helped the Republicans more than it hurt them . . ." (" 'Why I Won'—'Why I Lost,' " *U.S. News & World Report*, XXIX [November 17, 1950], 30).

Before 1938 the virulence of right-wing invective had not decreased the La Follette Committee's stature. For two years the committee had basked in the approval of liberals, radicals, and civil libertarians. On August 11, 1938, the committee had concluded its second and apparently final series of hearings without serious challenge to its authority. But on August 12 a Special Committee on Un-American Activities, chaired by Representative Martin Dies of Texas, held its first public hearing.

The accidental juxtaposition of the two committees—one symbolizing the aspirations of those who looked to the New Deal for social and economic justice, the other soon to symbolize the antithesis of all that the New Deal represented—had a particularly ironic quality that went unappreciated at the time. Suddenly, the La Follette Committee found itself not merely overshadowed but actually threatened. The Dies Committee attracted those—and in 1938 there were many—who had failed to find a home in the New Deal and wanted to believe the worst about it. It quickly became the investigative counterweight to the La Follette Committee. From this intramural congressional struggle emerged a microcosmic facsimile of the larger battle between the New Deal and its political enemies.

The Dies Committee, more than any other single institution, abetted the charge that the La Follette Committee's origins, composition, and direction evinced affinity for communism. During its second day of hearings, John P. Frey, president of the Metal Trades Department of the American Federation of Labor, presented a sweeping indictment of the C.I.O., tying it and the La Follette Committee to a Communist conspiracy. According to Frey, "There have been numerous reports of close contacts between investigators for the [La Follette] committee and members of the Communist Party. . . ." [35] Frey charged that Vincent Favorito, a star committee witness during hearings on the Little Steel strike, was a member of the Communist Party. "In our estimation," noted Frey, who had accumulated files filled with allegations of conspiratorial activities, "this is one of the most rotten angles of the La Follette Committee that has ever been brought to the public's attention." [36] One correspondent complained that Frey's statements were too moderate. "I do not think," he wrote, that La Follette "would withhold from Communists any data that might come into the Committee but in case he should be . . . inclined to do so, there

[35] Investigation of Un-American Propaganda Activities, I, 106.
[36] Memo, August 3, 1938, John P. Frey Papers, "Communism: No. 21," Box 5; New York Times, August 14, 1938; August Raymond Ogden, The Dies Committee, p. 54.

are people in the employ of the Committee in his office to pass that information along." Frey later reminisced: "In the beginning the [La Follette] Committee was doing a fairly good job, but after about one third of its existence, it was a Communist affair." [37]

Frey's testimony before the Dies Committee opened the floodgates to those who nurtured grievances against the La Follette Committee. William T. Gernaey testified that as an undercover agent for a Detroit company he had joined the Young Communist League and the Communist Party. In January 1937 the party had expelled him as a labor spy; after his expulsion trial, he claimed, two committee investigators who had cooperated with the party, Harold A. Cranefield and Benjamin Allen, came to party offices and served him with a subpoena. Cranefield, according to Gernaey, turned to the other Communists present and stated, "Comrades, this man's life is not worth two cents. He is of no more use to the capitalist class, and he will be destroyed." [38]

John M. Barringer, city manager of Flint in 1937, insisted that the sit-down strike, which he claimed Communists had instigated, would not "have developed so seriously if it had not been for the attitude of the members of the La Follette Committee" and Governor Frank Murphy's "treasonable action." According to Barringer, Cranefield and Allen had demanded the names of his special deputies; Barringer, expecting that the UAW would be the beneficiary of this information, had refused to divulge it. Furthermore, the committee had publicized the union side of the Flint dispute, but it had not called to Washington "any of the men on our side . . . the side of law and order." [39]

Robert B. Barker, a Dies Committee investigator, incorporated into the record the substance of a bill in equity filed by the Silver Shirt Legion of America, and long since dismissed by two federal courts, asking for an injunction against the La Follette Committee. The bill reiterated the Dilling–*Herald Tribune* misstatements about the Cosmos Club dinner,

[37] James E. Cassidy to Frey, August 13, 1938, Frey Papers, "Dies Committee Hearings," Box 8; Frey, COHC, p. 580. Frey nurtured a grievance against the New Deal, which he later expressed; speaking of the Wage-Hour bill, he said, "I had a little knowledge of how we went about drafting a bill and securing the advice that we felt we needed. . . . All of a sudden this is changed, and a group, some of whom are quite young men not long out of . . . Columbia and Harvard, came to [Washington]. They were the ones who were drafting this legislation affecting labor, that we knew nothing about" (COHC, p. 572).

[38] *Investigation of Un-American Propaganda Activities*, II, 1482–84. Cranefield wired a vigorous denial to Dies (*ibid.*, p. 1537).

[39] *Ibid.*, II, 1689–91.

charged the committee with retaining investigators, "some of whom could not speak the English language," and accused committee secretary Robert Wohlforth of being a Communist.[40]

Before long, Dies himself threw down the gage to the La Follette Committee. In June 1938 he had requested Attorney General Cummings to assign investigators and lawyers from the Justice Department to his staff. Cummings refused, but Wohlforth offered Dies the services of two La Follette Committee investigators. Before their arrival, according to Dies, he received "a telephone tip that they were Communist Party members." Questioned in executive session, they admitted, Dies claimed, "enough to convince us that they were either Communists or Communist sympathizers. Their admissions made it evident that someone high in the Administration wanted to plant them for the purpose of sabotaging our investigation." [41]

In November rumors circulated in the press that the Dies Committee would consider a proposal to determine if "well-known Communists" had conspired to create the La Follette Committee. The proposal, offered by Dies Committee member Harold G. Mosier (D-Ohio), was considered briefly and dropped; Dies explained that he doubted whether his committee had jurisdiction to investigate another congressional body.[42] Several months later, during his defense of further appropriations for the Un-American Activities Committee, Dies accused the La Follette Committee of placing on the witness stand "certain well-known Communists to attack American businessmen." Recounting his committee's achievements, Dies, according to an article in the St. Louis *Post-Dispatch*, claimed to have offset the La Follette Committee's revelations and caused the Senate to cut its appropriation.[43]

Within the atmosphere of the 1930's, the charges made by the Dies Committee seemed ridiculous and malevolent. After World War II, how-

[40] *Ibid.*, VI, 4251, 4254. Jacob Spolansky, a former labor spy for the Fisher Body division of General Motors, also testified before the Dies Committee, charging that the La Follette Committee was tainted with communism (memo of conference at Fisher Body Division Executive Offices, 11/10/36, LFC, Box 124; *Investigation of Un-American Propaganda Activities*, II, 1444-60).

[41] Martin Dies, *Martin Dies' Story*, p. 61; *New York Times*, November 1, 1938. According to Wohlforth, the two staff members were offered as a courtesy gesture, well in advance of Dies' first hearing (Wohlforth, COHC, pp. 29-30).

[42] *New York Times*, November 16, 17, 1938. Mosier made his proposal after reading the Silver Shirt distortion of the *Fight* article on the Cosmos Club dinner.

[43] *Congressional Record*, 76th Cong., 1st Sess., 1939, Vol. 84, p. 1126; *Progressive*, February 11, 1939; Ogden, *The Dies Committee*, p. 152.

ever, it became apparent that "red herring" countercharges obscured the involvement of La Follette Committee staff members with the Communist Party. Evidence indicated that some of the La Follette Committee's most active and most crucially placed staff members had been warmly sympathetic to the objectives of the Communist Party. Whittaker Chambers, testifying before the House Un-American Activities Committee in 1948, indicated that counsel John Abt and investigator Charles Kramer had been members of a Communist cell during their tenure in the Department of Agriculture. Its purpose, Chambers said, "was the Communist infiltration of the American Government." Abt, according to Chambers, succeeded Nathan Witt as cell leader. In the summer of 1950 Lee Pressman, who had been a member of the cell, confirmed Abt's and Kramer's presence in the AAA group; Nathaniel Weyl, also a member, concurred. "They were there," he stated, referring to the entire group, "because they believed in revolution." [44]

Gardner Jackson, the La Follette Committee's devoted ally, admitted in retrospect, "I was certainly guilty . . . of being an instrument of the Communists in . . . the staffing of [the La Follette] committee." Jackson, who had complied with Lee Pressman's suggestion to propose Abt as counsel, believed that Abt "brought into that staff quite a good many Communists." La Follette subsequently told Jackson that he, La Follette, had "been hoodwinked at the time the . . . staff was set up, . . . having taken on fellows [whom] he now, looking back, realized were active Communists." "I just haven't any doubt of the Communist activity there," Jackson concluded. [45]

During 1952–1953 four former members of the La Follette Committee staff—John Abt, Charles Kramer, Allen Rosenberg, and Charles Flato—refused to answer questions posed by congressional committees about their alleged Communist affiliations. They claimed, in part, that their answers might tend to incriminate them. Kramer, in particular, was harassed for having "worked with" persons identified by the Chicago

---

[44] U.S. House of Representatives, Committee on Un-American Activities, *Hearings Regarding Communist Espionage in the United States Government*, 80th Cong., 2d Sess., 1948, pp. 565–566; Whittaker Chambers, *Witness*, pp. 332, 334, 342; U.S. House of Representatives, Committee on Un-American Activities, *Hearings Regarding Communism in the United States Government*, 81st Cong., 2d Sess., 1950, IV, 2850, 2853, 2855, 2886; "I Was in a Communist Unit with Hiss," *U.S. News & World Report*, XXXIV (January 9, 1953), 23–24.

[45] Gardner Jackson, COHC, pp. 741–743; interview with Gardner Jackson, December 3, 1963, copy in COHC, p. 13.

police department as Communist participants in the Memorial Day incident. The counsel to the Senate Judiciary Committee made the erroneous charge that "Communists were the source for the films and for [the] files" assembled by the La Follette Committee during its investigation of the Memorial Day violence.[46]

In 1947 La Follette himself had dredged up the Communist issue. In an article in *Collier's*, he wrote: ". . . when I was chairman of the Senate Civil Liberties Committee, I was forced to take measures in an effort to stamp out [Communist] influences within my own committee staff." But John Abt, in a later comment upon La Follette's article, stated: "I don't know to what he referred, I really don't. Certainly, during the period of my tenure as counsel, there was no such problem. I just don't know what he was talking about."[47]

The "purge" to which La Follette referred occurred in the spring of 1937, and it did not involve any committee staff member later questioned about his alleged Communist affiliations. La Follette directed Robert Wohlforth to examine the record of every staff member on loan from another government agency. "We went down the list," Wohlforth recalled, "and turned up a couple of Trotskyites and some people who had rather questionable records, and then we asked for replacements." At least one Trotskyite was dropped, together with several investigators whose blatant affinity for the *New Masses* or the *Daily Worker* might have jeopardized the committee's reputation.[48] When La Follette learned that one investigator, assigned to the committee by the NLRB, had released information and documents to a representative of the *People's Press*, the senator summarily discharged him. "Such conduct on the part of a staff member," La Follette wrote in a curt letter of dismissal, "cannot and will not be tolerated by the Committee."[49]

[46] *Hearings Regarding Communism in the U. S. Government*, pp. 2952–54 and *passim; Hearings Regarding Communist Espionage*, pp. 819–833; U.S. Senate, Committee on the Judiciary, *Hearings on Interlocking Subversion in Government Departments*, 83rd Cong., 1st Sess., 1953, pp. 345–353, 378–379; U.S. House of Representatives, Committee on Un-American Activities, *Hearings on Methods of Communist Infiltration in the United States Government*, 82d Cong., 2d Sess., 1952, pp. 3418, 3427, 3430; *Interlocking Subversion*, pp. 488–490.

[47] Robert M. La Follette, Jr., "Turn the Light on Communism," *Collier's*, CXIX (February 8, 1947), 22; Abt, COHC, p. 11.

[48] Wohlforth, COHC, pp. 20, 22, 23, 24.

[49] La Follette to ———, March 10, 1937, LFC, Box 5. John P. Frey's charge that the committee, "after about one third of its existence, . . . was a communist affair," was patently false. Frey could more accurately have argued the reverse, for by the summer of 1937 the purge had occurred and Abt, Kramer, and Rosenberg were no longer with the committee.

Unchallenged testimony before congressional committees, La Follette's and Jackson's statements, and evidence of the purge point unerringly toward the conclusion that Communists sought and secured places on the La Follette Committee staff. If Chambers, La Follette, Pressman, and Jackson were correct—and there is no convincing evidence to the contrary—the committee, particularly during its most productive first phase, included a number of party members and sympathizers. Its counsel and its chief investigator in Detroit during the sit-down strike, to cite only the most prominent, apparently had been members of a Communist cell. The very nature of the investigation, of course, encouraged Communists to join the staff. Haphazard hiring procedures reinforced this tendency. Prospective investigators were never questioned about their political beliefs. As Robert Wohlforth stated: "If the Labor Board or the Bureau of Labor Statistics sent me somebody, I wasn't going to put him in a corner under a bright light and beat him with a rubber hose." [50]

Documenting the presence of Communists on the committee staff is less difficult than measuring the influence they exerted on the committee's choice of topics and on its findings. With few exceptions—the most conspicuous being the Barton-Gelders hearing early in 1937—C.I.O. organizing drives determined the committee's focus. Within this framework, however, Communists on the committee staff enjoyed considerable freedom to maneuver. The personal predilections of staff members found numerous opportunities for expression. With a nucleus of at least half a dozen staff members sympathetic to Communist Party doctrine, it is not surprising that incidents were selected, witnesses chosen, and reports drafted that stressed the theme of class warfare and placed responsibility for it squarely on the shoulders of American capitalists. Industrial tyranny was a fact—and the La Follette Committee performed a genuine service in exposing it. Yet the committee, by producing a composite portrait of the American industrialist as an armed practitioner of class violence, probably did more to buttress the Communist Party line than any other New Deal institution.[51]

The altercation between the Dies and the La Follette Committees, which the Communist issue exacerbated, spread to the press and, before long, entangled the administration. These committees, observed the New

[50] Wohlforth, COHC, p. 26.
[51] See Bernard Karsh and Phillips L. Garman, "The Impact of the Political Left," *Labor and the New Deal*, ed. Milton Derber and Edwin Young, pp. 109–111; Max M. Kampelman, *The Communist Party vs. the C.I.O.*; Kempton, *Part of Our Time*, pp. 332–334.

Orleans *Times-Picayune*, "are working at cross purposes. Neither makes full use of its opportunity for constructive service. . . . The country is missing an opportunity to get a full and fair presentation of the issues raised by today's industrial controversies." [52] Richard L. Strout, writing in the *Christian Science Monitor*, described a bitter conflict between the two committees. While the Dies Committee heard the former secretary of the Associated Farmers, a West Coast employers' association, testify to Communist infiltration in the California labor movement, La Follette Committee staff members conducted an investigation of the Associated Farmers. Dies, referring to deportation proceedings then pending against Harry Bridges, leader of the San Francisco longshoremen, publicly criticized La Follette for guiding a Senate attack on Dies's bill to make the membership of aliens in the Communist Party an offense punishable by deportation.[53]

Whereas the respective merits of the two investigations were endlessly debated, the Roosevelt administration never hesitated about bestowing its allegiance. Roosevelt had given at least tacit approval of the La Follette Committee since early 1937. In January of that year, the House Appropriations Committee had inserted in the Deficiency bill a proviso depriving congressional committees of personnel from independent government agencies. Tommy Corcoran hurried to the Department of the Interior to express his displeasure to Harold Ickes; the Secretary, understanding that Corcoran spoke for the President, made a number of telephone calls in an effort to have the proviso stricken. Referring to the La Follette and Wheeler investigations, Ickes noted in his diary, "They have been so restricted by lack of funds that these two investigations would have had to close down long ago if it had not been for the help that we have given them." [54]

Roosevelt praised the La Follette Committee when the occasion permitted. At White House parties he told Robert Wohlforth to "keep going," and during a press conference in March 1938 he proposed that a permanent committee be established to continue the La Follette Committee's work. Roosevelt generally did not emphasize his sympathies, however, until the Dies investigation sparked his appreciation of the La Follette Committee's usefulness as a political instrument. At a cabinet meeting in January 1939, when proposals for restraining the Dies Committee were considered, Ickes suggested that an additional appropriation for La Fol-

[52] New Orleans *Times-Picayune*, August 5, 1939.
[53] Reprinted in the Washington *Post*, November 2, 1938.
[54] Harold L. Ickes, *The Inside Struggle, 1936–1939* (Vol. II of *The Secret Diary of Harold L. Ickes*), pp. 58, 63.

lette would be "our best method" for curbing Dies. "I laid particular stress," he wrote in his diary, "on the necessity of investigating certain economic and fascist conditions in California, important evidence concerning which is already in the hands of La Follette's committee." [55]

When the Dies Committee received a sizable new appropriation, Ickes complained, "Here was another example of a complete falling down of the so-called Democratic leadership of the House." If that investigation could not be "cut off sharp," as Roosevelt wanted, the President's alternative suggestion was, Ickes recorded, "either a combination with La Follette's Senate committee . . . or an enlarged [Un-American Activities] committee on which some friends of the Administration could be placed." [56] While the incompatibility of the two committees made a merger impossible, further investigations by the La Follette Committee might be expected to parry the Dies Committee's anti-administration thrusts. But La Follette's pledge to the Senate, made the previous spring, to conclude his investigation within eight months had to be circumvented without arousing sufficient opposition to thwart the administration's plan.

During the early weeks of 1939 the La Follette Committee verged on disintegration. After the hearings on citizens' committees and employers' associations, committee investigators had flocked to California, where left-wingers had long detected signs of imminent agrarian fascism. Staff members sifted evidence indicating that agricultural workers in the Imperial Valley had been deprived of their civil liberties. But, as committee funds evaporated, their work ground to a halt. "From all appearances," Roger Baldwin learned, the committee "will fold up within [a] few days. . . ." [57]

While La Follette remained aloof from maneuvers to resuscitate the committee—either from a sense of propriety or from sheer weariness—Senator Lewis B. Schwellenbach of Washington assumed the brunt of the responsibility for securing an additional appropriation. Schwellenbach tried to restrain public agitation on the committee's behalf, fearing offense to Senator Byrnes, who, as chairman of the Audit and Control Committee, still controlled the purse strings. Only pressure from the President,

[55] Wohlforth, COHC, p. 55; Roosevelt press conference, March 22, 1938, transcript in FDRL; Ickes, *The Inside Struggle*, pp. 548–549.

[56] *Ibid.*, pp. 573–574.

[57] *Progressive*, February 11, 1939; Jack Spivak to Roger Baldwin, January 13, 1939, and Drex Sprecker to Baldwin, January 21, 1939, ACLU, Vol. 2081. At the end of January, J. Raymond Walsh agreed to serve as chairman of a National Committee to Save the La Follette Committee, which included Bruce Bliven, Robert Lynd, Langdon Post, and Oswald Garrison Villard (National Consumers League to ACLU, January 27, 1939, *ibid.*).

Schwellenbach believed, would save the La Follette investigation.[58] "Strictly speaking," Roosevelt told Schwellenbach, "it is, of course, none of my business to say anything out loud about the continuation of the Senate Civil Liberties Committee. I can, however, tell you personally of my real interest in it and my belief that I think it should be continued." The President suggested that Schwellenbach inform Elbert Thomas and Alben Barkley of his wishes.[59]

In March Schwellenbach, encouraged by Roosevelt, introduced a resolution authorizing an appropriation of $100,000 for the La Follette Committee to investigate interference with labor's rights in California, Washington, and Oregon.[60] In an angry editorial the *Nation*, demanding "Funds for La Follette," branded as "inexcusable" the "apathy of progressives toward the committee's fate." It warned that "reaction could win no greater victory at this session than to choke off the inquiry. . . . Democracy has found no more effective or appropriate weapon against reaction. The inquiry has served to call attention . . . to major forces that threaten freedom in this country." [61]

The decisive pressure, however, was exerted by Roosevelt. At a press conference on July 11 the President was asked if he favored continuation of the La Follette investigation; he replied, "I have all along." On July 26 he dispatched an unequivocal statement to Senator Byrnes: "From the point of view of the preservation of civil liberties, I recommend it [the request for funds] strongly—and from the point of view of good politics, I recommend it equally strongly. Can I," Roosevelt asked Byrnes, "make a stronger statement to you?" Within the week, at another press conference, the President stated: "I have said it before and I want to make it just as strong as I possibly can, that I hope that amount [$100,000] will be given by the Senate Committee to extend the work of that Civil Liberties Committee." [62]

[58] Roger Baldwin memo, February 16, 1939, ACLU, Vol. 2081. "It is understood," Baldwin noted, "that the President is definitely interested in the continuation of the Committee's work on the West Coast. . . ."

[59] Roosevelt to Lewis B. Schwellenbach, March 8, 1939, FDRL, OF 1581.

[60] *Congressional Record*, 76th Cong., 1st Sess., 1939, Vol. 84, p. 3143.

[61] "Funds for La Follette," *Nation*, CXLIX (July 15, 1939), 61. "A combination of politics and punctilio," the article continued, "has led [La Follette] to pull his punches in the fight for his own inquiry. His political advisers in Wisconsin fear that the powerful enemies the investigation has made will spare no expense to defeat him for reelection [in 1940]."

[62] Roosevelt press conference, July 11, 1939, transcript in FDRL; Roosevelt to Byrnes, July 26, 1939, FDRL, OF 1581; Roosevelt press conference, August 1, 1939, transcript in FDRL.

Roosevelt's support probably saved the La Follette investigation. It did not, however, prevent the Audit and Control Committee from slicing the appropriation in half before recommending Schwellenbach's resolution to the Senate. In an acrimonious debate in August, La Follette, with support from administration Democrats, defended his committee from its detractors. Senator Edward R. Burke (D-Neb.) charged that the La Follette investigation "has been an investigation aimed solely to carry out a particular point of view, and not with the attempt to investigate the violation of civil liberties for all the people of this country. . . ." Burke demanded an enlarged committee, with senators "who have somewhat of a different philosophy" from La Follette and Thomas. Senator Hiram Johnson of California, defending the Associated Farmers of his home state, also insisted upon the addition of at least one new senator to the committee.[63]

"Cotton Ed" Smith of South Carolina delivered one of his characteristic tirades against "state socialism" and federal power. "We are setting a precedent," he warned, "which will result in eliminating the initiative of the officers of the States." Smith declared his preference for suffering "the ills of bloody Kentucky, or the tremendous scandals of Teapot Dome, than to have to give up the key by which can be opened the door to centralization and Federal control. . . ." When Alben Barkley praised the La Follette Committee's Harlan investigation, Smith paid homage to states' rights and warned of the consequences of protecting civil liberty (Pennsylvania, he observed irrelevently, "obtained so much civil liberty that she wanted to open the door of public places of amusement and entertainment to our brothers in black"). Responding to this harangue, Champ Clark (D-Mo.), who had favored the reduced appropriation, announced that the "very eloquent speech by a very dear friend of mine . . . completely convinced [me] on the other side"; Clark was now "perfectly willing to vote for an appropriation of $200,000 if it is necessary." But the Senate was not. After two hours of debate it approved Schwellenbach's resolution, and the $50,000 appropriation, 36–17.[64]

[63] *Congressional Record*, 76th Cong., 1st Sess., 1939, Vol. 84, pp. 11044, 11045, 11046.

[64] *Congressional Record*, 76th Cong., 1st Sess., 1939, Vol. 84, pp. 11050–51, 11053, 11054. The vote reflected a sharply divided Democratic party. Twenty-nine Democrats favored the appropriation; thirteen Democrats, including seven from the South, opposed it. The Republicans, most of whom did not vote, split 4–4. Senate approval, noted the Madison (Wis.) *Capital Times* on August 13, 1939, occurred "only after President Roosevelt expressed a strong desire to see the committee's work go on . . ." (clipping in Legislative Reference Library, Madison). "Mr. Roosevelt deserves credit," declared TRB in the *New Republic*, "for his single-handed conversion of Senator Byrnes . . ." (*New Republic*, C [August 30, 1939], 102). On August 11 Senator Thomas announced that a third senator would be appointed to the La Follette Com-

The La Follette Committee prepared for the final phase of its investigation with its luster considerably dimmed. Having once reflected the exuberant optimism of the labor movement and of the New Deal itself, it had become the inevitable target of antilabor and anti–New Deal onslaughts. As the committee had ridden the crest of the New Deal tide, so its strength ebbed when the New Deal's surge diminished. Critics of the committee lacked the power to terminate its investigation (indeed, their attacks ensured its continuation), but they succeeded in stripping from the committee its veneer of libertarian impartiality, and they argued convincingly that the committee, as Senator Burke had alleged, "aimed solely to carry out a particular point of view."

The committee's bias had two major sources. Robert Wohlforth, the committee's secretary, constituted one; the Communists and Party sympathizers, the other. Wohlforth, for all his apparent contradictions (he was a Republican in a Democratic administration, a West Pointer turned antimilitarist), was thoroughly consistent in one respect: his government service during the New Deal years evinced strong anti-big-business convictions. The Nye Committee had been preoccupied with the influence exerted by powerful economic interests on American intervention in World War I. After three years with the La Follette Committee, Wohlforth moved on to the Justice Department, where he served in the Antitrust Division under Thurman Arnold, America's most diligent trust buster. Helping to curb the antisocial power of businessmen seemed to be Wohlforth's personal destiny.

Communists on the committee staff not only reinforced, but significantly extended, Wohlforth's kind of antipathy toward American capitalists. Wohlforth's antagonism was *ad hoc;* theirs was ideological. They translated business irresponsibility into class warfare; they interpreted the principles and actions of business according to their own Marxist predilections. In so doing they made a generous contribution to the dualism of the New Deal years; both Left and Right eschewed moderation, each perceiving malevolent intent that only intensified its own extremism. The La Follette Committee, with the assistance of its Communist members, became a pawn in this struggle. Its moderate objectives and modest

---

mittee. Lister Hill of Alabama was asked, but he declined; David I. Walsh of Massachusetts accepted, but he took no part in subsequent committee business (*New York Times,* August 12, September 15, 1939; Thomas to Lister Hill, August 11, 1939, Thomas to David I. Walsh, August 17, 1939, Walsh to Thomas, September 9, 1939, Thomas Papers, "Civil Liberties," Box 17).

achievements notwithstanding, it came to symbolize an inevitable clash between the forces of Light and Darkness.

The committee, viewed from the perspective of its left-wing defenders or its right-wing assailants, demonstrated the popularity of the theme of class struggle during the New Deal decade. Few New Dealers found a haven in ideology, but many of them seemed to accept the premises of the Left when it suited their reformist instincts to do so. Class warfare, however, was a double-edged weapon. The New Deal and the La Follette Committee had wielded it adroitly, but by 1938 they were suffering from its painful counterthrusts. The committee, in particular, barely escaped dying by the sword it had lived by so successfully.

ᨠᨠ VIII ᨠᨠ

The Committee and Farm Factories

FOR nearly half a century California had witnessed recurrent bitter confrontations between labor and management. During the Progressive era Los Angeles was known as the "scab city." Harrison Gray Otis, influential owner of the Los Angeles *Times,* labeled unions "industrial vampires," and his newspaper won national notoriety for its anti-union diatribes. In 1910 labor responded: the McNamara brothers dynamited the *Times* building, killing twenty-one employees. In San Francisco, employers tried to emulate the Los Angeles open-shop record. The city was divided into warring camps: "Against . . . regimented capital," historian George E. Mowry has written, "labor itself mobilized on a city-wide basis." The campaign to eradicate unionism reached its peak in 1916, after a bomb explosion during a preparedness day parade killed ten people and injured forty others. Labor radicals Tom Mooney and Warren K. Billings were arrested for the bombing, which became a *cause célèbre* of considerable publicity value to both sides. Employers used the incident to rally support for the open shop, and Mooney and Billings became martyrs to the union cause.[1]

During the 1930's California's most virulent outbursts of labor-management intransigence occurred inland. Although California growers employed fewer than 5 per cent of the country's farm laborers, the state suffered 140 agricultural labor strikes, involving 127,000 workers; its nearest competitor, Oregon, had 17 strikes involving 8,000 workers. In each of 34 California strikes at least one thousand workers left the fields. Intensive, large-scale farming, and the dependence of growers upon a quantity of seasonal workers hired for short periods, helped to account for this unenviable record. Unyielding employers and militantly left-wing unions—first the Cannery and Agricultural Workers Industrial Union, and then the United Cannery, Agricultural, Packing and Allied Workers of America—brought California to a condition verging on class warfare.[2]

[1] George E. Mowry, *The California Progressives,* pp. 46–48, 50, 257–260; Robert G. Cleland, *California In Our Time,* pp. 69–71, 88–92.
[2] Stuart Jamieson, *Labor Unionism in American Agriculture,* pp. 1, 27, 31, 38.

Perhaps nowhere else in the country were labor and management so sharply divided; certainly in no other state were the problems of industrial unionization so exacerbated by the related issue of agricultural unionism. Employers in factories and in the fields equated unionization with communization; workers equated anti-unionism with fascism. Given this bifurcation, violence was inevitable. A decade of violence, particularly in California's fertile valleys, yielded the La Follette Committee investigation a rich harvest.

As early as November 1936 the committee had been asked to investigate the state of civil liberties in California agriculture. A. L. Wirin, loaned to the committee by the National Labor Relations Board, found Robert Wohlforth sympathetic to the idea and NLRB member Edwin S. Smith "strongly enthusiastic."[3] But the committee's small initial appropriation and its preoccupation with antilabor practices in industry precluded any West Coast ventures at that time. For the next two years, however, the NLRB importuned the committee to go west. Towne Nylander, NLRB regional director on the coast, asked Heber Blankenhorn to try to persuade the committee to study California labor relations. "It would be of utmost interest," Nylander wrote, "to obtain the information as to where funds are coming from for all these [vigilante] activities, even if the exposé is not of a more startling nature."[4]

Late in 1938 an NLRB examiner, investigating charges of unfair labor practices against a Washington packing company, submitted a supplementary report to the board documenting the vigilante activities of the Associated Farmers, a California employers' association. Spurred by this report, a small contingent of La Follette Committee staff members conducted a limited inquiry, which the exhaustion of funds abruptly terminated. Their evidence interested the NLRB; the committee, Nylander believed, possessed information "which will be of a great deal of help to us in the administering of the [Wagner] Act in this Region if the same becomes public." If the committee did not expect to conduct public hearings in California, would it, Nylander asked, convene long enough

[3] Wirin to Clinton J. Taft, November 5, 1936, NLRB *Hearings*, XXIV, 5631. Taft, an NLRB staff member, had broached the idea of a committee investigation to Wirin, who suggested that Taft secure letters and resolutions from California liberals.

[4] Nylander to Blankenhorn, July 14, 1938, *ibid.*, p. 5637. Nylander continued, "We know, but we can't prove that there is a very definite tie-up between the Associated Farmers, Inc. and the employing interests in Southern California, and possibly a tie-up with the Bank of America."

to introduce its California material into the record so that the NLRB might use it? [5]

Although the preliminary investigation by the committee was made in response to the labor board's stimulus, this probe and the full investigation that followed also had political overtones. In 1938 Californians elected Culbert Olson, their first Democratic governor in the twentieth century. Olson had waged a vigorous and successful campaign against Proposition No. 1, an antilabor initiative severely restricting picketing, forbidding "hot cargo" and secondary boycotts, and rendering unions liable for the actions of their members. Elected with overwhelming labor support, Olson further endeared himself to the labor movement by pardoning Tom Mooney during the first week of his administration.[6]

The new governor had no objections to a thorough congressional investigation of civil liberties infractions in California labor relations. According to journalist Marquis Childs, La Follette Committee staff members obtained evidence indicating that spies had infiltrated several important campaign meetings of Democratic party leaders. Soon after these meetings had adjourned, Republican governor Frank Merriam had apparently learned everything that had transpired.[7] Many California liberals, Governor Olson among them, hoped that an investigation in California by the La Follette Committee would redound to the Democrats' advantage.[8] California Senator Sheridan Downey cosponsored the Schwellenbach resolution for an additional appropriation, which Olson strongly supported and the California legislature endorsed.[9]

While the La Follette Committee awaited senatorial determination of its fate, the publication of two books during the spring and summer of 1939 evoked nationwide interest in the plight of California farm laborers. *The Grapes of Wrath*, John Steinbeck's affecting, bitter saga of the Joads, epitomized for an entire generation the human toll of the Depression. The urgency of its message was equaled only by the intensity of the opposition it aroused. Kern County, California, banned the book from its public libraries; numerous Oklahoma libraries refused to cir-

[5] *Progressive*, November 12, 1938; Nylander to Blankenhorn, January 13, 1939, NLRB *Hearings*, XXIV, 5638.

[6] Robert E. Burke, *Olson's New Deal for California*, pp. 31–33, 48.

[7] *Progressive*, February 11, 1939, citing an article by Marquis Childs in the St. Louis *Post-Dispatch*.

[8] Interview with Carey McWilliams, February 28, 1964, copy in COHC, p. 3. Those close to Olson wanted the committee in California even before the election, to ensure his victory.

[9] Items in FDRL, OF 1581.

culate it; the Kansas City Board of Education declared it "obscene" and removed it from school bookshelves.[10] But Highway 66, the migrant road, wound its way into the American conscience.

Three months later, in July, appeared Carey McWilliams' *Factories in the Field*. McWilliams, Chief of the California Division of Immigration and Housing, had visited the San Joaquin Valley in 1935 to gather material for a series of articles on farm labor. His book, the product of that visit, described a revolution in agriculture that had taken Americans by surprise and bred a new class of disinherited citizens. In California, McWilliams wrote, "a new type of agriculture has been created: large-scale, intensive, diversified, mechanized." Many farms had become "industrial enterprises conducted on factory lines"; McWilliams called them "farm factories." Their owners, he alleged, exploited field workers, violently opposed their organization, and resisted federal and state regulatory legislation. In California, McWilliams wrote bitterly, "the mechanism of fascist control has been carried to further lengths than elsewhere in America. . . ." The only effective solution, he suggested, "involves the substitution of collective agriculture for the present monopolistically owned and controlled system." [11]

Requests from the NLRB, and the vicissitudes of California and national politics, had given the La Follette Committee a new *raison d'être*.[12] The warnings of Steinbeck and McWilliams provided the final thrust necessary to bring the committee to California and focus its investigation on impediments to farm labor organization.[13] Fortified with $50,000, the committee organized a staff of thirty-five, including attorneys, investigators, economists, and stenographers, and opened offices in Los Angeles and San Francisco.

Guiding the investigation was Henry H. Fowler, a thirty-two-year-old lawyer from Virginia who had served for five years as counsel to the Tennessee Valley Authority. Fowler, under explicit instructions from La Follette to expedite and conclude the committee's investigation, gave the committee a more conservative posture than it had previously displayed. La Follette confronted a campaign for re-election in 1940, and he evidently

[10] New York *Post*, August 18, 1939; Carey McWilliams, *Ill Fares the Land*, p. 43.

[11] Carey McWilliams, *Factories in the Field*, pp. 4, 5, 9, 236–238, 324; McWilliams, *Ill Fares the Land*, p. 20.

[12] McWilliams was told that the pressure from California tipped the scales in favor of the committee's continuance (McWilliams, COHC, p. 3).

[13] *Ill Fares the Land*, p. 47; Henry H. Fowler to Roger Baldwin, November 28, 1939, ACLU, Vol. 2081.

decided to fend off charges circulating in Wisconsin that his committee was contemplating a vendetta against farm organizations. There is also evidence that he may have been disturbed by the affinity of some staff members for California's left-wing agricultural unionists.[14] La Follette's reluctance notwithstanding, his committee went to California with "pencil in hand, taking notes on a social revolution." [15]

Popular myth and national policy had perpetuated a distinction between agriculture and industry that no longer seemed to have validity. In California industrialized agriculture—meaning large-scale operations, concentrated ownership, distant markets, and a sizable labor force—presented many of the same labor problems that "pure" industrialization created elsewhere in the United States. But there was one significant difference: Organizing farm workers into viable unions had proved to be virtually impossible. American agricultural organizations traditionally had been composed of farm owners, not field laborers. Not even the presence of large-scale farming enterprises, producing cash crops for distant markets, dissipated the myth of the independent farm owner-operator who succeeded by dint of his own and his family's labor.[16]

Throughout the 1930's the labor movement failed to duplicate in agriculture its gains in industry. It faced imposing obstacles. Farm laborers generally were widely and thinly dispersed. Racial and cultural heterogeneity divided workers with common economic interests. The unskilled nature of field work meant that one worker could easily be substituted for another; workers found it difficult to maintain organized control over their own labor supply. Federal and state legislation protecting the right to organize usually excluded farm workers; most field hands did not benefit from New Deal wage and social security measures. Workers were inexperienced in union affairs and could rarely afford the financial contributions necessary to sustain a labor organization. The Depression and the drought displaced thousands of farm laborers and produced a chronic labor surplus. Finally, the living and

[14] Madison (Wis.) *Capital Times*, December 28, 1939, clipping in Legislative Reference Library, Madison; interview with Henry H. Fowler, September 16, 1963; Blankenhorn to Wohlforth, September 18, 1939, Wohlforth Papers. See also McWilliams, COHC, p. 4.

[15] Arthur Eggleston, "Industrial Farming—Preview," *Nation*, CL (January 27, 1940), 96.

[16] Sidney C. Sufrin, "Labor Organization in Agricultural America, 1930–35," *American Journal of Sociology*, XLIII (January 1938), 544–549; Jamieson, *Labor Unionism*, pp. 4–6.

working conditions of casual migratory workers left them at their employers' mercy. They could not depend upon a sympathetic community or upon their own resources to protect their rights; their farm was their community, and their resources were virtually nonexistent.[17]

California, where factory farms constituted an additional irritant, presented "a case study of rural class conflict." Nowhere else in the country, concluded one student of farm labor organization, "have farm labor problems been so acute, or the antagonisms so intense and manifest."[18] Workers smoldered with rage at their conditions of employment, but to no avail. In the Imperial Valley, a "below-sea-level, sweated, overpopulated, 130-degrees-Fahrenheit Eden," the migratory cycle began. Okies and Arkies from the east and Mexicans from the south harvested vegetables and fruit, toiling during the peak of the season from four in the morning until ten at night. At night carrot-pullers slept between the rows to hold their places in the field so that they might earn 60¢ for a day's work. "They're aimin' at keeping fellows such as me right down on our knees—aimin' at making slaves of us," complained one worker. "We've got no more chance than a one-legged man in a footrace."[19]

Many migrants fled to the north, but they could not escape exploitation. In the Salinas Valley, the "Salad Bowl of America," working conditions were no better. A man, Steinbeck wrote, "must crawl like a bug beneath the rows of lettuce, he must bend his back and pull his long bag between the cotton rows, he must go on his knees like a penitent across a cauliflower patch."[20] In the San Joaquin Valley workers lived in tarpaper shanties without plumbing and crowded the streets

[17] Alexander Morin, *The Organization of Farm Labor in the United States*, pp. 31–72; Witt Bowden, "Freedom for Wage Earners," *Annals of the American Academy of Political and Social Science*, CC (November 1938), 185; Jamieson, *Labor Unionism*, pp. 15, 21, 39; Harry Schwartz, *Seasonal Farm Labor in the United States*, pp. 12–22.

[18] Morin, *Organization of Farm Labor*, pp. 81, 82. Morin points out that there were never very many farm factories in this country; nevertheless, where they appeared they had a powerful effect on the farm labor force. The La Follette Committee, according to Morin, expressed "the extreme form of the forebodings" arising from this agricultural pattern (*ibid.*, p. 2).

[19] "I Wonder Where We Can Go Now," *Fortune*, XIX (April 1939), 114; James Rorty, "Lettuce—with American Dressing," *Nation*, CXL (May 15, 1935), 575–576; Dorothea Lange and Paul S. Taylor, *An American Exodus*, pp. 114, 115.

[20] Frank J. Taylor, "Hot Lettuce," *Collier's*, XCVIII (September 26, 1936), 33; John Steinbeck, *The Grapes of Wrath*, pp. 316–317.

of Stockton, hoping to be hired. Every morning, before sunrise, trucks rolled into the "slave market" at Market and Center Streets, their drivers looking for fruit pickers and packers to work a seven-day week at 17¢ per hour. The valley was beautiful in May, at harvest time: "Vast hay meadows and alfalfa fields wave and ripple high and ripe in the breeze. Asparagus and beets need hoeing. There are onions, peas, potatoes, carrots. And cherries are red and must be picked in a hurry." But field workers, justifying a rebellion that disturbed the valley's tranquility, insisted, "It is better to die on your feet than to live on your knees." [21]

Everywhere in California workers spoke of degradation and hardship. A fruit tramp told how "the prunes get hot [and] they get sticky and your hands are covered with gummy mud. Your knees hurt like hell. . . . Your back never gets used to prune picking." Berry pickers in Sonoma County worked on hillsides where, even when they stood erect, their faces were only two feet from the ground "and the heat reflects back into your face till you can hardly breathe." A picker of wine grapes explained, "The hazards are sunstroke, cuts from the knife and starvation. . . . We got five cents a box." [22]

Unions tried repeatedly to capitalize on unrest among workers. The Cannery and Agricultural Workers Industrial Union, established in 1930 by the Communist Party's Trade Union Unity League, launched the first great organizing drive in the state. It survived until 1934, when strikes in San Francisco and in the Imperial Valley served as pretexts for its suppression. Union headquarters in Sacramento were raided, and seventeen union leaders were arrested under California's criminal syndicalism law. Imperial Valley growers, declared federal mediator Pelham Glassford, "have welcomed labor agitation, which they could brand as 'Red,' as a means of sustaining supremacy and mob rule. . . ." [23]

New organizing campaigns culminated in 1937 with establishment of

[21] Paul Y. Anderson, "California's Blackshirts," *Nation*, CXLVII (August 6, 1938), 122–123; "No Jobs in California," *Saturday Evening Post*, CCXI (November 12, 1938), 18–19, 40, 44; Louis Adamic, "Cherries Are Red in San Joaquin," *Nation*, CXLII (June 27, 1936), 840–841; Clarke A. Chambers, *California Farm Organizations*, p. 78.

[22] Daniel Mainwaring, "Fruit Tramp," *Harper's Magazine*, CLXIX (July 1934), 235–236; State Relief Administration of California, *Migratory Labor in California*, pp. 178–181.

[23] *Hearings*, Pt. 55, p. 20148. As Superintendent of Metropolitan Police in Washington, D.C., Glassford had been extremely considerate of the Bonus Army in 1932.

the C.I.O.-chartered United Cannery, Agricultural, Packing and Allied Workers of America. Avowedly left-wing like its predecessor, it suffered similar repression. The mere presence of a union blinded many California employers to the vexing problems responsible for its birth. "We on the land," wrote a member of the Los Angeles Chamber of Commerce, "have always recognized that California agricultural labor requirements made impossible to those people so employed the full efforts of American citizenship and the possibilities of partaking of our normal standards of life." [24]

The La Follette Committee took for its central theme "the existence of the National Labor Relations Act, the reaction of employee or employer organizations to its application, and their long struggle to realize or frustrate the benefits which it promised." [25] It knew, of course, that farm labor was not covered by the Wagner Act, but much of its California investigation was an attempt to demonstrate that this unjustifiable exemption had unsettled employer-employee relations in industry and in agriculture. The committee argued that powerful employers' associations had extended the influence of the business community to agricultural labor relations. This practice, it alleged, resulted in the "continued conspiratorial nullification and destruction of civil rights." [26] By stressing conflict on comparatively few but large and economically powerful farm factories, the committee made plausible its contention that farm workers should enjoy the full benefits of federal labor legislation.

During December 1939 and January 1940 the committee held twenty-eight days of public hearings in San Francisco and Los Angeles, called approximately four hundred witnesses, and amassed a voluminous record to document the changing pattern of agricultural labor relations. Its inquiry focused on five interrelated subjects: the structure and history of California agriculture; the activities of employers' associations hostile to collective bargaining; the concern of these associations with farm labor; the impact of their labor policies upon specific organizing drives and strikes; and the co-operation of agricultural and industrial associ-

[24] Jamieson, *Labor Unionism*, pp. 19–20, 107, 113–114, 134–135, 149, 165; *Hearings*, Pt. 53, p. 19544.

[25] U. S. Senate, Committee on Education and Labor, *Employers' Associations and Collective Bargaining in California*, Report No. 1150, Pt. 1, 77th Cong., 2d Sess., 1942, p. 42.

[26] *Ibid.*, Pt. 4, pp. 408–410; U. S. Senate, Committee on Education and Labor, *Employers' Associations and Collective Bargaining in California*, Report No. 398, Pt. 1, 78th Cong., 1st Sess., 1943, p. 702.

ations to frustrate organization and collective bargaining in both agricultural and nonagricultural employment.[27]

The California hearings did not generate much excitement, either locally or nationally. The investigation, wrote one columnist, "is a sapping operation, a digging in and under and around. . . ." It was neither sensational nor dramatic, but a painstaking attempt, in La Follette's words, "to produce a record . . . [containing] all the possible information and sidelights and points of view that are obtainable. . . ." International developments, and the more spectacular findings of the Dies Committee, overshadowed this phase of the La Follette investigation; the press gave the La Follette Committee skimpy coverage. Even West Coast businessmen did not view the hearings with alarm. *Business Week* reported their conviction that the committee would do little damage.[28]

If the committee's findings were virtually ignored at the time, they were not insignificant. The committee grappled with problems that would continue to unsettle California labor relations for decades to come. University of California economist Paul S. Taylor told the committee that farm laborers "bear increasingly the mark of a class as chances of ascending the agricultural ladder, or of finding outlets into industry, grow more difficult." Taylor asked the crucial question: "Can a large farm labor class be reconciled with democracy?"[29]

The committee discovered that, in Carey McWilliams' words, "the industrial revolution has finally hit the farmer." Violently unstable labor relations, and alarming indifference to civil liberties, had accompanied this revolution ever since the federal government had guaranteed to other workers the right to organize. In January 1934 a strike called by the Cannery and Agricultural Workers Industrial Union had ignited three months of anti-union repression in the Imperial Valley. Attorney A. L. Wirin, scheduled to chair a union meeting under ACLU auspices, was abducted from his hotel by an angry mob and driven twenty miles into the desert. A district attorney in the San Joaquin Valley justified

[27] *Employers' Associations*, Report No. 1150, Pt. 1, pp. 13, 14; *Hearings*, Pt. 53, p. 19486.

[28] Arthur Eggleston in San Francisco *Chronicle*, cited in *Progressive*, December 23, 1939; *Hearings*, Pt. 53, p. 19486; "La Follette Quiz Lacks Fireworks," *Business Week* (January 13, 1940), 38–39.

[29] *Hearings*, Pt. 47, p. 17283.

the eviction of cotton pickers from their camps by declaring, "If it isn't the law, it ought to be." [30]

In Salinas the organization of a *posse comitatus*, according to its sponsor, made "every member of the labor union or group on strike or in resistance to the employer commit a crime against the State." He conceded, "That is a certain deprivation of civil liberties." When the California Highway Patrol discovered red flags on the highways leading into Salinas its chief imagined an imminent Communist assault and acted accordingly. Two days later the San Francisco *Examiner* revealed that the State Planning Commission had installed the flags to designate checking stations for a traffic count.[31]

Paul S. Taylor described the essential characteristics of California's farm labor troubles for the La Follette Committee: "Ardent organizers agitate and lead, incensed 'vigilantes' organize and act, growers, officials, and laborers each overstep the law, and citizens finally cry to the State authorities for peace, if necessary at the hands of troops." [32] The pivotal organization in this pattern, according to the committee, was the powerful employers' association called the Associated Farmers.[33] Launched in 1934, it culminated a statewide effort to repress attempts by farm workers to organize and bargain collectively. Its activities ranged from anti-union publicity to sponsorship of antipicketing ordinances and initiation of criminal prosecutions against strike leaders. Associated Farmers became dormant in 1935, when Dust Bowl refugees ensured a labor surplus and the conviction of union leaders for criminal syndicalism discouraged further organizing efforts. When the Wagner Act stimulated renewed union activity on the coast, particularly among teamsters and longshoremen, industrial interests revived Associated Farmers to repulse the union onslaught.[34]

Like its predecessors, who had crushed the Industrial Workers of the World, Associated Farmers ignored the grievances responsible for the strikes that it fought. The "Bible" of the Associated Farmers, explained Samuel Parker Frisselle, its first president, was "to protect agriculture from subversive groups. . . ." The organization looked to industry for guid-

[30] McWilliams, *Ill Fares the Land*, p. 3; *Employers' Associations*, Report No. 1150, Pt. 4, pp. 455–456; *Hearings*, Pt. 54, p. 19964.

[31] *Employers' Associations*, Report No. 398, Pt. 4, pp. 1372–76.

[32] *Hearings*, Pt. 54, p. 19947.

[33] Cf. Richard L. Neuberger, "Who Are the Associated Farmers?" *Survey Graphic*, XXVIII (September 1939), 517–521, 555.

[34] *Employers' Associations*, Report No. 1150, Pt. 4, pp. 426–430, 573–574.

ance; industrial assistance, Frisselle declared, "made us effective enough in enforcing law and order." "Since the establishment of the Associated Farmers of Los Angeles County," wrote a member of the Los Angeles Chamber of Commerce, "we have been able to handle every single strike within the industries of the organization. . . ." [35]

Associated Farmers rallied its members to the standard of "Americanism." Its cries of patriotism, declared the La Follette Committee, "are used to cloak moves by employer groups to frustrate the right of employees to organize and bargain collectively." The Monterey County unit of Associated Farmers pledged itself to "oppose and combat all doctrines or practices which imperil the maintenance of constitutional liberties." But in Monterey County this organization itself posed the most serious menace to constitutional liberties. In Sutter County deputized members of Associated Farmers functioned as a vigilante group to intimidate labor organizers. The Associated Farmers of Yuba County secured the adoption of an antipicketing ordinance. Its secretary insisted that the ordinance did not proscribe peaceful picketing. When Senator La Follette asked for his definition of peaceful picketing he replied, "I would say there isn't any such thing." [36]

Various chapters of Associated Farmers utilized blacklists, espionage, strikebreaking, pressure for antipicketing legislation, and vigilante tactics in order to stifle organization by farm workers. This record, the La Follette Committee reported, indicated a conspiracy "designed to prevent the exercise of their civil liberties by oppressed wage laborers in agriculture, [which] was executed ruthlessly with every device of repression that antiunionism could muster." Where Associated Farmers successfully implemented its policies, the committee concluded, "local fascism was the result." [37]

The Brentwood Plan, sponsored by Associated Farmers in 1934 after a strike of apricot workers in Contra Costa County, illustrated the association's tactics at their peak of efficiency. Execution of the plan required law enforcement officers to co-ordinate their actions with the labor policy of the association. The plan, designed to retain for the growers complete control over wages and workers, provided for com-

[35] *Hearings*, Pt. 49, pp. 17938, 17945, Pt. 55, pp. 20277.

[36] *Employers' Associations*, Report No. 398, Pt. 4, pp. 1410, 1462, 1470; *Hearings*, Pt. 74, p. 27109, Pt. 48, pp. 17526–27.

[37] *Employers' Associations*, Report No. 1150, Pt. 1, p. 47, Report No. 398, Pt. 4, p. 1612.

mittees of ranchers and growers to meet prior to the harvest season to establish uniform wage scales, camp conditions, and publicity policy. Each worker in the district was registered; each received an identification card. No unregistered worker could expect to find employment in Contra Costa County.[38]

Sheriff John A. Miller introduced the Brentwood Plan when he took office in the fall of 1934. He spoke personally to every prospective worker and issued an identification card when he was satisfied "that that person had been peaceful in his years . . . there." Miller told workers who hesitated to register that the community did not need them. He registered union sympathizers and sent their names to employers with the suggestion that they not be hired. Miller boasted that his registration list "gives me and my officers complete surveillance over every fruit worker in the district. . . . We have complete control of the situation . . . ." The sheriff took his responsibilities seriously; during the picking season he donned work clothes and picked fruit with the field hands whose activities he controlled. He tried, he explained, to give every picker "a happy smile," realizing "the value of a smile given to the fruit worker under conditions which he operates, and in this way we tend to inject contentment and happiness." [39]

The Brentwood Plan empowered Sheriff Miller to formulate and implement his own definition of free speech. Union organizers, he told the La Follette Committee, "have a right to come in and talk to individuals, or they have a right to hire a hall to speak to them, but where they get up on soap boxes and address a group from a street corner or in the open, the people of Brentwood take the position that these [organizers] are inciting riot. . . ." Miller did not interrupt a soap-box orator: "We allow him to finish; we watch him carefully, and when he gets alone somewhere away from the scene, we place him under arrest and take him to the County Jail." [40]

By 1936 Sheriff Miller was prepared for any contingency. In June Associated Farmers notified him of the expected return to Brentwood of labor organizer Julius B. Nathan, a participant in the 1934 strike which had been responsible for the adoption of the Brentwood Plan. Four days later Sheriff Miller learned of Nathan's imminent arrival from the young district attorney of Alameda County, Earl Warren. Miller expected

[38] Report No. 398, Pt. 4, pp. 1308–9.
[39] Ibid., p. 1313; Hearings, Pt. 49, pp. 18004, 18007.
[40] Ibid., p. 18146.

Nathan "to pull an agitation. . . ." He acted on the theory that "since the people of the district were peaceful and desired to work . . . any one coming in here to disturb them was guilty of Disturbing the Peace and such would be arrested."[41]

Sheriff Miller formulated plans for "hiding out" Nathan by moving him "from jail to jail ahead of bail or a writ, for a couple of days until the peak of the crop was over and then it would be too late for agitation." But this elaborate scheme proved superfluous. The sheriff warned Nathan to leave town by midnight of the day of his arrival, under penalty of arrest. Nathan departed so quickly that Miller had no opportunity to follow him; discovered in a neighboring town, the organizer was watched overnight and escorted from town the following morning. With some pride Sheriff Miller told the La Follette Committee, "We had ridded ourselves of a serious menace, with[out] the necessity of placing him in jail, or without intimidating him in any way."[42]

Sheriff Miller justified his actions on the ground of community peace. "We haven't had a strike," he said, "we haven't pulled a trigger, and we have had nothing but friendship with the workers."[43] The La Follette Committee concluded that the price of peace was exorbitant. The migrant worker, prevented from organizing and deprived of collective bargaining, "is forced to accept a wage, however small, which has been set by a united front of growers and to submit to a system of regimentation which includes the inspection of his past history and political, economic, and social beliefs." Union organizers suffered from similar discrimination. They could not speak freely in public; warrants for their arrest were issued in anticipation of their acts; evictions and jail sentences removed them, and the position they represented, from every labor controversy. The Brentwood Plan, in the words of the La Follette Committee, was "a gross denial of democratic liberties."[44]

Members of Associated Farmers did not disguise their militant anti-unionism. "We have an excellent formula," wrote the secretary of the Imperial Valley affiliate, "for getting rid of cockroaches, grasshoppers and CIO agitators." "There is no justification at all for organized union

---

[41] *Employers' Associations*, Report No. 398, Pt. 4, pp. 1319–20; *Hearings*, Pt. 49, p. 18173.

[42] *Employers' Associations*, Report No. 398, Pt. 4, pp. 1320–21; *Hearings*, Pt. 49, p. 18174.

[43] *Ibid.*, p. 18004.

[44] *Employers' Associations*, Report No. 398, Pt. 4, p. 1329.

agricultural labor," the La Follette Committee was told. Senator Thomas asked the field secretary of the Associated Farmers of Los Angeles whether any unionization of farm workers was desirable. That official replied, "Not to the point where the farmer loses control of the workers." [45]

The La Follette Committee's examination of the policies and practices of the Associated Farmers dominated its West Coast investigation. Like the Republic Steel Corporation during the hearings on the Little Steel strike, Associated Farmers became the villain in a sharp class struggle. The committee insisted that the anti-union tactics of the Associated Farmers pointed to the desperate need for revision of traditional agricultural policy; it warned of the imminence of agrarian fascism if changes were not forthcoming.[46]

"The unchecked force of finance capitalism and the efficiency of large-scale and mechanistic operation," declared the La Follette Committee, "are rapidly eliminating the prosperous 'family farm,' the institution around which our rural democracy has functioned." The committee stressed the correlation between "areas of large-scale agriculture based on antidemocratic traditions" and strongholds of fascism. "It is more than coincidence," it observed, "that Germany, Italy, Spain, and Hungary have areas of this character." The committee did not propose the abolition of industrialized agriculture; rather, it insisted that such agriculture "should not be permitted to operate outside our normal system of democratic employer-employee relationships." It feared that anti-union agricultural areas might jeopardize the implementation of national labor policy. Existing legislation permitted such organizations as Associated Farmers to "proceed . . . with impunity to perpetuate a system of economic tyranny which should be a cause of national shame and concern." [47]

The La Follette Committee proposed that control over labor re-

[45] *Hearings*, Pt. 55, p. 20347, Pt. 49, p. 17977, Pt. 58, p. 21367.

[46] General comments on the La Follette Committee's California hearings may be found in the following: Eggleston, "Industrial Farming—Preview," *Nation*, CL (January 27, 1940), 96–98; Ella Winter, "La Follette in California," *New Masses*, XXXIV (February 20, 1940), 11–13; Carey McWilliams, "La Follette Hearings: Final Sessions," *New Republic*, CII (March 25, 1940), 400–403; Carey McWilliams, "Civil Rights in California," *New Republic*, CII (January 22, 1940), 108–110; Katherine Douglas, "West Coast Inquiry," *Survey Graphic*, XXIX (April 1940), 227–231, 259–261.

[47] *Employers' Associations*, Report No. 1150, Pt. 1, p. 61, Report No. 398, Pt. 4, pp. 1614–15, 1617.

lations in industrialized agriculture pass from employers' associations to government. "Collective action by the hired workers . . . , supplemented by social action of governmental agencies . . . must become the order of the day." No longer should farm workers be unprotected by the Wagner Act, the Fair Labor Standards Act, social security, and state labor legislation. "We stand at the threshold of decision," the committee proclaimed. "We must either sacrifice the economies and efficiencies inherent in large-scale, specialized, commercialized agriculture or devise and protect a pattern of economic democracy in which the individual hired workers . . . may effectively exercise his civil rights. . . ." [48]

The La Follette Committee gave the approval of the national government to *The Grapes of Wrath* and *Factories in the Field*. But documenting the industrial revolution in agriculture had not been the committee's primary task. Its concern with factory farming emanated from its mandate to investigate civil liberties infractions in labor disputes. The West Coast investigation elicited the committee's most thorough examination of this problem and the most comprehensive statement of its philosophy of civil liberty.

Before the California hearings opened, chief investigator Henry Fowler had requested information from the governors of western states regarding the proper role of the federal government in assisting states to protect the civil liberties of their workers. The replies of two governors, Charles A. Sprague of Oregon and Culbert Olson of California, delineated the approximate boundaries within which the committee could conduct its search for principles. Sprague opposed federal action unless a state "is flagrantly derelict in protecting the rights of its citizens. . . ." [49] But Olson, testifying before the committee, welcomed its efforts "to focus public attention upon the many interferences with civil liberties that have occurred in the past." The California governor linked the exercise of civil liberties to the ability of farm labor to organize. "If we would prevent the crystallization within the rural communities of rigid groups," he said, "then ways and means must be found to afford farm labor an opportunity for advancement consistent with American democratic ideals." [50]

In California a favorite device for squelching incipient unionism was

[48] *Ibid.*, Report No. 1150, Pt. 4, p. 671, Pt. 1, p. 61; see also Pt. 3, pp. 394–396.
[49] *Hearings*, Pt. 47, p. 17237; Charles A. Sprague to Henry H. Fowler, December 5, 1939, *ibid.*, p. 17239.
[50] *Ibid.*, Pt. 47, pp. 17252, 17265–66.

the antipicketing ordinance. Picketing, more than any other civil liberties issue in labor relations during the New Deal, substantively stretched the meaning of free speech. Traditional forms of expression simply did not meet union needs; workers relied upon picket lines to advertise their side of labor disputes. Throughout the thirties picketing confronted state and federal courts with a difficult challenge: to bring the First Amendment into line with the exigencies of modern industrial relations. The Supreme Court did not rule decisively on this issue until 1940, when it held that peaceful picketing enjoyed the protection given to free speech by the First Amendment. Before the *Thornhill* decision, however, antipicketing legislation crippled many union organizing campaigns.

Between 1934 and 1938 thirty-four counties and nineteen municipalities in California enacted at least sixty antipicketing laws. By the fall of 1938, the La Follette Committee discovered, the entire state, with the exception of San Francisco, "was blanketed by antipicketing ordinances. . . ." [51] These ordinances generally permitted "peaceful" picketing, but authorities responsible for their enforcement frequently interpreted this phrase as self-contradictory.

The La Follette Committee assigned most of the blame for these ordinances to "those associations of employers who . . . sought to pervert public authority to their own private use in preventing employees from publicizing the existence of a labor dispute." The Associated Farmers circulated copies of model antipicketing ordinances for the benefit of counties lacking them. Ben Hayes, president of the Madera County Associated Farmers, reported to headquarters: "The District Attorney said our antipicketing ordinance was too weak, and was requested by the supervisors to draw up a new one with plenty of teeth in it. . . . I would appreciate it very much if you would send me copies of the best antipicketing ordinance you have. . . ." [52]

Notwithstanding the plethora of local ordinances, a campaign to enact statewide antipicketing legislation had been launched during the summer of 1938. An antipicketing initiative, Proposition No. 1, was submitted to California voters. According to the La Follette Committee, Proposition No. 1 provided "a perfect case history of an attempt by

[51] *Employers' Associations*, Report No. 398, Pt. 5, p. 1645. For a review of the Supreme Court's decisions on picketing, see Osmond K. Fraenkel, *Our Civil Liberties*, pp. 223–230.

[52] *Employers' Associations*, Report No. 398, Pt. 5, p. 1657; *Hearings*, Pt. 51, p. 18637, Pt. 61, p. 22271.

organized antiunionism, posing as a disinterested citizenry, to stifle the rights of labor. . . ." Industrial, commercial, and banking interests drafted this legislation; they and the associations in which they were active financed the campaign for its enactment.[53]

Proposition No. 1 made picketing, peaceful or otherwise, illegal except when conducted during the course of a strike for higher wages, shorter hours, or better physical conditions of employment. In a strike for union recognition no picketing would be tolerated. Only striking employees were permitted to picket. No more than one picket (designated by his fellow strikers) could march in front of a factory or farm entrance. The initiative expressly prohibited picketing to induce a person to join or refrain from joining any labor organization. Its advocates waged a vigorous and expensive campaign for adoption up and down the West Coast. Oregon and Washington submitted similar measures to their voters, but only the Oregon measure was approved, and two years later the state supreme court struck it down. Proposition No. 1, the La Follette Committee declared, constituted prior restraint on free expression that was blatantly contradictory to the mandate of the First Amendment.[54]

Campaigns for antipicketing legislation in California generally proceeded through legitimate channels, even if the results did not meet constitutional standards of free expression. But farm workers striving to organize faced an additional and more serious threat, one that was extralegal: the doctrine that the collective popular will need not tolerate civil liberties guarantees that thwarted its objectives. During a cotton strike in 1939 in Madera County, the Madera *Daily Tribune* reminded the "radicals": "Enthusiasm for the I.W.W. ceased when a few were found suspended from a bridge. . . . So far as anyone has ever been able to prove, they were letting themselves down with ropes, the ropes slipped and became tangled about their heads." O. L. Baker, a director of Associated Farmers, met with representatives of Governor Olson during the strike. "My statement there at this meeting," he told the La Follette Committee, "was that the people were the Government. . . . We, the people, elect competent people to the head of our Government to administer the laws, and when they cease to do that, . . . the people had to take it in their own hands. . . ."[55]

[53] *Employers' Associations*, Report No. 398, Pt. 5, pp. 1674, 1693.
[54] *Ibid.*, pp. 1646, 1663–6.
[55] *Hearings*, Pt. 51, pp. 18655, 18679.

Byron C. Hanna, former president of the Los Angeles Chamber of Commerce, insisted that labor activity "would be determined and controlled by public sentiment. . . . I felt that if the people of Los Angeles could know what was going on, and the public could be educated upon the subject, that we could depend upon the judgment of public sentiment to control the situation." To educate the public, the Chamber of Commerce helped to organize the Southern Californians, Inc., which spearheaded the successful campaign in Los Angeles for antipicketing legislation. Maintenance of the open shop, Hanna claimed, constituted "preservation of one of the civil liberties of workers." [56] In California, as in Ohio and Pennsylvania during the Little Steel strike, the boundaries of the First Amendment were set by organized private interests.

The inquiry in California culminated the La Follette Committee's efforts to square the Bill of Rights with American labor relations.[57] California presented the committee with as stringent a test of its commitment to First Amendment principles as it encountered during the entire life of its investigation. Early in the hearings Philip Bancroft, former president of the Associated Farmers of Contra Costa County, accused La Follette of "giving aid and comfort to the Communists . . . by trying to smear the farmers and the law-enforcement officers of the State." [58] The undisputed presence and power of Communists in the California labor movement had long served as a convenient justification for opposing every effort of labor to organize. With left-wingers on its staff, the La Follette Committee had an obvious interest in extending the limits of tolerance for ideas that were anathema to many Americans. But the committee was also committed to libertarian ideals, and, as its investigation drew to a close, it enunciated this commitment.

In California as elsewhere, the committee refused to investigate the

[56] *Ibid.*, Pt. 56, pp. 20474–75, 20477.

[57] The California hearings ended on January 29, 1940. Between May 2 and June 4, 1940, the committee held supplementary hearings in Washington, D.C., on the national farm labor problem. It limited these hearings to testimony from expert witnesses. See U. S. Senate, Subcommittee of the Committee on Education and Labor, *Supplementary Hearings*, 77th Cong., 1st Sess., 1941; McWilliams, *Ill Fares the Land*, pp. 91, 300, 384.

[58] *Hearings*, Pt. 49, p. 18051. La Follette replied: "In the conduct of these hearings every effort has been made . . . to give every witness . . . full opportunity to present any relevant material which he desired to present. . . . The committee has not been here with any other objective than the sole one, to carry out the instructions given to it by the Senate, and to carry them out impartially, and to carry them out so as to obtain all of the facts . . . " (*ibid.*).

political affiliations and sympathies of participants in labor disputes. Whether it was motivated by libertarian convictions, or by the self-interest of its left-wing staff members, or both, is uncertain. Whatever the reason, the committee extended to Communists the same privileges that they enjoyed under the law at the time of the committee's investigations. The committee declared unequivocally "that a person possesses certain rights of free speech and assembly under the Constitution which must be observed, regardless of his political affiliations, no matter how strongly these political affiliations may be disapproved." [59] Too often, in the committee's experience, strikebreaking and union-busting had become "a patriotic crusade for home, country, property, church, and all that men hold dear." The committee conceded that "a number of Communists" had been involved in organizing activities in California. But it deemed of even great importance the fact that

"the civil rights of strikers, unions, union organizers, outsiders, and many of the agricultural laborers in California to speak, assemble, organize into unions, and bargain collectively are repeatedly and flagrantly violated, and that these illegal and ofttimes criminal violations of the rights of others are excused, condoned, defended, and constantly induced by a repeated emphasis and publicity on the alleged communism of a few of the labor leaders and their followers." [60]

Toward the end of the California hearings Senator Thomas had pondered federal responsibility for safeguarding civil liberties. "There has to be a line between Federal and State power in this vexed field," he said. "The committee is confined to treating local crimes and violence not as something in themselves, but as incidents of Federal citizenship, or as part of a large trend, of a conspiracy or design or economic movement or something that Federal power can constitutionally and profitably be applied to." [61] With the right to organize and bargain collectively guaranteed by federal legislation, the La Follette Committee affirmed the extension of federal power at least to those civil liberties deriving from this right.

"The guarantees which the Constitution throws around civil liberties," the committee declared, "are neither pious declarations nor

[59] *Employers' Associations*, Report No. 1150, Pt. 1, pp. 28–29.
[60] *Ibid.*, p. 30.
[61] *Hearings*, Pt. 57, p. 20910.

archaic echoes of the historic past; they are the ground plan for the healthy functioning of an industrial society. Their infraction will shatter our democratic society upon its internal conflicts; their fulfillment will enable it to achieve a strength and unity which no domestic or foreign enemy can challenge." Particularly where economic inequalities exist, "frequent intervention by the Government" was justified to protect civil liberties and restrain the exercise of private power. The committee did not care to weigh property and personal rights; "where rights of persons do not exist," it stated, "rights of property are in danger." [62]

The committee regarded the right of workers to associate as "more than an abstract civil liberty. It has a fundamental bearing upon the economic, social, and political welfare of the people to whom the right is confided by our institutions of law and government." When employers dominated labor relations, the results were "economic injustice, industrial unrest, class violence as distinct from group cooperation, and the myriad evils that flow from industrial autocracy." The history of California labor relations taught "that a democratic government must aggressively maintain adequate safeguards of the right of labor to organize and bargain collectively." That history, the committee observed, must also deter Congress from "relaxing the vigilance [which] the Government should exercise over the civil liberties of its citizens." [63]

The La Follette Committee findings raised two questions: Did the federal government possess the power to enforce the Bill of Rights? If it did, would it exercise that power? The committee answered both questions in the affirmative. Economic tyranny, it concluded, "can only be restrained by . . . a democratic government zealous in the protection of the civil rights of its citizens and in the furtherance of social justice." [64] The committee's sole remaining task was to translate its libertarian rhetoric into operative legal sanctions.

[62] *Employers' Associations*, Report No. 1150, Pt. 1, pp. 9, 57, Report No. 398, Pt. 4, p. 1617.

[63] *Ibid.*, Report No. 1150, Pt. 3, p. 157, Pt. 2, p. 142.

[64] *Ibid.*, Pt. 4, p. 671.

Securing the Blessings of Liberty

THE mandate originally given to the La Follette Committee had empowered it to make recommendations "for the enactment of any remedial legislation it may deem necessary." This provision of Senate Resolution 266 posed a difficult challenge. Legislation protecting civil liberties or civil rights had rarely emerged from Congress; even more rarely had it alleviated the distress that inspired it. Courts, not Congress, were the most vigilant defenders of the Bill of Rights. On the strength of its investigation, the La Follette Committee enjoyed a unique opportunity to redress this balance.

As early as 1938 the committee had begun to look toward a legislative solution of the problem of protecting civil liberties in industrial relations. During the summer of that year, after the end of the second phase of its investigation, staff members attempted to write the committee's findings into law. The committee was expected to recommend its own continuation as a permanent Senate body and to propose a stringent bill combating oppressive labor practices. But La Follette's pledge to the Senate earlier in the year to terminate committee activities by January 1939 left the labor-practices bill as the sole legislative objective.[1]

In November 1938 La Follette gave his provisional approval to the drafting of an omnibus bill. He received administration blessings for the project; Tom Corcoran and Ben Cohen assigned government attorneys to co-operate with lawyers on the committee staff. "Everybody has new ideas," Heber Blankenhorn told J. Warren Madden, "but everybody is tentatively agreed on trying to put it in one big bill."[2] After Thanksgiving, committee lawyers David Lloyd and Daniel Margolies met with Labor and Justice Department personnel three evenings each week to

[1] Milwaukee *Journal*, August 14, 1938, clipping in Legislative Reference Library, Madison. The C.I.O. was very much in favor of a permanent independent bureau in the government empowered primarily to investigate civil liberties infractions in labor disputes (*C.I.O. News*, August 13, 1938; C.I.O., *Proceedings of the First Constitutional Convention* [1938], p. 189).

[2] Blankenhorn to Madden, November 18, 1938, NLRB *Hearings*, XXI, 4407.

draft the measure. Margolies also directed a comprehensive study of state legislation pertaining to industrial espionage, detective and strike-breaking agencies, utilization of armed guards, and deputization of private police. Blankenhorn, still serving as unofficial liaison between the National Labor Relations Board and the committee, correlated various proposals and relayed them to committee lawyers.[3]

On March 28, 1939, La Follette introduced S. 1970, a bill "to eliminate certain oppressive labor practices affecting interstate and foreign commerce. . . ." The bill prohibited the four anti-union practices investigated by the committee during 1936–1937: espionage, strikebreaking, the use of gas munitions or automatic weapons, and the use of armed guards beyond an employer's premises. It empowered the Secretary of Labor to investigate complaints and apply for injunctions; the Department of Justice would prosecute. Violators were subject to a maximum fine of $10,000, or six months imprisonment, or both.[4] In a press release the committee explained that S. 1970 was the product of its discovery that "the most persistent and significant violations of civil liberties occurred in the field of labor and arose principally from a labor relations policy hostile to collective bargaining and the organization of unions."[5]

One month later Representative Reuben T. Wood (D-Mo.), who had entered Congress after twenty years as president of the Missouri State Federation of Labor, introduced a companion bill in the House of Representatives. Wood described S. 1970 as "by far the most important legislative proposal that this Congress could pass for the benefit of the working people of this country. . . . Even more directly than the Wagner Act, this bill makes for industrial peace." From Secretary of Labor Perkins came an equally strong endorsement. The La Follette Committee hearings, she noted, left "a monumental record of the need for such legislation as this." Implementation of New Deal labor policy depended upon the elimination of oppressive labor practices. Secretary Perkins told Senator Thomas, chairman of the Committee on Education and Labor, "I deem this proposed bill of primary importance and urge your committee to report favorably upon it as soon as possible."[6]

[3] David D. Lloyd to La Follette and Thomas, December 10, 1938, Elbert Thomas Papers, "Civil Liberties," Box 17; NLRB *Hearings*, XX, 4268–71.

[4] *Congressional Record*, 76th Cong., 1st Sess., 1939, Vol. 84, pp. 3395–98. The committee's precise definitions of "industrial espionage," "industrial munitions," and "strikebreaker" may be found on page 3396.

[5] La Follette Committee Press Release, March 28, 1939, copy in Wohlforth Papers.

[6] *Congressional Record*, 76th Cong., 1st Sess., Vol. 84, pp. 4864–65; David D. Lloyd to Wohlforth, April 12, 1939, Wohlforth Papers; Frances Perkins to Elbert Thomas, May 12, 1939, Secretaries of Labor Papers, Box 9 (Perkins).

A subcommittee of the Committee on Education and Labor held hearings on S. 1970 during May and June.[7] Recapitulating the high points of his investigation, La Follette vigorously urged the enactment of legislation based upon the committee's work. "This bill is several decades overdue," he insisted. The committee's recommendations, La Follette said, "are not novel. They echo the findings of past governmental investigations conducted periodically over the past 40 years. . . . To make these [oppressive labor] practices illegal is in a sense to add the capstone to the legislation buttressing the national labor policy. The bill will stand with the Wagner Act and the Walsh-Healey Act as a guidepost to liberty and industrial freedom." [8]

Chairman Madden of the National Labor Relations Board spoke of his agency's "vital interest" in the enactment of S. 1970. "My appearance is not to be regarded as a routine response," Madden told the subcommittee. The Wagner Act, he observed, authorized the NLRB to issue orders only against employers. But enactment of the La Follette bill would curb the antilabor activities of those whom the Wagner Act did not directly restrain. Vigorous enforcement "will remove a serious infection which is poisoning the labor relations of large areas of this country." [9]

Representatives of both major labor organizations pledged their enthusiastic support. The American Federation of Labor, president William Green testified, was "unqualifiedly in favor" of S. 1970. Joseph A. Padway, A.F. of L. counsel, declared, "It is not only labor's privilege, but it is labor's right, to be protected in the exercise of the right to free speech and assemblage." John L. Lewis expressed the "wholehearted support" of the C.I.O. Pointing to the mildness of NLRB sanctions, Lewis demanded federal criminal legislation to "restore basic rights to the American people that are essential to their free existence, rights that have been consistently denied to them by the giant corporations that control the economic life of the Nation." [10]

While many of the bill's advocates defended it as a logical and necessary extension of congressional power to regulate interstate commerce, Attorney General Frank Murphy insisted "that the Federal Government has a definite role to play in the preservation of civil liberties."

[7] The subcommittee comprised La Follette, Thomas, Claude Pepper (Fla.), Lister Hill (Ala.), and William E. Borah (Idaho).

[8] U. S. Senate, Subcommittee of the Committee on Education and Labor, *Hearings on S. 1970*, 76th Cong., 1st Sess., 1939, pp. 8, 10.

[9] *Ibid.*, pp. 61, 67.

[10] *Ibid.*, pp. 87, 89, 97–100.

S. 1970, Murphy said, "bears vitally on the question of civil liberties. One of its chief objectives is to prevent the invasion of civil rights by private interests." The bill, he predicted, would take its place "in the line of legislation defensive of the civil rights guaranteed by the Constitution." [11]

Representative Clare E. Hoffman of Michigan, long the committee's archfoe, alone appeared in opposition to S. 1970. Hoffman attacked the La Follette Committee for conducting a biased investigation. It "was more interested in disclosing the violation of civil liberties on the part of the employers than . . . on the part of the strikers, labor organizers, and unions." S. 1970 erroneously assumed "that there must inevitably be strife and discord between employer and employee." If enacted, Hoffman insisted, it would "not only place industry but the individual workers at the mercy of the labor organizer, labor organizations, and the professional labor politicians. . . ." Hoffman thought that the bill would prove even "more destructive to civil liberties" than the Wagner Act and the La Follette Committee investigation. "The day has come," he declared, "when the people of this land will not much longer submit to the insidious inroads which of late have been made upon our liberties." [12]

Hoffman's tirade was muted by the bill's many supporters—even a former strikebreaker and two former labor spies testified on its behalf. But his testimony portended bitter wrangling over the merits of the bill when the Senate considered the measure. La Follette, however, felt "almost certain" that the bill would be acted upon favorably, and he terminated hearings on it after eight days.[13] On July 20 his subcommittee approved the bill; two days later the Committee on Education and Labor voted to report it favorably; and on July 24 it was placed on the Senate calendar. But Senator Wallace H. White, Jr., of Maine blocked its consideration on the Senate's final consent call of the session, and S. 1970 remained on the calendar until the next session of Congress.[14]

Before the labor-practices bill finally reached the Senate floor in the spring of 1940, its opponents had ample time to muster their attack. The National Association of Manufacturers argued that S. 1970 was

[11] *Ibid.*, pp. 75–77.

[12] *Ibid.*, pp. 169, 173, 175, 178–179, 190–91.

[13] Sol Alpher to Roger Baldwin, May 29, 1939, ACLU, Vol. 2081.

[14] *New York Times*, July 21, 23, 25, 1939; Sol Alpher to Jerome Britchey, August 8, 1939, ACLU, Vol. 2081.

"drastic and unfair." None of the enumerated practices, the NAM contended, were so widely used as to justify such stringent federal legislation. Furthermore, the bill was "based upon an investigation which failed even to consider the activities of organized labor which in many cases have made these practices necessary or justifiable. . . ." Only the "blind or prejudiced," announced the association, "can view this legislation as designed to protect civil liberties or civil rights." [15]

The United States Chamber of Commerce believed that the bill's "real purpose is not to protect or preserve civil liberty but to assure the success of strikes called by labor organizations and conducted under their auspices." The American Legion announced its opposition to S. 1970, and Congressman Hoffman inserted still another attack on the bill in the *Congressional Record*. By May 15, 1940, on the eve of Senate consideration of the bill, La Follette, Roger Baldwin was told, was "not very hopeful of the outcome, [and conceded] the bill less than an even chance of passage by the Senate." [16]

La Follette's pessimism was probably attributable less to the thrusts of the bill's opponents than to Senate and national hypersensitivity to the worsening international situation. One month earlier Germany had invaded Denmark and Norway; a week before Senate debate began, the Nazi blitzkrieg battered Belgium, Luxembourg, and the Netherlands. Americans became concerned mainly with defense; according to a news magazine, La Follette could have chosen "no worse time" to introduce his bill. "With the people of this country depending on our manufacturers to carry out the government's defense program," observed the Milwaukee *Journal*, "Senator La Follette's bill is strangely out of step." [17] In Manhattan, leaders of the National Legion of Mothers of America organized the Molly Pitcher Rifle Legion to defend against descending parachutists. Chicago's Sportsmen's Defense Reserve mobilized an army of minute men to protect the city from invaders.[18] The oppressive-labor-practices bill, under consideration at a time of maximum anxiety over European developments, became the pawn in a debate on national defense.

[15] *Hearings on S. 1970*, pp. 201, 202, 208.

[16] *Progressive*, January 20, 1940; *New York Times*, September 29, 1939; *Congressional Record*, 76th Cong., 1st Sess., 1939, Vol. 84, pp. 2579–80; Sol Alpher to Baldwin, May 15, 1940, ACLU, Vol. 2087.

[17] *Time*, June 10, 1940; Milwaukee *Journal*, May 25, 1940, clipping in Legislative Reference Library, Madison.

[18] *Time*, June 3, 1940; see also Brig. Gen. Robert E. Wood to Senator Alexander Wiley, *Congressional Record*, 76th Cong., 3d Sess., 1940, Vol. 86, p. 6365.

The Senate shrugged aside rousing appeals by La Follette and Thomas on behalf of their bill.[19] Debate was punctuated by frequent references to "Trojan horses" and "fifth columns." Wisconsin's junior senator, Alexander Wiley, argued that "the present is no time to think about hamstringing defense. In the last few years we have had enough of hamstringing of initiative, vision, and energy." Wiley insisted that the bill should exclude companies with government contracts from its coverage; these employers must be free to scrutinize the affiliations and activities of their workers in order to prevent espionage and sabotage. "My business," Wiley declared, "stands for American principles, American ideals. I want to know whether the employee believes in the ideas of Hitler or Stalin." [20]

Wiley's colleagues embellished his attack. Robert A. Taft of Ohio argued that S. 1970 was "one-sided" and "unnecessary." It would "deliberately hamper the preparations of the United States for war" and would "open industrial plants to sabotage. . . ." Taft conjured up a picture of German troops, knowing that American employers could not arm, preparing to invade the country. Josiah W. Bailey of North Carolina warned of Communists who "are boring in everywhere they can. They bore into the churches. . . . They bore into the Congress. . . . They bore into the offices down the street. . . . They bore into the missionary societies. . . . And they bore into the labor unions." The country, he insisted, must prepare for war and must strike all shackles from industry. "Happy" Chandler of Kentucky, speaking on behalf of the American Legion, predicted mournfully, "If this bill were enacted, one of my fellow citizens back in the hills at home could not take a shotgun and shoot a parachutist in his yard if he landed there suddenly." [21]

Two amendments proposed by Senator Robert R. Reynolds (D-N.C.) transformed S. 1970 from a labor to a defense measure. The first provided that no company covered by the bill could employ aliens in excess of 10 per cent of its working force. The second prohibited the employment

[19] Ibid., pp. 6213–16, 6227. On May 17 La Follette asked Roosevelt to do everything possible to ensure that the bill would not be put aside without a vote (La Follette to FDR, May 17, 1940, FDRL, OF 407-B).

[20] Congressional Record, 76th Cong., 3d Sess., 1940, Vol. 86, p. 6367. La Follette replied that nothing in the bill prevented an employer from investigating an employee's affiliations and activities, provided the employee was notified in advance and consented to the investigation. The worker could be discharged without penalty to the employer if he refused his consent.

[21] Ibid., pp. 6682–83, 6690–91, 6693, 6707.

of "any Communist or member of any Nazi Bund organization." Reynolds' amendments became Titles II and III of the bill; Title I still proscribed the four oppressive labor practices. Amended in this fashion, the bill was passed, 47—20. But, the *New York Times* observed, the Senate had altered S. 1970 "to a fragment of its original form. . . ." Reynolds' amendments, the *Times* complained, carried "in every syllable the mark of bigotry and injustice." The United States, declared *Time*, was "less concerned with the immediate future of civil liberties than with the immediate future of the U.S." The oppressive-labor-practices bill, it announced, was "smothered in aliens." [22] The companion version to S. 1970 never even came to a vote in the House of Representatives. The vain fight for the measure marked the La Follette Committee's final effort to aid the American industrial worker. In a twist of irony its investigation culminated in blatantly antilibertarian legislation that best served the libertarian cause by failing to be enacted.[23]

As a civil liberties measure even the original version of the La Follette bill left much to be desired. The committee tried to institutionalize a mood of revulsion against oppressive labor practices. But one of the basic lessons of its investigation was the ineffectuality of weak unions in restraining employers from infringing the civil liberties of their members. With union legitimacy, however, workers could utilize their own resources to terminate antilabor practices. As a means of protecting workers' civil liberties, union power loomed as a more effective weapon than oppressive-labor-practices legislation.

The La Follette Committee's legislative failure should not dim the luster of its earlier investigative achievements. The committee had nudged the executives of United States Steel toward a prestrike collective bargaining agreement; it had encouraged automobile workers and miners in their efforts to organize and had enabled them to publicize their grievances and mobilize support for their cause; and it had countered sentiment hostile to the sit-down strike by stressing the legiti-

[22] *Congressional Record*, 76th Cong., 3d Sess., 1940, Vol. 86, pp. 6379, 6904–6; *New York Times*, May 28, 29, 1940; *Time*, June 10, 1940.

[23] See *New York Times*, June 1, 6, 9, 16, 1940, for letters commenting on S. 1970; *Amalgamated Journal*, June 6, 1940; "A Good Bill Gone Wrong," *New Republic*, CII (June 17, 1940), 809; Harry A. Millis and Emily Clark Brown, *From the Wagner Act to Taft-Hartley*, p. 337. On April 3, 1942, La Follette introduced S. 2435, a revised oppressive-labor-practices bill, which included sanctions against the activities of citizens' committees and employers' associations. It expired in committee (*Congressional Record*, 77th Cong., 2d Sess., 1942, Vol. 88, pp. 3308–14; *New York Times*, April 4, 1942).

macy of union complaints. Furthermore, the committee left an exhaustive account of labor's perspective on labor-management relations during the New Deal, and it dispelled the aura of respectability surrounding unethical antilabor practices. Perhaps most significantly, it perceived the menace to civil liberties from the concentration of power in private hands. For liberty to flourish, the committee's record indicated, the federal government must take steps to secure the Bill of Rights against private encroachment.

The committee's achievements depended, of course, upon the concurrent determination and power of the National Labor Relations Board and the Congress of Industrial Organizations. Given sustenance by other institutions, the committee flourished; without their support its work would have been, in Heber Blankenhorn's phrase, another piece of labor research down the drain.[24] For the La Follette investigation, Blankenhorn wrote in 1937, "was no more than the expansion of a phase of the [Interchurch] inquiry, fulfillment of the Church's specific demand once (1921) laid, uselessly, before the Senate." The many venomous attacks on the committee missed this point completely. "Everything we did," Robert Wohlforth recalled, "had been said or done before by some government body." The reports of the Industrial Relations Commission and the Interchurch inquiry, in particular, presaged the La Follette Committee's findings. But the committee luxuriated, as its predecessors had not, in a climate of union and government opinion warmly sympathetic to its efforts. Only this climate saved the committee from withering like the Interchurch inquiry, for, as Heber Blankenhorn knew, "the general findings were dishearteningly similar, two milestones close together on a road of little progress." [25]

Even with fullest co-operation from the administration, the La Follette investigation produced salutary results only in those industries in which powerful unions fought for and secured the rights of their members. The committee could not by itself halt oppressive labor practices, which were manifestations of a system of absolute employer power. Only countervailing power could end them; neither publicity nor legislation sufficed. At best, the committee contributed to the increase of public tolerance of unions sufficiently strong to protect themselves.[26]

[24] Mrs. Ann Blankenhorn to Jerold S. Auerbach, June 23, 1963.

[25] Blankenhorn, "The Struggle of Labor," *Religion and Public Affairs*, ed. Rall, p. 37; Robert Wohlforth, COHC, p. 40.

[26] The C.I.O. regional director for eastern Pennsylvania wrote in 1939: "Every experienced trade union leader knows that while a very great deal has been done

Where unions could not establish a foothold, oppressive labor practices flourished despite congressional exposure. In 1952, for example, a subcommittee of the Senate Committee on Labor and Public Welfare found "concerted opposition" to organization in Southern textile mills, and "nullification" of national labor policy. It reported:

"In stopping a union organizing campaign employers will use some or all of the following methods: surveillance of organizers and union adherents; propaganda through rumors, letters, news stories, advertisements, speeches to the employees; denial of free speech and assembly to the union; organization of the whole community for antiunion activity; labor espionage; discharges of union sympathizers; violence and gunplay; injunctions; the closing or moving of the mill; endless litigation. . . ." [27]

Quite obviously, the La Follette investigation did not by itself usher in a new era of labor-management relations.

The committee's work did, however, have important consequences for the status of civil liberties. The executive branch was receptive to the warning that private power threatened constitutional rights. On February 3, 1939, Attorney General Frank Murphy issued Order No. 3204, announcing the establishment of a Civil Liberties Unit in the Department of Justice which would "direct, supervise and conduct prosecutions of violations of the Constitution or Acts of Congress guaranteeing civil rights to individuals." That day Murphy wrote to Roger Baldwin, "I am anxious that the weight and influence of the Department of Justice should be a force for the preservation of the people's liberties." [28]

Prior to establishment of the unit, the Justice Department had displayed little interest in prosecuting civil liberties or civil rights cases. Its two major efforts during the New Deal were the indictment and trial of Harlan County coal operators and sheriffs, and a grand jury investigation of the abysmal conditions in Mayor Hague's Jersey City.

---

by the La Follette Committee to check the evil of industrial espionage that labor spies still continue to operate in all types of industry . . . " (John W. Edelman to Senator Joseph Guffey, January 13, 1939, copy in Elbert Thomas Papers, Box 17).

[27] U. S. Senate, Subcommittee of the Committee on Labor and Public Welfare, *Report on Labor-Management Relations in the Southern Textile Industry*, 82d Cong., 2d Sess., 1952, pp. 54–55.

[28] Office of the Attorney General, Order No. 3204, February 3, 1939, copy in ACLU, Vol. 2070; Frank Murphy to Roger Baldwin, February 3, 1939, copy in *ibid.*

In both instances the civil liberties of workers were at stake; the Harlan proceedings, of course, followed the La Follette Committee's highly publicized exposures.

The Justice Department was handicapped by the existence of few statutes—and those dating from Reconstruction days—making federal crimes of civil liberties or civil rights violations. Section 51 of Title XVIII of the United States Code prohibited conspiracies to deprive any citizen of rights or privileges secured by the Constitution or by federal statutes. Comparatively few such rights or privileges, however, extended to private action; most were secured only against the actions of officials or instrumentalities of government itself. Section 52 prohibited actions "under color of any law, statute, ordinance, regulation, or custom" to deprive any inhabitant of constitutional or statutory rights. It, too, seemed applicable only to infringements of distinctly federal rights, invariably narrowly construed.[29] Even more inhibiting than statutory deficiencies was the prevailing attitude that government was powerless to intervene to protect civil liberties. Former Attorney General Homer S. Cummings, for example, "could see no way out, no relief from Washington under our Federal Constitution" for the Arkansas sharecroppers who had been treated as though the Bill of Rights did not exist.[30]

The shibboleth of federal nonintervention meant little to Frank Murphy. As governor of Michigan during the hectic days of the sit-down strike, Murphy learned that "in times of social unrest," as he later expressed it, "there is an increased necessity for vigilance in those charged with the protection of constitutional privileges and immunities." [31] He was firmly convinced that the menace of dictatorship abroad could best be counteracted by an infusion of democracy at home. Murphy, an admirer has written, was by temperament "a fighter who was aroused by seeming injustice"; intellectually, he was an instrumentalist

[29] Henry A. Schweinhaut, "The Civil Liberties Section of the Department of Justice," *Bill of Rights Review,* I (Spring 1941), 206–216; Francis Biddle, "Civil Rights and the Federal Law," *Safeguarding Civil Liberty Today,* Carl L. Becker, *et al.,* p. 134; Robert K. Carr, *Federal Protection of Civil Rights: Quest for a Sword.*

[30] Sherwood Eddy to Roger Baldwin, April 15, 1936, ACLU, Vol. 925. Eddy wrote to Baldwin after a visit to Arkansas: "I never met such conditions of lawlessness, such menace of violence and of terror, such possibility of a race war . . . during all my years in India and China as I found in these Southern states." Eddy "took the matter up" with Cummings, his former classmate, but to no avail. See also Cummings to Norman Thomas, June 23, 1934, Norman Thomas Papers, Box 11, regarding federal nonintervention in the Imperial Valley.

[31] Russell Porter, "Our No. 1 Trouble-Shooter," *New York Times,* April 16, 1939.

who knew "that law is at root an instrument for the achievement of social goals." [32]

The record of the La Follette Committee was well known to Murphy and may have served as a model for him. During negotiations between UAW representatives and General Motors, he had confronted company officials with the committee's espionage findings. He cited its work in a number of gubernatorial addresses, returning always to the theme that private property must serve the higher purposes of social justice and human fulfillment. Murphy stated his own goal and credo: "a zealous regard for the preservation of liberty in every crisis, [so that] human life will have its proper security and dignity." [33]

"The weight of the Department of Justice," Murphy said shortly after his appointment to Roosevelt's cabinet, "ought to be active, alert and defensive of civil liberties in this country." He instructed a Justice Department lawyer to study the Reconstruction civil rights statutes "to determine whether the Department of Justice should have a unit of administration to preserve civil liberties, to determine the effect of these statutes under modern conditions in local communities." Murphy's diligence, the *New York Times* stated, "is an assurance that henceforth the right of citizens to meet and express opinions, however unpopular, will be consistently defended by the Federal Government." [34] The attorney general's Order No. 3204 evinced Murphy's commitment to civil liberties; it also marked a milestone in the transition from federal apathy to federal concern for the Bill of Rights—a transition to which the La Follette Committee made a significant contribution.

A United Press release on February 3, 1939, declared, "Establishment of a permanent civil liberties bureau was in line with suggestions by members of the Senate Civil Liberties Committee." Murphy told reporters that he planned to confer with La Follette about the establishment of the unit.[35] "In the aftermath of our Civil Liberties investigations and as a result of our work and our findings," Elbert Thomas wrote,

[32] J. Woodford Howard, Jr., "Frank Murphy: A Liberal's Creed" (unpublished doctoral dissertation), pp. 149–157; John P. Roche, "The Utopian Pilgrimage of Mr. Justice Murphy," *Vanderbilt Law Review*, X (February 1957), 393–394; Richard D. Lunt, "The High Ministry of Government: The Political Career of Frank Murphy" (unpublished doctoral dissertation), pp. 264–269, 290, 292, 312, 314.

[33] St. Louis *Post-Dispatch*, July 21, 1939; *Selected Addresses of Frank Murphy, Governor of Michigan, January 1, 1937, to September 30, 1938*, pp. 20, 29, 44–45, 67.

[34] *Progressive*, February 4, 1939; *New York Times*, January 26, 1939.

[35] United Press clipping in ACLU, Vol. 2068; *New York Times*, February 3, 1939; *Progressive*, February 4, 1939.

"Frank Murphy . . . organized a Civil Liberties unit in the Justice Department." [36] During its first months the unit appeared eager to continue the work begun by the La Follette Committee. Every week the Justice Department received several hundred complaints, the majority of which described allegedly illegal acts committed by employers in labor disputes. Department officials expected to spend considerable time investigating complaints that rights guaranteed by the Wagner Act had been denied, even after the NLRB had issued cease-and-desist orders. O. John Rogge, a Justice Department attorney, told a committee of the American Bar Association: "One of the types of situation which the . . . unit will watch closely concerns labor. We propose to enforce the 1870 law to the fullest extent, and to the end that labor may organize and secure the power of collective bargaining and all other rights. . . ." [37]

"These are great days for civil liberties," proclaimed *Unity Magazine* in March 1939. "When the government itself actually undertakes the job of protecting the rights of the people, something is happening." [38] Attorney General Murphy hammered persistently at the theme of federal responsibility for enforcing federal rights. "The Federal Government today is determined . . . to protect civil liberties by all means available to it," he said. "Until public opinion *does* reach the point where it will not tolerate violation of civil liberties," he told a New York audience, "there can and will be violation—*unless government takes a hand and refuses to permit it.*" [39] Reviewing his first six months in office, Murphy informed President Roosevelt: ". . . for the first time in our history the full weight of the Department will be thrown behind the effort to preserve in this country the blessings of liberty, the spirit of tolerance, and the fundamental principles of democracy." Murphy proudly acknowledged that this "is one of the most significant happenings in American legal history." [40]

[36] Thomas to Mark Anderson, October 17, 1939, Thomas Papers, "Civil Liberties," Box 17. But see Carr, *Federal Protection of Civil Rights:* ". . . there is no evidence that the unit was set up at the direct request of the La Follette Committee or along lines suggested by it" (p. 28).

[37] T.R.B., "Washington Notes," *New Republic*, XCVIII (March 8, 1939), 128; A.F. of L. *Weekly News Service*, February 11, 1939; *New York Times*, July 14, 1939; *Progressive*, March 4, 1939.

[38] Quoted in *Progressive*, March 25, 1939.

[39] Address of Frank Murphy, March 27, 1939, *Congressional Record*, 76th Cong., 1st Sess., 1939, Vol. 84, Appendix, p. 1196; Frank Murphy, "Civil Liberties and the Cities," *Vital Speeches*, V (June 15, 1939), 544.

[40] Murphy to FDR, July 7, 1939, FDRL, OF 2111. In this report Murphy stressed the Justice Department's interest in protecting "the civil liberties of the individual citizen and of minority groups. . . ." This statement approximates the distinction be-

The attorney general's Order No. 3204 officially rejected the Jeffersonian creed of American civil libertarians. The Depression and the New Deal, however, had already precipitated a reappraisal of the relationship between the federal government and liberty. Libertarians ceased to measure liberty by governmental self-restraint; private incursions on individual rights, they came to realize, required more, not less, government intervention. "The history of liberty," Woodrow Wilson had said in 1912, "is the history of the limitation of governmental power. . . ." The New Deal wrote a new chapter to that history: the constructive use of governmental power to extend the benefits of the Bill of Rights to millions of citizens.[41]

Years before the New Deal some libertarians had anticipated, or at least hoped for, this development. In 1928 Horace M. Kallen wrote, "In the decade since the world has been made safe for democracy, it seems to have been made very unsafe for freedom." Noting that nineteenth-century liberalism prescribed little and forbade much, Kallen suggested that freedom be defined as "a positive, intrinsic quality. . . ." Zechariah Chafee, Jr., asked for more than the adjustment of "negative forces which restrain liberty. We should also consider the development of positive forces which will encourage it. . . ." And John Dewey insisted upon "positive and constructive changes in social arrangements" to hasten the attainment of freedom.[42]

The Depression years intensified these pleas and made alternatives to traditional libertarian dogma more palatable. Libertarians reacted sharply to the "freedom from . . ." approach espoused by those seeking to escape New Deal regulation. They demanded "freedom to . . ."; the state should not only provide social and job security, but should protect the right of an individual to act on his own behalf by safeguarding the liberties on

----

tween civil liberties and civil rights that has been observed in the present volume. Murphy, however, occasionally used these terms interchangeably. In June 1941 Victor Rotnem became chief of the Civil Liberties Unit and asked that its name be changed to the "Civil Rights Section." Rotnem, according to Carr, wished to avoid confusion between the Civil Liberties Unit and the American Civil Liberties Union. Rotnem also believed that "civil rights" suggested less radical activities than "civil liberties" (Carr, *Federal Protection of Civil Rights*, p. 24).

[41] See Merrill D. Peterson, *The Jefferson Image in the American Mind*, pp. 330, 344; Oscar and Mary Handlin, *The Dimensions of Liberty*, pp. 14–22; Leonard W. Levy, *Jefferson and Civil Liberties*. Before the New Deal only nineteenth-century abolitionists had consistently linked protection of civil liberties to the expansion of federal power.

[42] Horace M. Kallen, "Why Freedom Is A Problem," *Freedom in the Modern World*, ed. Horace M. Kallen, pp. 1–2, 22; Zechariah Chafee, Jr., "Liberty and Law," *ibid.*, p. 113; John Dewey, "Philosophies of Freedom," *ibid.*, p. 250.

which such action depended. Dewey argued that the "only hope for liberalism" was the realization that social control "is necessary in order to render secure the liberties of the individual, including civil liberties." [43] Other observers advised liberals to shed their outworn concepts of freedom and pay attention to antilibertarian forces more dangerous than government power. "While we have been so busy defending a traditional . . . concept of freedom from governmental control," wrote a professor of social science, "we have succumbed to the restrictive efforts of nongovernmental forces possessing power more effective and more dangerous to most of us than the authority of the state." He suggested, "Perhaps it is time to think of civil liberty as protection *by* the state rather than protection *against* the state." [44] Americans had been content "to build up sanctions against the deprivation of civil liberties by the public power of the state," declared a contributor to the *Yale Law Journal*. But, he continued, "we have given little thought . . . to the importance of providing sanctions against the use of the private power of the employer to the same end." [45]

The New Deal years witnessed the first explicit recognition by the federal government that traditional definitions of liberty were inadequate in a modern industrial society. If nonintervention by government meant liberty, in the nineteenth-century sense of the word, it also had come to mean unlimited opportunity for private power to destroy liberty. The Roosevelt administration circumscribed this opportunity and simultaneously enlarged the bounds of liberty. The federal government discovered that the Bill of Rights, the shield protecting individual rights against government encroachment, required a complementary weapon: the sword of federal intervention to restrain local governments and local majorities.[46] "Collectivist liberalism," in the words of one analyst, replaced "individualist liberalism." [47]

[43] John Dewey, "Liberalism and Civil Liberties," *Social Frontier*, II (February 1936), 138.

[44] Frederic Heimberger, "Our Outworn Civil Liberties," *Christian Century*, LIII (April 22, 1936), 599–600.

[45] T. Richard Witmer, "Civil Liberties and the Trade Union," *Yale Law Journal*, L (February 1941), 622.

[46] Hans J. Morgenthau, "The Dilemmas of Freedom," *The Essentials of Freedom*, ed. Raymond English, p. 137. The shield-sword metaphor was used by Mr. Justice Robert H. Jackson in *Pollock* v. *Williams*, 322 U.S. 4, 8 (1944); Robert K. Carr, *Federal Protection of Civil Rights*, pp. 5–7, and "Civil Rights in America," *Annals of the American Academy of Political and Social Science*, CCLXXV (May 1951), viii.

[47] Harry W. Jones, "Freedom and Opportunity as Competing Social Values: Mill's Liberty and Ours," *Liberty*, ed. Carl J. Friedrich, pp. 234–235, 241.

During the New Deal federal intervention to safeguard liberty was less an articulated policy than a series of improvised responses to specific needs. But institutional innovations—such as the National Labor Relations Board, the La Follette Committee, and the Civil Liberties Unit of the Justice Department—indisputably made the Bill of Rights the concern of the federal government. Civil liberties, once privileges granted by a community to its members, became rights enforceable against local majorities.[48] By assuming responsibility for protecting civil liberties, the federal government *made* certain rights inalienable, empirically rather than metaphysically.[49]

Civil libertarians, caught off balance by the constructive exercise of federal power, quickly regained their equilibrium and savored their many noteworthy gains. "I did not appreciate," Roger Baldwin recalled, "how much further the New Dealers were prepared to go than we in federalizing the protection of civil rights." During the New Deal, he acknowledged, the American Civil Liberties Union "basked in the light of understanding as never before." Roosevelt and his cabinet, Baldwin said, "were civil liberty minded. . . . Access to the President was simple; his secretaries were of our persuasion." Roosevelt's smashing victory in 1936 marked the beginning of "a new chapter in the story of civil liberties in this country," wrote ACLU secretary Lucille Milner. "The next few years from the liberals' viewpoint [were] the most glowing in our history."[50] Civil libertarians took their cue from the federal government and accepted federal power as the keystone of a new libertarian creed.

The link between the reorientation of government and of libertarians was the labor movement. "It was when labor sought to exercise its 'right' to organize or strike," wrote NLRB attorney Joseph Rosenfarb, "that the most fruitful soil was prepared for the wholesale violation of our civil liberties." The need to protect labor's right to organize thrust the federal government into the civil liberties domain. The Wagner Act, perhaps the single most important civil liberties statute ever passed by Congress, extended, in theory at least, the guarantees of the First Amendment to American workers who had grown accustomed to enjoying their

---

[48] John P. Roche, "The Curbing of the Militant Majority," *Reporter*, XXIX (July 18, 1963), 38. See Roche, *The Quest for the Dream, passim,* and "Civil Liberty in the Age of Enterprise," *University of Chicago Law Review*, XXXI (Fall 1963), 103–105.

[49] Christian Bay, *The Structure of Freedom*, p. 76.

[50] Roger Baldwin, COHC, pp. 182, 197; Lucille Milner, *Education of an American Liberal*, p. 242.

civil liberties on the sufferance of their employers. That statute, a California state senator told the La Follette Committee, "is the greatest gain for civil liberties since Thomas Jefferson and the Democrats of his day forced adoption of the Bill of Rights as an essential part of the Constitution." The National Labor Relations Act, Roger Baldwin believed, stood as the New Deal's "major achievement" in the protection of civil liberties. And the *Jones & Laughlin* decision which upheld it, more than any other Supreme Court decision in Baldwin's experience, "affected civil liberties in the one major area where they had been most grossly violated." [51]

The Wagner Act stretched the First Amendment by extending its sanctions and by expanding the scope of its free-speech clause. Advocacy of unionism, previously consigned to the mercy of local statutes and community tolerance, now enjoyed an ample measure of constitutional protection. Significantly, the Wagner Act applied First Amendment prohibitions to private persons. It prohibited *employers* from abridging their workers' freedom of speech. "It was by proceeding against the very source of anti-unionism," wrote Joseph Rosenfarb, "that the Act and the Board were able to liberate whole communities from the feudal control of the dominant economic interest." As a result, he concluded in 1945, "the incidence of violations of civil liberties is much less now than ... before the Act was adopted." [52]

No accurate appraisal of the status of civil liberties in the United States, argued the International Juridical Association in 1938, "can fail to recognize the decisive role played in their defense" by the Wagner Act and the National Labor Relations Board. The rights to organize and to bargain collectively, embracing the freedoms of speech, press, and assembly, had been "crystallized as fundamental liberties. . . ." [53] NLRB chairman Madden often stressed the same point; the "most significant result" of the Wagner Act, he said, "is that it has created a new and important civil liberty and has given new vitality to

[51] Joseph Rosenfarb, "Protection of Basic Rights," *The Wagner Act*, ed. Silverberg, p. 93; *Hearings*, Pt. 60, p. 21952; Baldwin, COHC, pp. 176, 201.

[52] Rosenfarb, "Protection of Basic Rights," p. 93. See also Bowden, "Freedom for Wage Earners," *Annals of the American Academy of Political and Social Science*, CC (November 1938), 185–209. Beyond the scope of this volume, but worth noting, is the fact that the Wagner Act, in practice, did much to curtail the freedom of speech of employers.

[53] "NLRB And Free Speech," reprinted in American Association for Economic Freedom, *Problems of the National Labor Relations Board*, p. 28.

the old civil liberties." Administration of the act, Madden believed, brought civil liberties to many communities for the first time. "When the principal employers in such communities have begun to obey the . . . Act and to keep their hands out of the union question," Madden stated, "the other civil liberties problems largely disappear." [54]

Characterization of the La Follette Committee as a "civil liberties" committee, and its focus on interference with labor's rights, also indicate the conjunction of labor's liberty and civil liberty during the New Deal. The committee's enabling resolution permitted scrutiny of a number of civil liberties issues; had any of them constituted as urgent a problem as did civil liberties infractions in labor relations, it is likely that the La Follette Committee would have pursued them. Its perpetually precarious existence and its instinct for self-preservation required it to respond to the most flagrant civil liberties violations. By 1940, after it had spent four years exposing antilibertarian practices in labor disputes, the wisdom of its choice was obvious.

The labor movement was also the vehicle for the reorientation of civil libertarians toward the federal government. The predecessor of the American Civil Liberties Union was born in protest against the exercise of federal power. Until 1935 the ACLU, which had adopted labor unionization as its primary civil libertarian crusade after World War I, distrusted the federal government. Confronted by the Wagner bill, however, it had to sacrifice either its allegiance to unionization or its distrust of the state; with federal power looming as the workers' major resource, the ACLU could not have it both ways. Its acceptance of the federal government as protector of civil liberties in labor relations paved the way for similiar acquiescence in other areas. For the past thirty years, in fact, defenders of civil liberties and civil rights have looked to Washington when local majorities have seemed indifferent to the guarantees of the First and Fourteenth Amendments.[55]

[54] Quoted in D. O. Bowman, *Public Control of Labor Relations*, p. 445; "NLRB and Free Speech," p. 29; "Symposium on Civil Liberties," *American Law School Review*, IX (April 1941), 897; *C.I.O. News*, July 16, 1938, calling the Wagner Act "the charter of civil liberties under which labor has been declared free to help itself . . ."; *Hearings*, Pt. 60, pp. 22062-63; Philip B. Willauer, "Civil Rights in Labor-Management Relations: A Management Viewpoint," *Annals of the American Academy of Political and Social Science*, CCLXXV (May 1951), 140-147. Willauer wrote: "The basic right through which the concept of civil liberty must find expression and application in our industrial system is the right of workers to bargain collectively with their employers" (p. 141).

[55] This is not to argue that the exercise of federal power is *ipso facto* beneficial to liberty. Of course it is not; in fact, as the Smith and McCarran Acts and various

The libertarian-labor alliance, however, had pitfalls as well as promises. The most dangerous was the tendency for civil liberties to be subsumed in the labor crusade, stripped of their identity, and manipulated for selfish purposes. The American Civil Liberties Union argued, for example, that the circumstances of industrial conflict forced it to champion the civil liberties of labor. But a convincing argument can also be made in support of the proposition that the sympathies of ACLU members for unionism conditioned their approach to civil liberties issues. "The one hope for a better world," Lucille Milner believed, "lay in strengthening organized labor. . . ." Some ACLU members, Arthur Garfield Hays recorded, "regarded free speech as merely a means toward a better social or economic end as against others of us who felt that the right of self-expression is an end in itself. . . ." [56]

The primary commitment of some ACLU members to labor organization created serious problems of allegiance that were not easily resolved. At the union's annual dinner in 1936, chairman Dr. Harry F. Ward declared that "the struggle for civil rights is entering a new phase. The question now is whether these rights may be used to accomplish fundamental social change without violence. In other words, the fight is to use these rights as tools for peaceful political evolution." For a time Roger Baldwin held similar notions. A few years earlier he had written: "Civil liberties, like democracy, are useful only as tools for social change." It was once said of Baldwin that when he invoked the Constitution and the Declaration of Independence, "it is because they are weapons conveniently left available by a dominating class. . . ." [57]

Sympathy for labor's liberty at the expense of civil liberties occasionally led the ACLU into embarrassing quandaries. During 1937–1938, for example, union members agonized over an NLRB directive to Henry Ford ordering him to cease cautioning his employees not to join the UAW. A special committee was appointed to determine whether the directive infringed Ford's freedom of speech. "The idea of the

government loyalty orders plainly show, federal power has continued to jeopardize civil liberties. Since World War II, in civil *rights* issues federal power has been exercised consistently on behalf of liberty; in civil *liberties* issues, involving the expression of individuals, the exercise of federal power has once again disturbed civil libertarians.

[56] Milner, *Education*, p. 92; Arthur Garfield Hays, *City Lawyer*, pp. 229–230.

[57] Copy of Ward speech, ACLU, Vol. 863; Roger Baldwin to Editor, *New York Times*, April 8, 1933, in *New York Times*, April 11, 1933; R. L. Duffus in *American Mercury*, quoted in Dwight Macdonald, "Profiles: The Defense of Everybody," *New Yorker*, XXIX (July 11, 1953), 31.

Civil Liberties Union collaborating with labor's enemy," wrote Lucille Milner, "was unthinkable to many on the Board." The ACLU avoided both horns of its dilemma by deciding that the directive left the status of Ford's freedom in doubt. Miss Milner, for one, was deeply disturbed. "Had something gone wrong with the old Civil Liberties Union, I asked myself. For nearly twenty years . . . the Union had championed the rights of labor . . . . Now a change was taking place. . . ." [58]

By no means all of the ACLU leaders shared the class consciousness of the Ward-Baldwin-Milner approach. The ACLU's vacillation on principles made Dr. John Haynes Holmes afraid "that little by little, step by step, almost without our realizing it, under the impact of our real sympathy for labor's cause, we are allowing ourselves to become mere advocates of the rights of labor to the denial of those rights as exercised by those who are against labor." Dr. Holmes warned of those "who are not fundamentally interested in civil liberties at all, but only in the question as to how the advocacy of civil liberties may now be used for the benefit of labor in the current struggle. . . . More reluctantly than I dare to confess, I find myself believing that our enemies have good reason for charging us with being partisan in the labor struggle, and using the civil liberties principle as a means of fighting labor's battles and the cause of radicalism generally." [59]

Dr. Holmes, deeply involved in an internecine struggle—one that, in another guise, would tear the ACLU apart in 1940—did not overstate his case; he may, however, have exaggerated its implications. Throughout American history the "civil liberties principle" had achieved maximum power when it merged with issues of immediate political consequence. Temporarily disadvantaged individuals had traditionally used "civil liberty" as an instrument to increase their power and realize their social and political objectives. Libertarian principles were invariably strengthened as a result of their efforts.

In colonial New York, for example, the Assembly favored freedom of the press as "a useful instrument for the expansion of legislative prerogative. . . ." In the battle over constitutional ratification, Antifederalists "used the issue of a bill of rights as a smokescreen for those objections to the Constitution that could not be dramatically popularized." Abandon-

[58] Milner, *Education*, pp. 252–255.
[59] Holmes to Dr. Harry F. Ward, February 8, 1938, ACLU, Vol. 1080. "We are interested in labor at the expense of liberty—and that's not our business!," Dr. Holmes stated on October 26, 1939 (ACLU, Vol. 2063).

ment of the Blackstonian concept of seditious libel, after the Alien and Sedition Acts, in favor of the principle of free political expression, represented "an expediency of self-defense on the part of a besieged political minority struggling to maintain its existence and right to function unfettered." [60] Nineteenth-century abolitionists learned to temper their moral intransigence with political opportunism; they found that abolitionism "must be linked with other, more material issues to reach its full political strength." [61] In sum, advocacy of civil liberties was often grounded in the quest for political advantage or in the desire to hasten social change.

Libertarian instrumentalism was particularly characteristic of the New Deal years, when civil liberties were used repeatedly in efforts to forge a new industrial society. Despite this blend of instrumentalism and idealism, or perhaps because of it, the New Deal left a glowing civil liberties record, which has not received the plaudits it deserves. This oversight is perhaps attributable to a reluctance to accept the major civil liberties issues of the 1930's as "genuine." Superficially, labor organization and civil liberties may seem unrelated. But any evaluation of the New Deal's civil liberties accomplishments must adhere to the New Deal's own definition of civil liberties issues. [62]

During the 1930's, John P. Roche has written, "the United States left the paths of tribalism for the high road of due process of law and substantive justice and equality. . . . [By 1940] civil liberties and minority rights had become part of American public policy." [63] The Supreme Court read provisions of the Bill of Rights into the Fourteenth Amendment; it overruled convictions in state courts that violated fundamental liberties; and it brought state criminal proceedings under federal scrutiny. Mr. Justice Cardozo, for the Court, held that the due process clause of the Fourteenth Amendment included not only First Amendment freedoms but also those other features of the Bill of Rights which are "of the very essence of a scheme of ordered liberty." [64] By the eve of

[60] Leonard W. Levy, *Legacy of Suppression*, pp. 49, 227, and *Jefferson and Civil Liberties*, p. 55.

[61] Richard Hofstadter, *The American Political Tradition*, p. 149.

[62] Failure to distinguish between civil liberties and civil rights blurs New Deal achievements in safeguarding the former. Civil rights, on the other hand, were subsumed in the economic recovery program. See Richard P. Longaker, *The Presidency and Individual Liberties*, pp. 8–9.

[63] Roche, *The Quest for the Dream*, pp. 134, 183.

[64] Roche, *The Quest for the Dream*, pp. 145–150; *Palko* v. *Connecticut*, 302 U.S. 319 (1937). Most significantly for labor's civil liberties, the Court brought picketing

World War II the federal government's commitment to the principle of protecting civil liberties seemed irrevocable.

This commitment is easier to document than to explain. Roche suggests the growth of "civil liberty elites" among important leadership groups in the United States; in particular, "we can see the Washington lawyer of the New Deal period as a force for regularized, impartial procedures which incorporated a new attitude toward civil liberty." [65] The La Follette Committee's reports and Frank Murphy's speeches indicate that the antilibertarian abuse of centralized power by Fascist nations strengthened the determination of some Americans to make their government responsible for protecting, rather than destroying, liberty. But the *sine qua non* of legislative and executive concern for civil liberties seems to have been the expansion of power to meet the economic crisis.[66] Once the New Deal made unionization the cornerstone of national labor policy and fostered labor organization as a recovery measure, sensitivity to civil liberties in labor relations was mandatory. Frank Murphy sought to extend this federal commitment to the entire Bill of Rights, for the benefit of all Americans. Depression problems made the exercise of federal power fashionable; the Bill of Rights was the residual beneficiary.

The La Follette Civil Liberties Committee made weighty contributions to libertarian instrumentalism and to the shift in attitude toward government and liberty. Its service to the cause of labor organization strengthened, rather than weakened, its contribution to safeguarding civil liberty. And, although it was originally a manifestation of concern for the American industrial worker, it came to justify a nascent governmental concern for the liberties of all Americans.

Yet, in regard to the status of civil liberties in an industrial society, the La Follette inquiry raised many more disturbing questions than it resolved. Its findings offered slight solace to civil libertarians. For four years it demonstrated that if civil liberties received their strongest defense from those who sought power, they were most flagrantly violated by those who held power. During periods of stress and dislocation any

---

within the free speech provision of the First Amendment. See *Senn* v. *Tile Layers Protective Union*, 301 U.S. 468 (1937); *Thornhill* v. *Alabama*, 310 U.S. 88 (1940); *Carlson* v. *California*, 310 U.S. 106 (1940).

[65] John P. Roche, "American Liberty: An Examination of the 'Tradition' of Freedom," *Aspects of Liberty*, ed. Milton R. Konvitz and Clinton Rossiter, pp. 157–158.

[66] *Progressive*, April 29, 1939.

latent commitment to the Bill of Rights seemed to disappear when confronted by competing demands. Americans may in fact be deeply committed to "civil liberties," but they frequently define that concept extremely narrowly at just the moment when those liberties most desperately need defending. Individual rights, notwithstanding the provisions of the First and Fourteenth Amendments, tend all too often to yield to community "needs."

The La Follette Committee left unresolved the problem of protecting the civil liberties of individuals for whom the government is not politically obligated to show concern. It reached no final decision regarding the boundary line between competing claims for liberty. Nor did its record inspire optimism for the fate of civil liberties in the absence of a national crisis that kindles interest in their preservation. The committee underscored a national paradox: American citizens had once restrained the power of their government in order to preserve liberty, but they themselves became in turn the most serious menace to liberty. Consequently, government emerged as liberty's most vigilant and reliable defender. In one of its final reports the La Follette Committee concluded: "It is now taken for granted that the public interest is so great in the preservation of civil rights that the Government, and the strongest governmental power available, should intervene to protect them." [67] In its statement the committee proclaimed a challenge no less than an achievement.

[67] *Employers' Associations*, Report No. 1150, Pt. 1, p. 57.

Bibliography

MANUSCRIPT COLLECTIONS

AGRICULTURAL ADJUSTMENT ADMINISTRATION PAPERS. National Archives.
WILL ALEXANDER MEMOIR. Oral History Collection, Columbia University.
AMERICAN CIVIL LIBERTIES UNION PAPERS. Princeton University.
ROGER BALDWIN MEMOIR. Oral History Collection, Columbia University.
JOHN BROPHY MEMOIR. Oral History Collection, Columbia University.
JOHN BROPHY PAPERS. Catholic University of America.
JOHN CARMODY MEMOIR. Oral History Collection, Columbia University.
C.I.O. PAPERS. Catholic University of America.
NICK DiGAETANO COLLECTION. Wayne State University Labor History Archives.
JOHN EDELMAN PAPERS. Wayne State University Labor History Archives.
THOMAS I. EMERSON MEMOIR. Oral History Collection, Columbia University.
CHARLES FAHY MEMOIR. Oral History Collection, Columbia University.
FEDERAL COUNCIL OF CHURCHES INDUSTRIAL DEPARTMENT PAPERS. Federal Council Archives, New York.
RICHARD FRANKENSTEEN PAPERS. Wayne State University Labor History Archives.
JOHN P. FREY MEMOIR. Oral History Collection, Columbia University.
JOHN P. FREY PAPERS. Library of Congress.
WILLIAM GREEN PAPERS. State Historical Society, Madison, Wisconsin.
CARL HAESSLER PAPERS. Wayne State University Labor History Archives.
GARDNER JACKSON MEMOIR. Oral History Collection, Columbia University.
LABADIE COLLECTION. University of Michigan.
LA FOLLETTE CIVIL LIBERTIES COMMITTEE PAPERS. National Archives.
BENJAMIN C. MARSH PAPERS. Library of Congress.
HARRY L. MITCHELL MEMOIR. Oral History Collection, Columbia University.
PHILIP MURRAY PAPERS. Catholic University of America.
NATIONAL LABOR RELATIONS BOARD CASE FILES. National Archives.
JOHN C. NICHOLS PAPERS. Division of Manuscripts, University of Oklahoma.
PRESIDENTS' FILE. University of Wisconsin.
LEE PRESSMAN MEMOIR. Oral History Collection, Columbia University.
VICTOR REUTHER PAPERS. Wayne State University Labor History Archives.
FRANKLIN D. ROOSEVELT PAPERS. Hyde Park.
SECRETARIES OF LABOR PAPERS. National Archives.
BORIS SHISHKIN MEMOIR. Oral History Collection, Columbia University.
SOCIALIST PARTY PAPERS. Duke University.
SOUTHERN TENANT FARMERS UNION PAPERS. Southern Historical Collection, University of North Carolina.

ELBERT D. THOMAS PAPERS. Hyde Park.
NORMAN THOMAS MEMOIR. Oral History Collection, Columbia University.
NORMAN THOMAS PAPERS. New York Public Library.
ROBERT F. WAGNER PAPERS. Georgetown University.
ROBERT WOHLFORTH PAPERS. In possession of Mr. Wohlforth.
WORKERS DEFENSE LEAGUE PAPERS. New York City.

UNPUBLISHED MATERIAL

ADAMS, GRAHAM, JR. "Age of Industrial Violence: Social Conflict on the Eve of the First World War as Revealed by the United States Commission on Industrial Relations." Doctoral dissertation, Columbia University, 1962.

BARBASH, JACK. "Employer Attitudes and Methods in Industrial Disputes." Master's thesis, New York University, 1937.

CLEVELAND, ALFRED S. "Some Political Aspects of Organized Industry." Doctoral dissertation, Harvard University, 1946.

CONRAD, DAVID EUGENE. "The Forgotten Farmers: The AAA and the Southern Tenants, 1933–36." Doctoral dissertation, University of Oklahoma, 1962.

GRUBBS, DONALD H. "The Southern Tenant Farmers Union and the New Deal." Doctoral dissertation, University of Florida, 1963.

HARBISON, FREDERICK H. "Labor Relations in the Iron and Steel Industry, 1936 to 1939." Doctoral dissertation, Princeton University, 1940.

HOWARD, J. WOODFORD, JR. "Frank Murphy: A Liberal's Creed." Doctoral dissertation, Princeton University, 1959.

HURD, WALTER C. "The Labor and Industrial Program of the Federal Council of Churches, 1932–1940." Master's thesis, Columbia University, 1954.

JOHNSON, DONALD. "The American Civil Liberties Union: Origins, 1914–1924." Doctoral dissertation, Columbia University, 1960.

LEOTTA, LOUIS, JR. "Republic Steel Corporation in the Steel Strike of 1937." Master's thesis, Columbia University, 1960.

LUNT, RICHARD D. "The High Ministry of Government: The Political Career of Frank Murphy." Doctoral dissertation, University of New Mexico, 1962.

RALSTON, CRAIG. "The La Follette Dynasty." Manuscript, Legislative Reference Library, Madison, Wisconsin.

RIKER, WILLIAM H. "The CIO in Politics, 1936–1946." Doctoral dissertation, Harvard University, 1948.

SOFCHALK, DONALD G. "The Little Steel Strike of 1937." Doctoral dissertation, The Ohio State University, 1961.

PUBLIC DOCUMENTS

REPORT OF THE PRESIDENT'S COMMITTEE. *Farm Tenancy*. Washington, D.C.: Government Printing Office, 1937.

U.S. COMMISSION ON INDUSTRIAL RELATIONS. *Final Report of the Commission on Industrial Relations*. Washington, D.C.: Government Printing Office, 1916.

————. *Final Report and Testimony Submitted to Congress by the Commission on Industrial Relations*. Document No. 415. 64th Cong., 1st Sess., 1916.

U.S. *Congressional Record*. Vols. LXXX-XC.

U.S. HOUSE OF REPRESENTATIVES. *Hearings Before the Special Committee to Investigate the National Labor Relations Board*. Vols. XIII, XX, XXI, XXIV. 76th Cong., 3d Sess., 1940.

U.S. HOUSE OF REPRESENTATIVES. COMMITTEE ON UN-AMERICAN ACTIVITIES. *Hearings on Methods of Communist Infiltration in the United States Government*. 82nd Cong., 2d Sess., 1952.

————. *Hearings Regarding Communism in the United States Government*. Vol. IV. 81st Cong., 2d Sess., 1950.

————. *Hearings Regarding Communist Espionage in the United States Government*. 80th Cong., 2d Sess., 1948.

U.S. HOUSE OF REPRESENTATIVES. SPECIAL COMMITTEE ON UN-AMERICAN ACTIVITIES. *Hearings, Investigation of Un-American Propaganda Activities in the United States*. 75–76th Congs., 1938–1939.

U. S. NATIONAL LABOR RELATIONS BOARD. *Decisions and Orders*. Vol. I. Washington, D.C.: Government Printing Office, 1936.

————. *First Annual Report*. Washington, D.C.: Government Printing Office, 1936.

————. *Second Annual Report*. Washington, D.C.: Government Printing Office, 1937.

U. S. SENATE. COMMITTEE ON EDUCATION AND LABOR. *The Chicago Memorial Day Incident*. Report No. 46., Part 2. 75th Cong., 1st Sess., 1937.

————. *Employers' Associations and Collective Bargaining in California*. Report No. 1150, Parts 1–4. 77th Cong., 2d Sess., 1942.

————. *Employers' Associations and Collective Bargaining in California*. Report No. 398, Parts 1–5. 78th Cong., 1st–2nd Sess., 1943–1944.

————. *Industrial Espionage*. Report No. 46, Part 3. 75th Cong., 2d Sess., 1937.

————. *Industrial Munitions*. Report No. 6, Part 3. 76th Cong., 1st Sess., 1939.

————. *Interim Report*. Report No. 46, Part 4. 75th Cong., 3d Sess., 1938.

————. *Labor Policies of Employers' Associations*. Report No. 6, Parts 4–6. 76th Cong., 1st Sess., 1939.

————. *Labor Policies of Employers' Associations*. Report No. 151. 77th Cong., 1st Sess., 1941.

————. *The "Little Steel" Strike and Citizens' Committees*. Report No. 151. 77th Cong., 1st Sess., 1941.

————. *Private Police Systems*. Report No. 6, Part 2. 76th Cong., 1st Sess., 1939.

————. *Report No. 2046*. 74th Cong., 2d Sess., 1936.

————. *Strikebreaking Services*. Report No. 6, Part 1. 76th Cong., 1st. Sess., 1939.

U. S. Senate. Committee on the Judiciary. *Hearings on Interlocking Subversion in Government Departments.* 83rd Cong., 1st Sess., 1953.

U. S. Senate. Subcommittee of the Committee on Education and Labor. *Hearings on S. 1970.* 76th Cong., 1st Sess., 1939.

———. *Hearings on S. Res. 266.* 74th Cong., 2d Sess., 1936.

———. *Hearings Pursuant to S. Res. 266, Violations of Free Speech and Rights of Labor.* Parts 1–75. 74th–76th Congs., 1936–1940.

———. *Preliminary Report Pursuant to S. Res. 266.* 75th Cong., 1st Sess., 1937.

———. *Supplementary Hearings.* Parts 1–3. 77th Cong., 1st Sess., 1941.

U. S. Senate, Subcommittee of the Committee on Labor and Public Welfare. *Report on Labor-Management Relations in the Southern Textile Industry.* 82nd Cong., 2d Sess., 1952.

U. S. Senate. Subcommittee of the Committee on the Judiciary. *Hearings to Investigate the Administration of the Internal Security Act and Other Internal Security Laws.* 82nd Cong., 2d Sess., 1952.

REPORTS

American Association for Economic Freedom. *Problems of the National Labor Relations Board.* Washington, D.C., n.d.

American Civil Liberties Union. *A Year's Fight for Free Speech.* New York, 1923.

———. *Eternal Vigilance! The Story of Civil Liberty, 1937–1938.* New York, 1938.

———. *Free Speech in 1924.* New York, 1925.

———. *How Goes the Bill of Rights? The Story of the Fight for Civil Liberty, 1935–36.* New York, 1936.

———. *In the Shadow of War: The Story of Civil Liberty, 1939–1940.* New York, 1940.

———. *Land of the Free: The Story of the Fight for Civil Liberty, 1934–35.* New York, 1935.

———. *Land of the Pilgrim's Pride, 1932–1933.* New York, 1933.

———. *Let Freedom Ring! The Story of Civil Liberty, 1936–1937.* New York, 1937.

———. *Liberty Under the New Deal: The Record for 1933–34.* New York, 1934.

———. *Sweet Land of Liberty, 1931–1932.* New York, 1932.

———. *The Bill of Rights 150 Years After: The Story of Civil Liberty, 1938–1939.* New York, 1939.

American Federation of Labor. *Report of Proceedings of the Annual Convention.* 55th–60th Conventions. 6 vols. Washington, D.C., 1935–1940.

American Liberty League. *The Labor Relations Bill.* Publication No. 27. N.p., n.d.

American Liberty League. National Lawyers Committee. *Report on the Constitutionality of the National Labor Relations Act.* Pittsburgh: Smith Brothers Co., 1935.

COMMITTEE FOR THE DEFENSE OF CIVIL RIGHTS IN TAMPA. *Tampa—Tar and Terror*. New York, 1937.

CONGRESS OF INDUSTRIAL ORGANIZATIONS. *Proceedings of the Constitutional Conventions*. 1st–3d Conventions. 3 vols. Washington, D.C., 1938–1940.

DILLING, ELIZABETH. *Dare We Oppose Red Treason?* N.p., 1937.

KAMP, JOSEPH P. *Join the C.I.O. and Help Build a Soviet America*. New Haven: Constitutional Educational League, 1937.

———. *The Hell of Herrin Rages Again*. New Haven: Constitutional Educational League, 1937.

NATIONAL COMMITTEE FOR THE DEFENSE OF POLITICAL PRISONERS. *Harlan Miners Speak*. New York: Harcourt, Brace and Co., 1932.

STATE RELIEF ADMINISTRATION OF CALIFORNIA. *Migratory Labor in California*. California, 1936.

WEINSTOCK, HARRIS. *Disturbances in the City of San Diego and the County of San Diego, California*. Report to Governor Hiram W. Johnson. Sacramento, 1912.

WEST, GEORGE P. *Report on the Colorado Strike*. Washington, D.C.: United States Commission on Industrial Relations, 1915.

WORKERS DEFENSE LEAGUE. *The Disinherited Speak*. New York, 1937.

———. *Labor, Defense and Democracy*. New York, 1941.

BOOKS

ADAMIC, LOUIS. *My America, 1928–1938*. New York, Harper & Brothers, 1938.

ALEXANDER, DONALD CRICHTON. *The Arkansas Plantation, 1920–1942*. New Haven: Yale University Press, 1943.

ALINSKY, SAUL. *John L. Lewis*. New York: G. P. Putnam's Sons, 1949.

APPEL, BENJAMIN. *The Power-House*. New York: E. P. Dutton & Co., 1939.

BALDWIN, ROGER, and CLARENCE B. RANDALL. *Civil Liberties and Industrial Conflict*. Cambridge: Harvard University Press, 1938.

BARBASH, JACK. *The Practice of Unionism*. New York: Harper & Brothers, 1956.

———(ed.). *Unions and Union Leadership*. New York: Harper & Brothers, 1959.

BARTH, ALAN. *Government by Investigation*. New York: Viking Press, 1955.

———. *The Loyalty of Free Men*. New York: Pocket Books, 1952.

BATES, ERNEST SUTHERLAND. *This Land of Liberty*. New York: Harper & Brothers, 1930.

BAY, CHRISTIAN. *The Structure of Freedom*. Palo Alto: Stanford University Press, 1958.

BEAL, FRED E. *Proletarian Journey*. New York: Hillman-Curl, 1937.

BECKER, CARL L., et al. *Safeguarding Civil Liberty Today*. Ithaca: Cornell University Press, 1945.

BELL, DANIEL (ed.). *The Radical Right*. New York: Doubleday & Co., 1963.

BERNHEIM, ALFRED L., and DOROTHY VAN DOREN (eds.). *Labor and the Government*. New York: McGraw-Hill Book Co., 1935.

BERNSTEIN, IRVING. *The Lean Years*. Boston: Houghton Mifflin Co., 1960.

————. *The New Deal Collective Bargaining Policy*. Berkeley: University of California Press, 1950.

BIDDLE, FRANCIS. *In Brief Authority*. New York: Doubleday & Co., 1962.

BLANKENHORN, HEBER. *Adventures in Propaganda*. Boston: Houghton Mifflin Co., 1919.

————. *The Strike for Union*. New York: H. W. Wilson Co., 1924.

BONNETT, CLARENCE E. *Employers' Associations in the United States: A Study of Typical Associations*. New York: Macmillan Co., 1922.

BOWMAN, D. O. *Public Control of Labor Relations*. New York: Macmillan Co., 1942.

BOYER, RICHARD O., and HERBERT M. MORAIS. *Labor's Untold Story*. New York: Cameron Associates, 1955.

BRADY, ROBERT A. *Business as a System of Power*. New York: Columbia University Press, 1943.

BRAEMAN, JOHN, ROBERT H. BREMNER, and EVERETT WALTERS (eds.). *Change and Continuity in Twentieth-Century America*. Columbus: Ohio State University Press, 1964.

BRISSENDEN, PAUL F. *The I.W.W.: A Study of American Syndicalism*. New York: Russell and Russell, 1920.

BRODY, DAVID. *Labor in Crisis: The Steel Strike of 1919*. Philadelphia: J. B. Lippincott Company, 1965.

————. *Steelworkers in America: The Nonunion Era*. Cambridge: Harvard University Press, 1960.

BROOKS, JOHN GRAHAM. *American Syndicalism: The I.W.W.* New York: Macmillian Co., 1913.

BROOKS, ROBERT R. *When Labor Organizes*. New Haven: Yale University Press, 1937.

BURKE, ROBERT E. *Olson's New Deal for California*. Berkeley: University of California Press, 1953.

BURNS, JAMES M. *Roosevelt: The Lion and the Fox*. New York: Harcourt, Brace and Co., 1956.

CALKINS, CLINCH. *Spy Overhead*. New York: Harcourt, Brace and Co., 1937.

CANTRIL, HADLEY (ed.). *Public Opinion, 1935–1946*. Princeton: Princeton University Press, 1951.

CARR, ROBERT K. *Federal Protection of Civil Rights: Quest for a Sword*. Ithaca: Cornell University Press, 1947.

————. *The House Committee on Un-American Activities*. Ithaca: Cornell University Press, 1952.

CARTER, PAUL A. *The Decline and Revival of the Social Gospel: Social and Political Liberalism in American Protestant Churches, 1920–1940*. Ithaca: Cornell University Press, 1954.

CAUGHEY, JOHN W. *Their Majesties the Mob*. Chicago: University of Chicago Press, 1948.

CHAFEE, ZECHARIAH, JR. *The Blessings of Liberty*. Philadelphia: J. B. Lippincott Co., 1954.

———. *Free Speech in the United States.* Cambridge: Harvard University Press, 1941.

CHAMBERS, CLARKE A. *California Farm Organizations.* Berkeley: University of California Press, 1952.

CHAPLIN, RALPH. *Wobbly.* Chicago: University of Chicago Press, 1948.

CLELAND, ROBERT G. *California in Our Time.* New York: Alfred A. Knopf, 1947.

COMMAGER, HENRY STEELE. *The American Mind.* New Haven: Yale University Press, 1950.

CORTNER, RICHARD C. *The Wagner Act Cases.* Knoxville: University of Tennessee Press, 1964.

CRAWFORD, KENNETH G. *The Pressure Boys.* New York: Julian Messner, 1939.

CUMMINGS, HOMER. *Liberty Under Law and Administration.* New York: Charles Scribner's Sons, 1934.

CUSHMAN, ROBERT E. *Civil Liberties in the United States.* Ithaca: Cornell University Press, 1956.

DERBER, MILTON, and EDWIN YOUNG (eds.). *Labor and the New Deal.* Madison: University of Wisconsin Press, 1957.

DETZER, DOROTHY. *Appointment on the Hill.* New York: Henry Holt and Co., 1948.

DIES, MARTIN. *Martin Dies' Story.* New York: Bookmailer, 1963.

———. *The Trojan Horse in America.* New York: Dodd, Mead & Co., 1940.

DIMOCK, MARSHALL E. *Congressional Investigating Committees.* Baltimore: The Johns Hopkins Press, 1929.

DOAN, EDWARD N. *The La Follettes and the Wisconsin Idea.* New York: Rinehart & Co., 1947.

DOWELL, ELDRIDGE FOSTER. *A History of Criminal Syndicalism Legislation in the United States.* "Johns Hopkins University Studies in Historical and Political Science," Series LVII. Baltimore: The Johns Hopkins Press, 1939.

DREISER, THEODORE (ed.). *Harlan Miners Speak.* New York: Harcourt, Brace and Co., 1932.

DULLES, FOSTER RHEA. *Labor in America.* New York: Thomas Y. Crowell Co., 1960.

DYKEMAN, WILMA, and JAMES STOKELY. *Seeds of Southern Change: The Life of Will Alexander.* Chicago: University of Chicago Press, 1962.

ENGLISH, RAYMOND (ed.). *The Essentials of Freedom.* Gambier, Ohio: Kenyon College, 1960.

FINE, SIDNEY. *The Automobile Under the Blue Eagle.* Ann Arbor: University of Michigan Press, 1963.

FRAENKEL, OSMOND K. *Our Civil Liberties.* New York: Viking Press, 1944.

FRANKFURTER, FELIX, and NATHAN GREENE. *The Labor Injunction.* New York: Macmillan Co., 1930.

FRIEDRICH, CARL J. (ed.). *Liberty.* New York: Atherton Press, 1962.

GALENSON, WALTER. *The CIO Challenge to the AFL.* Cambridge: Harvard University Press, 1960.

GAMBS, JOHN S. *The Decline of the I.W.W.* New York: Columbia University Press, 1932.

GINZBURG, ELI, and HYMAN BERMAN. *The American Worker in the Twentieth Century.* New York: Free Press of Glencoe, 1963.

GIRDLER, TOM M., in collaboration with BOYDEN SPARKES. *Boot Straps.* New York: Charles Scribner's Sons, 1943.

GOODELMAN, LEON. *Look at Labor.* New York: Modern Age Books, 1940.

GREGORY, CHARLES O. *Labor and the Law.* New York: W. W. Norton and Co., 1949.

HALLGREN, MAURITZ. *Landscape of Freedom.* New York: Howell, Soskin and Co., 1941.

HANDLIN, OSCAR, and MARY HANDLIN. *The Dimensions of Liberty.* Cambridge: Harvard University Press, 1961.

HARRIS, HERBERT. *Labor's Civil War.* New York: Alfred A. Knopf, 1940.

HAYS, ARTHUR GARFIELD. *City Lawyer.* New York: Simon & Schuster, 1942.

———. *Let Freedom Ring.* New York: Boni and Liveright, 1928.

———. *Trial by Prejudice.* New York: Covici, Friede, 1933.

HOFSTADTER, RICHARD. *The American Political Tradition.* New York: Vintage Books, 1955.

HOWARD, SIDNEY. *The Labor Spy.* New York: Republic Publishing Co., 1924.

HUBERMAN, LEO. *The Labor Spy Racket.* New York: Modern Age Books, 1937.

HUTCHISON, JOHN A. *We Are Not Divided.* New York: Round Table Press, 1941.

ICKES, HAROLD L. *The Inside Struggle, 1936–1939.* Volume II of *The Secret Diary of Harold L. Ickes.* New York: Simon & Schuster, 1954.

INTERCHURCH WORLD MOVEMENT. *Public Opinion and the Steel Strike.* New York: Harcourt, Brace and Co., 1921.

———. *Report on the Steel Strike of 1919.* New York: Harcourt and Howe, 1920.

JAMIESON, STUART. *Labor Unionism in American Agriculture.* U. S. Department of Labor, Bureau of Labor Statistics, Bulletin No. 836. Washington, D.C.: Government Printing Office, 1945.

JENKIN, THOMAS PAUL. *Reactions of Major Groups to Positive Government in the United States, 1930–1940.* "University of California Publications in Political Science," Vol. I. Berkeley: University of California Press, 1945.

JENSEN, VERNON H. *Heritage of Conflict.* Ithaca: Cornell University Press, 1950.

JOHNSON, CHARLES S., EDWIN R. EMBREE, and WILL W. ALEXANDER. *The Collapse of Cotton Tenancy.* Chapel Hill: University of North Carolina Press, 1935.

JOHNSON, DONALD. *The Challenge to American Freedoms.* Lexington: University of Kentucky Press, 1963.

JONES, ALFRED WINSLOW. *Life, Liberty, and Property.* Philadelphia: J. B. Lippincott Co., 1941.

KALLEN, HORACE M. (ed.). *Freedom in the Modern World.* New York: Coward-McCann, 1928.

KAMPELMAN, MAX M. *The Communist Party vs. the C.I.O.* New York: Frederick A. Praeger, 1957.

KAUPER, PAUL G. *Civil Liberties and the Constitution.* Ann Arbor: University of Michigan Press, 1962.

KEFAUVER, ESTES, and JACK LEVIN. *A Twentieth-Century Congress.* New York: Duell, Sloan and Pearce, 1947.

KELLY, ALFRED H. (ed.). *Foundations of Freedom in the American Constitution.* New York: Harper & Brothers, 1958.

KEMPTON, MURRAY. *Part of Our Time.* New York: Simon & Schuster, 1955.

KESTER, HOWARD. *Revolt Among the Sharecroppers.* New York: Covici, Friede, 1936.

KONVITZ, MILTON R., and CLINTON ROSSITER (eds.). *Aspects of Liberty.* Ithaca: Cornell University Press, 1958.

KORNHAUSER, ARTHUR, ROBERT DUBIN, and ARTHUR M. Ross (eds.). *Industrial Conflict.* New York: McGraw-Hill Book Co., 1954.

LA FOLLETTE, BELLE CASE, and FOLA LA FOLLETTE. *Robert M. La Follette.* 2 vols. New York: Macmillan Co., 1953.

LANE, ROBERT E. *The Regulation of Businessmen.* New Haven: Yale University Press, 1954.

LANGE, DOROTHEA, and PAUL S. TAYLOR. *An American Exodus.* New York: Reynal and Hitchcock, 1939.

LASKI, HAROLD J. *Liberty in the Modern State.* London: Faber & Faber, 1930.

LEIGHTON, ISABEL (ed.). *The Aspirin Age.* New York: Simon & Schuster, 1949.

LEISERSON, WILLIAM M. *Right and Wrong in Labor Relations.* Berkeley: University of California Press, 1938.

LEUCHTENBURG, WILLIAM E. *Franklin D. Roosevelt and the New Deal, 1932–1940.* New York: Harper & Row, 1963.

——. *The Perils of Prosperity, 1914–32.* Chicago: University of Chicago Press, 1958.

LEVIN, MEYER. *Citizens.* New York: Viking Press, 1940.

LEVINSON, EDWARD. *I Break Strikes!* New York: Robert M. McBride & Co., 1935.

——. *Labor on the March.* New York: Harper & Brothers, 1938.

LEVY, LEONARD W. *Jefferson and Civil Liberties.* Cambridge: Harvard University Press, 1963.

——. *Legacy of Suppression.* Cambridge: Harvard University Press, 1960.

LITWACK, LEON. *The American Labor Movement.* Englewood Cliffs, N.J.: Prentice-Hall, 1962.

LONGAKER, RICHARD P. *The Presidency and Individual Liberties.* Ithaca: Cornell University Press, 1961.

LORWIN, LEWIS L., and ARTHUR WUBNIG. *Labor Relations Boards.* Washington, D.C.; Brookings Institution, 1935.

McGEARY, M. NELSON. *The Developments of Congressional Investigative Power.* New York: Columbia University Press, 1940.

McWILLIAMS, CAREY. *Factories in the Field.* Boston: Little, Brown and Co., 1939.

————. *Ill Fares the Land*. Boston: Little, Brown and Co., 1941.

MACDONALD, LOIS. *Labor Problems and the American Scene*. New York: Harper & Brothers, 1938.

MARSH, BENJAMIN C. *Lobbyist for the People*. Washington, D.C.: Public Affairs Press, 1953.

MATTHEWS, DONALD R. *U. S. Senators and Their World*. Chapel Hill: University of North Carolina Press, 1960.

MEYER, DONALD B. *The Protestant Search for Political Realism, 1919–1941*. Berkeley: University of California Press, 1961.

MILLER, ROBERT MOATS. *American Protestantism and Social Issues, 1919–1939*. Chapel Hill: University of North Carolina Press, 1958.

MILLIS, HARRY A. (ed.). *How Collective Bargaining Works*. New York: Twentieth Century Fund, 1942.

————, and EMILY CLARK BROWN. *From the Wagner Act to Taft-Hartley*. Chicago: University of Chicago Press, 1950.

————, and ROYAL E. MONTGOMERY. *Organized Labor*. New York: McGraw-Hill Book Co., 1945.

MILNER, LUCILLE. *Education of an American Liberal*. New York: Horizon Press, 1954.

MITCHELL, BROADUS. *Depression Decade*. New York: Rinehart & Co., 1947.

MORIN, ALEXANDER. *The Organization of Farm Labor in the United States*. "Harvard Studies in Labor in Agriculture," No. 2-HL. Cambridge: Harvard University Press, 1952.

MOWRY, GEORGE E. *The California Progressives*. Chicago: Quadrangle Books, 1963.

MURRAY, ROBERT K. *Red Scare*. Minneapolis: University of Minnesota Press, 1955.

MYERS, JAMES, and HARRY W. LAIDLER. *What Do You Know About Labor?* New York: John Day Co., 1956.

MYRDAL, GUNNAR. *An American Dilemma*. Twentieth Anniversary Edition. New York: Harper & Row, 1962.

NIXON, HERMAN C. *Forty Acres and Steel Mules*. Chapel Hill: University of North Carolina Press, 1938.

NOURSE, EDWIN G., JOSEPH S. DAVIS, and JOHN D. BLACK. *Three Years of the Agricultural Adjustment Administration*. Washington, D.C.: Brookings Institution, 1937.

OAKES, EDWIN STACEY. *The Law of Organized Labor and Industrial Conflicts*. Rochester: Lawyers Cooperative Publishing Co., 1927.

OGDEN, AUGUST RAYMOND. *The Dies Committee*. Washington, D.C.: Catholic University of America Press, 1945.

OLDS, MARSHALL. *Analysis of the Interchurch World Movement Report on the Steel Strike*. New York: G. P. Putnam's Sons, 1922.

PALMER, FRANK I. *Spies in Steel: An Exposé of Industrial War*. Denver: Labor Press, 1928.

PARTON, MARY FIELD (ed.). *Autobiography of Mother Jones*. Chicago: Charles H. Kerr & Co., 1925.

PERKINS, FRANCES. *The Roosevelt I Knew.* New York: Viking Press, 1946.

PERLMAN, SELIG, and PHILIP TAFT. *History of Labor in the United States, 1896–1932.* Vol. IV of *History of Labor in the United States,* ed. JOHN R. COMMONS, 4 vols. New York: Macmillan Co., 1918–1935.

PETERSON, MERRILL D. *The Jefferson Image in the American Mind.* New York: Oxford University Press, 1960.

PINKERTON, ALLAN. *Strikers, Communists, Tramps and Detectives.* New York: G. W. Dillingham Co., 1878.

POPE, LISTON. *Millhands and Preachers.* New Haven: Yale University Press, 1942.

PRESTON, WILLIAM, JR. *Aliens and Dissenters: Federal Suppression of Radicals, 1903–1933.* Cambridge: Harvard University Press, 1963.

PRINGLE, HENRY F. *The Life and Times of William Howard Taft.* 2 vols. New York: Farrar & Rinehart, 1939.

PROTHRO, JAMES W. *Dollar Decade: Business Ideas in the 1920's.* Baton Rouge: Louisiana State University Press, 1954.

RALL, HARRIS FRANKLIN. *Religion and Public Affairs.* New York: Macmillan Co., 1937.

RAPER, ARTHUR F., and IRA DE A. REID. *Sharecroppers All.* Chapel Hill: University of North Carolina Press, 1941.

RICHARDS, HENRY I. *Cotton Under the Agricultural Adjustment Act.* Washington, D.C.: Brookings Institution, 1934.

ROCHE, JOHN P. *The Quest for the Dream.* New York: Macmillan Co., 1963.

ROOSEVELT, ELLIOTT (ed.). *The Roosevelt Letters.* Vol. III, 1928–1945. London: George G. Harrap and Co., 1952.

ROSENFARB, JOSEPH. *The National Labor Policy and How It Works.* New York: Harper & Brothers, 1940.

ROSENMAN, SAMUEL I. (comp.) *The Public Papers and Addresses of Franklin D. Roosevelt.* 13 vols. New York: Random House (Vols. I–V, X–XIII): The Macmillan Co. (Vols. VI–IX), 1938–1950.

SALTER, JOHN T. (ed.) *The American Politician.* Chapel Hill: University of North Carolina Press, 1938.

SAPOSS, DAVID J., and ELIZABETH T. BLISS. *Anti-Labor Activities in the United States.* New York: League for Industrial Democracy, 1938.

SCHLESINGER, ARTHUR M., JR. *The Age of Roosevelt.* 3 vols. (*The Crisis of the Old Order, 1919–1933; The Coming of the New Deal; The Politics of Upheaval.*) Boston: Houghton Mifflin Co., 1957, 1959, 1960.

SCHROEDER, THEODORE. *Free Speech for Radicals.* Riverside, Conn.: Hillacre Bookhouse, 1916.

SCHWARTZ, HARRY. *Seasonal Farm Labor in the United States.* New York: Columbia University Press, 1945.

SEIDMAN, JOEL. *Union Rights and Union Duties.* New York: Harcourt, Brace & Co., 1943.

Selected Addresses of Frank Murphy, Governor of Michigan, January 1, 1937 to September 30, 1938. Lansing, Michigan, 1938.

SILVERBERG, LOUIS G. (ed.). *The Wagner Act: After Ten Years.* Washington, D.C.: Bureau of National Affairs, 1945.

STEINBECK, JOHN. *The Grapes of Wrath*. New York: Viking Press, 1939.

STOLLBERG, BENJAMIN. *The Story of the CIO*. New York: Viking Press, 1938.

STOUFFER, SAMUEL A. *Communism, Conformity, and Civil Liberties: A Cross-Section of the Nation Speaks Its Mind*. New York: Doubleday & Co., 1955.

SUTTON, FRANCIS X., et al. *The American Business Creed*. Cambridge: Harvard University Press, 1956.

TAYLOR, TELFORD. *Grand Inquest*. New York: Simon & Schuster, 1955.

THOMAS, ELBERT D. *Thomas Jefferson*. New York: Modern Age Books, 1942.

THOMAS, NORMAN. *The Plight of the Share-Cropper*. New York: League for Industrial Democracy, 1934.

TIPPETT, TOM. *When Southern Labor Stirs*. New York: Jonathan Cape & Harrison Smith, 1931.

TRUMAN, DAVID B. *The Governmental Process*. New York: Alfred A. Knopf, 1957.

TUCKER, RAY, and FREDERICK R. BARKLEY. *Sons of the Wild Jackass*. Boston: L. C. Page & Co., 1932.

VANCE, RUPERT B. *Farmers Without Land*. New York: Public Affairs Committee, 1937.

VORSE, MARY HEATON. *Labor's New Millions*. New York: Modern Age Books, 1938.

WALSH, J. RAYMOND. *C.I.O.* New York: W. W. Norton & Co., 1937.

WHIPPLE, LEON. *Our Ancient Liberties*. New York: H. W. Wilson Co., 1927.

———. *The Story of Civil Liberty in the United States*. New York: Vanguard Press, 1927.

WILSON, EDMUND. *The American Earthquake*. New York: Doubleday & Co., 1958.

WILTZ, JOHN E. *In Search of Peace: The Senate Munitions Inquiry, 1934–36*. Baton Rouge: Louisiana State University Press, 1963.

WITTE, EDWIN E. *The Government in Labor Disputes*. New York: McGraw-Hill Book Co., 1932.

WOLFSKILL, GEORGE. *The Revolt of the Conservatives*. Boston: Houghton Mifflin Co., 1962.

WOLMAN, LEO. *The Growth of American Trade Unions, 1880–1923*. New York: National Bureau of Economic Research, 1924.

WOOD, CLEMENT, and MCALISTER COLEMAN, in collaboration with ARTHUR GARFIELD HAYS. *Don't Tread On Me*. New York: Vanguard Press, 1928.

ARTICLES

"Activities of National Labor Relations Board, 1936–37," *Monthly Labor Review*, XLVI (May 1938), 1144–1147.

ADAMIC, LOUIS. "Cherries Are Red in San Joaquin," *Nation*, CXLII (June 27, 1936), 840–841.

"All Clear on the Labor Front," *Business Week* (December 13, 1941), 72–73.

"All Around the Liberty Pole," *Survey Graphic*, XXV (July 1936), 426–427.

AMIDON, BEULAH. "Employers and the Spy Business," *Survey Graphic*, XXVI (May 1937), 263–266, 305–306.

ANDERSON, PAUL Y. "California's Blackshirts," *Nation*, CXLVII (August 6, 1938), 122–123.

———. "La Follette Pulls His Punches," *Nation*, CXLVII (August 20, 1938), 170.

AUERBACH, JEROLD S. "Southern Tenant Farmers: Socialist Critics of the New Deal," *Labor History*, VII (Winter 1966), 3–18.

———. "The Influence of the New Deal," *Current History*, XLVIII (June 1965), 334–339, 365.

———. "The La Follette Committee and the CIO," *Wisconsin Magazine of History*, XLVIII (Autumn 1964), 3–20.

———. "The La Follette Committee: Labor and Civil Liberties in the New Deal," *Journal of American History*, LI (December 1964), 435–459.

BALDWIN, ROGER N. "Civil Liberties: Losses and Gains," *Social Work Today*, IV (April 1937), 15–16.

BASSO, HAMILTON. "Strike-Buster: Man Among Men," *New Republic*, LXXXI (December 12, 1934), 124–126.

"The Battle for Civil Rights," *Nation*, CXLI (July 31, 1935), 116.

BELL, LAIRD. "Probes," *Atlantic Monthly*, CLX (July 1937), 23–31.

BLACK, RUBY A. "Give Me Liberty!," *Independent Woman*, XV (September 1936), 282, 302–303.

BLACK, WILSON. "The Fight Against Civil Liberties," *Social Work Today*, III (October 1935), 22–23.

BOWDEN, WITT. "Freedom for Wage Earners," *Annals of the American Academy of Political and Social Science*, CC (November 1938), 185–209.

BROWN, FRANCIS. "La Follette: Ten Years a Senator," *Current History*, XLII (August 1935), 475–480.

BURLINGAME, ROGER. "Freedom and the Lone Wolf," *Harper's Magazine*, CLXIX (June 1934), 82–90.

"Business and Senate Subpoenas," *Business Week* (July 23, 1938), 20–21.

CARR, ROBERT K. Foreword to "Civil Rights in America," *Annals of the American Academy of Political and Social Science*, CCLXXV (May 1951), vii–ix.

"Civil Rights in America," *Annals of the American Academy of Political and Social Science*, CCLXXV (May 1951), 1–154.

COEBURN, EUGENE. "The Reign of Terror in Harlan County," *Worker's Age*, VI (May 29, 1937), 3, 5.

"The Coming Open-Shop War," *Literary Digest*, LXVII (November 27, 1920) 18–19.

"The Committee Should Go On," *New Republic*, XCIV (April 27, 1938), 344.

"The Conditions of Civil Liberty," *New Republic*, LXXXII (February 27, 1935), 60–62.

"Congress and the Sit-Down Strikes," *Congressional Digest*, XVI (May 1937), 133.

"Congressional Investigations," *University of Chicago Law Review*, XVIII (Spring 1951), 421–661.

"Current Queries," *Commonweal*, XVIII (May 12, 1933), 33–34.

CUSHMAN, ROBERT E. "Civil Liberties," *Encyclopaedia of the Social Sciences*. 15 vols.; New York: Macmillan Co., 1930. Vol. III, pp. 509–513.

DANIELL, F. RAYMOND. "Behind the Conflict in 'Bloody Harlan,'" *New York Times Magazine* (June 26, 1938), 1–2, 11.

DAVENPORT, WALTER. "Fighting Blood," *Collier's*, LXXXIX (April 23, 1932), 10–11, 46–48.

DAVIS, ELMER. "The Wisconsin Brothers," *Harper's Magazine*, CLXXVIII (February 1939), 268–277.

DEWEY, JOHN. "Liberalism and Civil Liberties," *Social Frontier*, II (February 1936), 137–138.

DOUGLAS, KATHARINE. "West Coast Inquiry," *Survey Graphic*, XXIX (April 1940), 227–231, 259–61.

D.S. "Industrial Spying in Trade Unions," *Worker's Age*, VII (January 15, 1938), 7.

EGGLESTON, ARTHUR. "Industrial Farming—Preview," *Nation*, CL (January 27, 1940), 96–98.

"Employer Interference with Lawful Union Activity," *Columbia Law Review*, XXXVII (May 1937), 816–841.

"Employers and Unions," *Business Week* (April 17, 1937), 72.

ERVIN, CHARLES W. "What's Going On in Washington?," *Advance*, XXII (May 1936), 21.

FERGUSON, OTIS. "It Reads Like Fiction," *New Republic*, XCIX (May 24, 1939), 78.

"Fifteen Businessmen," *Fortune*, XVII (March 1938), 71–74.

FINE, SIDNEY. "The General Motors Sit-Down Strike: A Re-examination," *American Historical Review*, LXX (April 1965), 691–713.

"The Fink Racket," *Nation*, CXLVIII (February 11, 1939), 165–166.

"Funds for La Follette," *Nation*, CXLIX (July 15, 1939), 61.

"The Gastonia Strikers' Case," *Harvard Law Review*, XLIV (May 1931), 1118–1124.

"The G - - D - - - Labor Board," *Fortune*, XVIII (October 1938), 52–57.

"A Good Bill Gone Wrong," *New Republic*, CII (June 17, 1940), 809.

GRAUMAN, LAWRENCE, JR. "That Little Ugly Running Sore," *Filson Club Historical Quarterly*, XXXVI (October 1962), 340–354.

GREEN, WILLIAM. "The Goals of Organized Labor," *Annals of the American Academy of Political and Social Science*, CLXXXIV (March 1936), 147–153.

HACKER, ANDREW. "The Indifferent Majority," *New Leader*, XLVI (March 18, 1963), 18–21.

HEIMBERGER, FREDERIC. "Our Outworn Civil Liberties," *Christian Century*, LIII (April 22, 1936), 599–601.

HOFFSOMMER, HAROLD. "The AAA and the Cropper," *Social Forces*, XIII (May 1935), 494–502.

HOPKINS, GORDON. "The Labor Spy," *Social Action*, III (June 15, 1937), 3–31.

HUBERMAN, LEO. "$80,000,000 a Year for Labor Spies," *New Masses*, XXIII (June 8, 1937), 3–5.

HYMAN, HERBERT H., and PAUL B. SHEATSLEY. "Trends in Public Opinion on Civil Liberties," *Journal of Social Issues*, IX (1953), 6–16.

ICKES, HAROLD L. "Nations in Nightshirts," *Vital Speeches*, IV (January 1, 1938), 180–181.

"Industrial Policing and Espionage," *Harvard Law Review*, LII (March 1939), 793–804.

"Industrial Strikebreaking—The Byrnes Act," *University of Chicago Law Review*, IV (June 1937), 657–666.

"The Industrial War," *Fortune*, XVI (November 1937), 104–110, 156–179.

"It Happened in Steel," *Fortune*, XV (May 1937), 91–94, 176, 179–180.

"I Was in a Communist Unit with Hiss," *U.S. News & World Report*, XXXIV (January 9, 1953), 22–40.

"I Wonder Where We Can Go Now," *Fortune*, XIX (April 1939), 91–120.

JACKSON, ROBERT H. "The Philosophy of Big Business," *Vital Speeches*, IV (January 15, 1938), 209–210.

JOHNSON, ALVIN. "The Labor Crisis," *Yale Review*, XXVII (September 1937), 1–11.

"Kentucky Feudalism," *Time*, XXIX (May 3, 1937), 13–14.

"Labor Espionage: Summary of Senate Inquiry," *Monthly Labor Review*, XLVI (March 1938), 693–698.

"Labor Should Have Civil Rights," *American Federationist*, XLVI (July 1939), 691–692.

"The Labor Spy," *New Republic*, XCIII (January 5, 1938), 241.

"La Follette Civil Liberties Committee Investigation," *Railroad Trainman*, LIV (September 1937), 532–537.

LA FOLLETTE, ROBERT M., JR. "Labor Spy Crushes Civil Liberties," *New Leader*, XXI (March 5, 1938), 11–13.

———. "Oppression of Labor," *American Federationist*, LI (August 1944), 27–28.

———. "Turn the Light on Communism," *Collier's*, CXIX (February 8, 1947), 22, 73–74.

"La Follette's Quiz Lacks Fireworks," *Business Week* (January 13, 1940), 38–39.

LESCOHIER, D.D. "Labor's Drive to Power, 1933–1937," *Harvard Business Review*, XV (Summer 1937), 406–416.

"Let La Follette Go On!," *Nation*, CXLIV (March 6, 1937), 256.

LEVIN, MEYER. "Chicago: Memorial Day Massacre," *Photo-History*, I (July 1937), 60.

LEVIN, RUBEN. "Big Business Finances War on Labor," *Railroad Telegrapher*, LVII (January 1940), 3–4.

LEVINSON, EDWARD. "Strikebreaking Incorporated," *Harper's Magazine*, CLXXI (November 1937), 77–82.

———. "The Right to Break Strikes," *Current History*, XLV (February 1937), 77–82.

LONDON, JACK. "Chicago Memorial Day Massacre—An Eye Witness' Account," *Lithographers Journal*, XXII (July 1937), 111, 181.

MACDONALD, DWIGHT. "Espionage, Inc.," *Nation*, CXLIV (February 27, 1937), 238–239.

———. "Profiles: The Defense of Everybody," *New Yorker*, XXIX (July 11, July 18, 1953), 31–55, 29–59.

MCMANUS, PAUL G. "What About the Civil Liberties Committee?," *New Masses*, XXX (March 7, 1939), 13–14.

MCWILLIAMS, CAREY. "Civil Rights in California," *New Republic*, CII (January 22, 1940), 108–110.

———. "La Follette Hearings: Final Sessions," *New Republic*, CII (March 25, 1940), 400–403.

MADDEN, J. WARREN. "Spy System Used to Wage War on Workers' Civil Liberties," *American Photo-Engraver*, XXVIII (August 1936), 623–624.

MAGRUDER, CALVERT. "A Half Century of Legal Influence upon the Development of Collective Bargaining," *Harvard Law Review*, L (May 1937), 1071–1117.

MAINWARING, DANIEL. "Fruit Tramp," *Harper's Magazine*, CLXXIX (July 1934), 235–242.

MANGOLD, WILLIAM P. "On the Labor Front," *New Republic*, CXXXIV (October 23, 1935), 297, 300; CXXXVI (February 26, 1936), 74–75.

MATTHEWS, J. B., and R. E. SHALLCROSS. "Must America Go Fascist?" *Harper's Magazine*, CLXIX (June 1934), 1–15.

MITCHELL, JONATHAN. "Civil Liberties Under Roosevelt," *New Republic*, LXXXI (December 26, 1934), 186–187.

MITCHISON, NAOMI. "White House and Marked Tree," *New Statesman and Nation*, IX (April 27, 1935), 585–586.

"More Spies on Labor," *New Republic*, LXXXVI (April 22, 1936), 303.

MUNRO, W. CARROLL. "Cameras Don't Lie," *Current History*, XLVI (August 1937), 37–40.

MURPHY, FRANK. "Civil Liberties and the Cities," *Vital Speeches*, V (June 15, 1939), 542–544.

NEUBERGER, RICHARD L. "Who Are the Associated Farmers?" *Survey Graphic*, XXVIII (September 1939), 517–521, 555–557.

"New Attacks Upon Liberties," *Social Action*, II (January 10, 1936), 18–24.

"New Deal Sharpens Civil Rights Fight," *Civil Liberties Quarterly*, IV (April 1934), 11–12.

"No Jobs in California," *Saturday Evening Post*, CCXI (November 12, 1938), 18–19, 40, 44.

"Oppressive Labor Practices: Summary of Senate Inquiry," *Monthly Labor Review*, XLVIII (May 1939), 1062–1069.

OWEN, BLAINE. "Night Ride in Birmingham," *New Republic*, LXXXIV (August 28, 1935), 65–67.

"Remove the Rat," *Nation*, CXLII (January 29, 1936), 117–118.

"Review by 'I.S.'" *Saturday Review of Literature*, XIII (December 28, 1935), 19–20.

ROCHE, JOHN P. "Civil Liberty in the Age of Enterprise," *University of Chicago Law Review*, XXXI (Fall 1963), 103–135.

———. "The Curbing of the Militant Majority," *Reporter*, XXIX (July 18, 1963), 34–38.

———. "The Utopian Pilgrimage of Mr. Justice Murphy," *Vanderbilt Law Review*, X (February 1957), 369–394.

ROOSE, KENNETH D. "The Recession of 1937–38," *Journal of Political Economy*, LVI (June 1948), 239–248.

SAYRE, FRANCIS BOWES. "Labor and the Courts," *Yale Law Journal*, XXXIX (March 1930), 682–705.

SCHWEINHAUT, HENRY A. "The Civil Liberties Section of the Department of Justice," *Bill of Rights Review*, I (Spring 1941), 206–216.

"Scraps of Paper," *Literary Digest*, CXXII (September 5, 1936), 9–10.

RORTY, JAMES. "Lettuce—with American Dressing," *Nation*, CXL (May 15, 1935), 575–576.

"Shape of Government," *New Republic*, CII (September 5, 1936), 701–702.

"The Shape of Things," *Nation*, CXLII (June 10, 1936), 731–732.

SILVERBERG, LOUIS G. "Citizens' Committees: Their Role in Industrial Conflict," *Public Opinion Quarterly*, V (March 1941), 17–37.

SLICHTER, SUMNER H. "The Current Labor Policies of American Industries," *Quarterly Journal of Economics*, XLIII (May 1929), 393–435.

SOFCHALK, DONALD G. "The Chicago Memorial Day Incident: An Episode of Mass Action," *Labor History*, VI (Winter 1965), 3–43.

SOULE, GEORGE. "Liberty League Liberty," *New Republic*, LXXXVI (September 9, 1936), 121–125.

SPOFFORD, WILLIAM B. "Talking It Over," *Witness*, VII (May 5, 1938), 4.

"Spy Profits," *Literary Digest*, CXXIII (March 27, 1937), 5–6.

"The State of Civil Liberties," *Nation*, CXLII (June 10, 1936), 731–732.

STEPHENS, OREN. "Revolt on the Delta," *Harper's Magazine*, CLXXXIII (November 1941), 656–664.

"Strikebreaking," *Fortune*, XI (January 1935), 56–61, 89–92.

"Strike Terrors," *Literary Digest*, CXXII (October 3, 1936), 8–9.

SUFFRIN, SIDNEY C. "Labor Organization in Agricultural America, 1930–35," *American Journal of Sociology*, XLIII (January 1938), 544–559.

"Symposium on Civil Liberties," *American Law School Review*, IX (April 1941), 881–901.

TAYLOR, FRANK J. "Hot Lettuce," *Collier's*, XCVIII (September 26, 1936), 14, 33–34.

T.R.B. "Washington Notes," *New Republic*, XCVIII (March 8, 1939), 128–129; C (August 30, 1939), 102.

"Two to Make a Rumor," *New Republic*, XCIV (May 4, 1938), 380.

VARNEY, HAROLD LORD. "Are the Capitalists Asleep?," *American Mercury*, XXXVII (March 1936), 266–272.

VENKATARAMANI, M. S. "Norman Thomas, Arkansas Sharecroppers, and the Roosevelt Agricultural Policies, 1933–1937," *Mississippi Valley Historical Review*, XLVII (September 1960), 225–246.

VILLARD, OSWALD GARRISON. "Issues and Men," *Nation*, CXLIX (July 1, 1939), 17.

———. "Pillars of Government: Robert M. La Follette, Jr.," *Forum*, XCVI (August 1936), 87–91.

WARD, PAUL W. "The State of Civil Liberties," *Nation*, CXLII (June 10, 1936), 731–732.

———. "Washington Weekly," *Nation*, CXLII (April 8, 1936), 440–441; (April 22, 1936), 503–504.

WESTIN, ALAN F. "Anti-Communism and the Corporations," *Commentary*, XXXVI (December 1963), 479–487.

"Where Civil Liberties Stand Today," *New Republic*, LXXXIII (June 26, 1935), 187–192.

"'Why I Won'—'Why I Lost,'" *U.S. News & World Report*, XXIX (November 17, 1950), 26–37.

WILLAUER, PHILIP B. "Civil Rights in Labor-Management Relations: A Management Viewpoint," *Annals of the American Academy of Political and Social Science*, CCLXXV (May 1951), 140–147.

WINTER, ELLA. "Fascism on the West Coast," *Nation*, CXXXVIII (February 28, 1934), 241–242.

———. "La Follette in California," *New Masses*, XXXIV (February 20, 1940), 11–13.

WITMER, T. RICHARD. "Civil Liberties and the Trade Union," *Yale Law Journal*, L (February 1941), 621–635.

WOLF, HERMAN. "And Southern Death," *Common Sense*, V (February 1936), 12–14.

ZON, HENRY. "La Follette's Work Should Continue," *Brewery Worker*, LIV (January 7, 1939), 6.

OTHER SOURCES

The following persons were interviewed by the author: John J. Abt (March 22, 1963); Mrs. Ann Blankenhorn (September 12, 1963); Mrs. Ethel Clyde (May 16, 1963); Henry H. Fowler (September 16, 1963); Gardner Jackson (December 3, 1963); Philip La Follette (July 10, 1963); Carey McWilliams (February 28, 1964); Luke Wilson (September 12, 1963); and Robert Wohlforth (November 6, 1963). Transcripts of the interviews with Abt, Jackson, McWilliams, Wilson, and Wohlforth are now part of the Oral History Collection at Columbia University.

For newspaper comments the author relied most heavily upon three collections: the voluminous clipping scrapbooks in the American Civil Liberties Union Papers; the clipping scrapbooks of Heber Blankenhorn, generously loaned by Mrs. Blankenhorn; and the labor espionage clipping files in the Legislative Reference Library, Madison, Wisconsin. The author followed the entire life of the La Follette Committee in four newspapers: *New York Times*, New York *Herald Tribune*, St. Louis *Post-Dispatch*, and Washington *Post*. Of the following periodicals, issues for the periods indicated were read:

Advance, 1936–1939; *Amalgamated Journal*, 1937–1940; American Federation of Labor *Weekly News Service*, 1936–1940; C.I.O. *News*, 1937–1940; *Civil Liberties Quarterly*, 1931–1938; *Current Biography*, 1942, 1944; Federal Council of Churches *Information Service*, 1935–1937; *Labor*, 1936–1938; *Nation*, 1935–1940; National Association of Manufacturers *Labor Relations Bulletin*, 1936–1940; *New Leader*, 1935–1940; *New Militant*, 1935–1936; *New Republic*, 1935–1940; *Progressive*, 1936–1940; *Socialist Call*, 1936; *Time*, 1936–1940; United Mine Workers *Journal*, 1935–1939.

Index